Fight for It Now

Also by David Wilkinson

Keeping the Barbarians at Bay:
The Last Years of Kenneth Allsop, Green Pioneer

Fight for It Now

John Dower and the Struggle for National Parks in Britain

David Wilkinson

Signal

Signal Books
Oxford

First published in 2019 by
Signal Books Limited
36 Minster Road
Oxford OX4 1LY
www.signalbooks.co.uk

A catalogue record for this book is available from the British
Library

ISBN 978-1-909930-79-7 Cloth

Cover Design: Tora Kelly
Typesetting: Tora Kelly
Cover Image: Roger Clegg
Printed and bound in the UK by TJ International, Padstow

Contents

Preamble

Walking in Wartime:
Advice from the Ramblers' Association
June 1940

During the War, and especially if the present anxiety about parachutists and 'fifth columnists' continues, it is inevitable that persons walking in the countryside for health and exercise will from time to time be stopped and questioned by the police or the military. It is quite understandable that in present circumstances strangers walking in the countryside and carrying maps, and perhaps cameras, may arouse suspicion. It is best not to carry a camera at all if you know that your walk will take you past, or very close to aerodromes, military camps etc...

We do not advise night walking at the present time. There is always the possibility that some other zealous person will fire first and ask questions afterwards. Try to finish your walks before nightfall...

In conclusion, we urge you to continue your recreation of country walking, even though it may be attended by inconvenience...

Sunday 11 July 1943, Truro, Cornwall

John Dower gave a wry smile as he tucked the dog-eared card into his ex-army rucksack, down among his sandwiches, several large-scale Ordnance Survey maps and his Leica camera. Outside the seventeenth-century Red Lion Hotel the weekday noise and bustle of Boscawen Street was stilled in the quiet of an early Sunday morning. Dower lit his first pipe of the day, shaded his eyes against the bright sunlight, and scanned the near-deserted street for signs of his companion.

Even on a busy market day, Dower would have been unmissable among the crowds. He was a commanding figure: at six foot four, he stood head and shoulders above the average Cornishman. Despite his forty-three years he remained wiry and athletic-looking, with an academic air enhanced by his round, tortoise-shell glasses. The few passers-by could easily guess how he was intending to spend this Sunday. The nailed boots, walking stick, generously cut plus-fours and the khaki blouson jacket gave it away. He had salvaged the jacket and removed the badges after he had been invalided from the Army three years before.

The church clock had just finished striking eight when (James) Alfred Steers walked briskly around the corner towards him. 'Beautiful morning, John. Good to start early. We should be able to cover quite a few miles of coast today,' he said in a quiet but enthusiastic voice. Remarkably, Steers was just as tall and commanding as Dower, was about the same age, and like him was a passionate conservationist. Unlike Dower, however, Steers was a *real* academic – and one of some distinction. As Dean of St Catharine's College Cambridge and University Lecturer in Geography, he had a national reputation in the physiography of Britain's coastline. His weather-beaten complexion – several shades darker than Dower's – was the consequence of six months' walking around the coastline of England and Wales on behalf of the new Ministry of Town and Country Planning,

Before their trip, Steers had sent Dower a note describing how he had approached these coastal surveys. Dozens of large scale, 1:25,000 maps were methodically highlighted in different colours, indicating industrial areas, residential districts, quarries and individual buildings. 'Particular notes were made of all the shacks, huts, ugly and misplaced buildings,' he noted. 'Good, well-built and even artistic houses may be quite as offensive as meaner dwellings, especially if they are on open cliffs or if the individual houses or groups are poorly planned and sited... It is the haphazard placing of buildings on the coast that forms one of the worst features of its desecration.'

The note continued: 'A necessary but regrettable feature of the war has been the taking over of certain coastal areas for military purposes, and the erection of defence works and other buildings on the foreshore of many sections of the coast. This suggests problems of control and restoration no less urgent than those arising from industry and unregulated shack building – but for obvious reasons, comment on it at present must be limited to the minimum.'

*

A large Humber Super Snipe painted in military camouflage pulled up outside the hotel. This was a Voluntary Coast Patrol (VCP) car which was to take the two of them to survey the north Cornwall coast, from Newquay to St Ives Bay. They soon established that the volunteer driver was a seventy-year-old retired vet – which helped explain the pervasive odour inside the car of wet dog.

As they pulled away from the western suburbs of Truro, the countryside became increasingly pockmarked with abandoned mine workings and waste heaps. 'Do you think there will ever be a National Park in Cornwall?' Steers asked, looking forlornly out of the window. 'Well, not here, for sure,' Dower replied. 'The idea is to protect it with a *coastal* National Park along the lines we're proposing for Pembrokeshire – but not all 300 miles of it. We'll have to work around the rash of bungalows and shacks, the derelict mine workings and the military bases. And there's bound to be a lot of opposition from the biggest landowner of all, the Duchy of Cornwall.'

'But we can't accept an *à la carte* National Park – neither here nor anywhere else along Britain's coast,' Steers interrupted. 'The entire British coastline should be regarded as a unit. It is neither a local, nor even a regional possession, but a *national* one. It should be enjoyed by the public and managed by a national body like the Ministry of Town and Country Planning. You need a central organisation which can visualise the whole, have access to complete statistics on the relative numbers visiting the various parts of the coast, and deal with the problems impartially.'

Dower was just about to reply when he noticed with some alarm that the Humber's speedometer was nudging eighty mph. 'It's good to put the car through its paces,' smiled the vet. 'A four-litre engine needs some exercise! And apart from a few military vehicles, there are hardly any cars about. Can't get the petrol coupons, you see. It was different before the war. Nose to tail on summer weekends. It took hours to get to the beaches, and when you did the cars were parked all over the headlands, so the view was completely spoiled. Then trying to get back from the beach to the main road along these narrow lanes was just a nightmare...'

Dower and Steers were relieved to be dropped off at Portreath, to walk the five miles south-west to Godrevy Island where they would be picked up. Dower later noted that this stretch of coast was 'first rate'. 'It is completely unspoilt (neither bungalows nor mine workings),' he wrote. 'There is a good road (B3301) pretty close to the cliffs most of the way, and the greater part of the land between the road and the shore is rough downland. The dark cliffs are very varied – some sheer, some terraced, some sloping – and there are many stacks and rocky beaches. The National Trust already holds a good deal of it, but the whole must be strictly preserved.'

One of the greatest delights of the walk was the profusion and variety of wild flowers. The thyme on the cliff lands and the honeysuckle in the stunted hedgerows scented the air for miles around. Even though Dower had no reference book with him, and very little time for noting and identifying species, he managed to compile a list of over 140 species in flower.

*

After a sandwich lunch they were picked up and driven northwards to Penhale Point – and to great disappointment. To the south, a long stretch of dunes four miles long and a mile wide was colonised by permanent War Office buildings and anti-aircraft artillery ranges. Spitfires roared low overhead towards the open Atlantic in their search for enemy submarines. Further down the coast, Dower noted that Perranporth was 'architecturally *very* sub-standard – a shapeless sprawl of villas and bungalows with a few hotels and boarding houses – but it is doubtless a splendid place for popular family holidays. It wants taking in hand as such, within fairly close limits of growth – and leaving out of the National Park...'

Beyond Perranporth, abandoned mine workings peppered the cliff tops. 'Some of the old stone mine-houses – gaunt ruins with their very standardised brick-topped chimney shafts – are of picturesque effect but there are too many of them and the old waste heaps scar the ground badly,' Dower recorded. 'In sum, a very desolate effect, both here and still more in the concentrated mining areas inland. It doesn't look as if anybody had ever had – or ever will have – the time and money or the desire to clear anything away or tidy anything up.'

It was while Dower and Steers were studying the maps and taking photographs of the landscape that they were interrupted by the unmistakable sound of a rifle being cocked, ready to fire. A solitary corporal with a Home Guard armband emerged from behind a sand dune, his battered First World War Lee-Enfield .303 rifle pointing straight at them.

'Drop everything. Stand up. Hands on heads,' the soldier barked as he moved towards the two startled men. Carefully, he shifted the maps, the camera and the drawings with his boot. 'Now what do we have here, I wonder?'

'Let me explain,' Dower responded quickly, trying to recover his composure. 'This is Dr Steers and my name is John Dower. We're surveying the coast on behalf of His Majesty's Government to determine whether we should establish a National Park here. Look, this is my identity card, and a letter of introduction from the Ministry of Town and Country Planning.'

'Keep your hands on your head!' ordered the corporal, ignoring the proffered paperwork. 'Don't you know that dozens of jerry submarines are hunting in packs just off this coast, sinking our convoys and throttling our vital supply lines. There's quite a few fifth columnists operating around here, feeding the Hun with information about our shipping movements. Perhaps you might know some of them.'

He paused, then looked Steers straight in the eye. 'And what, pray, is a "National Park"?'

'Well, it's a large area of especial natural beauty which we must permanently protect from unsightly developments, and open up for the enjoyment of the public,' Steers replied, automatically. 'Er... after the war, of course.'

The soldier gave a hint of a smile and in an exaggerated gesture slowly turned his head to take in the features of the landscape about him – the concrete blocks, the barbed wire, the corrugated iron huts, the new tarmac roads, the abandoned waste tips. He waited until the roar of the next Spitfire had subsided, and then said, 'I think you'd better come along with me.'

*

Dower shielded his eyes from the bright sun that suddenly streamed through the opening door of the Watch House. He and Steers had been 'informally detained' there for a few hours until several telephone calls to the War Office, the Ministry of Town and Country Planning and the Volunteer Coast Patrol at last confirmed their innocence. They were free to go.

During their confinement Dower had had plenty of time to ponder that there was more than one war to be won here. But in the letter to his wife Pauline, at home in the Yorkshire Dales, he barely mentioned the incident, referring to it as 'a brief misunderstanding over a right of way'. He did, however, tell her about twisting his ankle on a hidden rock, which had made it 'stiff and puffy', but not bad enough to interfere with his walking. In fact, 'I felt myself getting fresher and fitter (and fatter?) as the sun and breeze and exercise played on me.' So much so that later, on the overnight train from Penzance to London, he managed to get seven hours' uninterrupted sleep.

As the train pulled into Paddington he was still tousled, wind-swept and dressed in his mud-spattered walking gear.

He had just enough time to get to his digs in Hampstead to pick up the dark suit and the gas-mask that Pauline had posted to him, together with his rations and a separate packet of bacon. Dower had become used to managing the two halves of his wartime life, split between city and countryside, London and Yorkshire. In a few hours he would be plunged into back-to-back meetings with senior officials in the corridors of Whitehall, followed by lunch with his friend the Revd. HH Symonds, chair of the Friends of the Lake District pressure group.

He was a man with a mission.

Introduction

Malham Cove is the sparkling jewel in the crown of the Yorkshire Dales – a huge curved amphitheatre of white limestone spanning 1,000 feet from end to end and towering 260 feet above the valley below. Thousands of walkers and cyclists following the Pennine Way labour their way up to the summit, many after a night's rest at the rather dour and functional Malham Youth Hostel, half a mile to the south. In the dining room of the hostel a modest plaque on the wall declares:

> *JOHN DOWER 1900-1947, architect and town planner, devoted his life to the cause of National Parks and preservation of the English Countryside. He designed and built this hostel which was dedicated to his memory in 1948.*

The plaque was unveiled in that year by a small group of Dower's friends and relatives, including GM Trevelyan – the distinguished historian, generous benefactor to the National Trust and founder of the Youth Hostels Association. It remains the only memorial to a man who became the driving force behind the establishment of National Parks in Britain.

Down the road from the youth hostel is the small village of Kirkby Malham, where Dower wrote his seminal report *National Parks in England and Wales* at his home 'The Rookery'.[1] It was a magisterial document described by one of his colleagues as 'a one-man White Paper'. It provided the basis for the 1949 National Parks and Access to the Countryside Act, which opened the way for the eventual designation of fifteen National Parks. They now cover 10 per cent of the land in England, 20 per cent in Wales and 7 per cent in Scotland. Five of the early English parks lie within a radius of seventy-five miles of Kirkby Malham.

---

1 John Dower, *National Parks in England and Wales, Report by John Dower*, Ministry of Town and Country Planning, Cmd. 6628, May 1945.

In his report, Dower defined a National Park as:

> an extensive area of beautiful and relatively wild
> country in which, for the nation's benefit and
> by appropriate national decision and action,
> (a) the characteristic landscape beauty is strictly
> preserved, (b) access and facilities for public open-
> air enjoyment are amply provided, (c) wildlife and
> buildings and places of architectural and historic
> interest are suitably protected, while (d) established
> farming use is effectively maintained. The several
> requirements and qualifications of this definition
> are all important...[2]

This was a tall order in a small crowded island like Britain,
where the land is densely populated (at least in England),
privately owned and highly developed for housing,
agriculture, forestry, shooting and mineral extraction.
Britain's first National Park – the Peak District – was not
formally designated until 1951. This was almost eighty years
after the world's first National Park had been established
by the United States at Yellowstone in Wyoming, covering
no less than two and a quarter million acres of wildland
– almost the size of Yorkshire. In contrast to the settled
character of Britain's landscape, the land of Yellowstone was
owned by the US Federal Government, and reserved 'for the
preservation from injury or spoliation of all timber, mineral
deposits, natural curiosities, or wonders within the said park,
and their retention in their natural condition'. Yellowstone
was to be 'withdrawn from settlement, occupancy or sale
under the laws of the United States, and dedicated and set
apart as a public park or pleasuring-ground, for the benefit
and enjoyment of the people; and all persons who shall
locate or settle upon or occupy the same, or any part thereof,
shall be considered trespassers and removed therefrom.'[3]

Such draconian measures may have been possible in the
wide open spaces of nineteenth-century America, Canada or

---

2 *Ibid*, para 4.
3 Harold Abraham (ed.), *Britain's National Parks*, Country Life
   Ltd, 1959, pp. 11-12.

South Africa – but not in crowded Britain. State intervention here was limited by the ruling doctrine of economic *laissez-faire* and the sanctity of private property. Wildlife and the beauty of the landscape remained inadequately protected, while access to much of Dower's 'relatively wild country' was denied to the thousands of ramblers seeking weekend escape from the cities. Yet public support for National Parks did not fully emerge in Britain until after the First World War. Before then, a few Members of Parliament had campaigned for 'Access to the Mountains'. One of them, James Brice (later Lord Brice), introduced a Bill (in relation to Scotland only) in 1884, and this was followed by six further Bills, all of which had to be withdrawn through lack of parliamentary support. By 1908, the baton had been passed to Labour MP Charles (later Sir Charles) Trevelyan, but his Access Bill was also kicked into the long grass.

Two key factors were to trigger popular demand for National Parks during the 1920s – the damaging invasion of the countryside brought about by expanding motor car ownership; and the election in 1924 of a Labour government headed by Ramsay MacDonald, himself a keen rambler. In 1929, after pressure from the newly-formed Council for the Preservation of Rural England (CPRE), MacDonald set up a government committee chaired by Christopher (later Lord) Addison to consider the case for National Parks. His report was completed in 1931, but at an inauspicious time. The onset of the Great Depression, the election of a Conservative-led government and savage cuts in government expenditure eventually led in 1934 to the shelving of Addison's report. It was a cautious document, and strangely prescient. It recommended the establishment of a National Authority to steer the development of what were then called 'National Reserves'. It also issued a caution:

> The task of the National Authority will not be an easy one. It will be attacked by those who think that any expenditure on the preservation of natural beauties of the country is unjustifiable; assailed by enthusiasts who wish to press their own fancies or look for action on some historic lines; importuned

by private individuals who see in the proposals an opportunity of private gain, and opposed by others who resent any interference with private interests. In many cases the Authority will be called upon to hold an even balance between conflicting interests – and at all times they must be prepared to take the long view and to leave it to time and a later generation to vindicate their actions...[4]

*

Dower was then in his early thirties, unusually tall and wiry, a great talker with a prodigious capacity for hard work. He was born in 1900 into a comfortable upper middle-class home in Ilkley, Yorkshire, and educated at The Leys School and St John's College in Cambridge, where he was awarded a good degree in history. Later he trained as an architect, and became an associate of the Royal Institute of British Architects (RIBA) and of the Town Planning Institute (TPI), setting up his own independent architectural practice.

A passionate walker from boyhood, he would go on long rambles through the Yorkshire countryside with Arthur, his younger brother. 'Walking had always been his recreation,' one of his colleagues observed. 'And walking for him was a study of geology and forestry, of landscape and rock formation, of access to mountains, ordnance maps, footpaths and farms.'[5] He went on extended walking tours in Brittany, the Pyrenees, the Ardennes and the Austrian Tyrol. But his heart remained in the Lakes and Dales. 'Watch my bias to the North country,' he wrote. 'Country rather than town, preservation of old rather than creation of new, an architect's approach to Town Planning...'

In 1929 his life took a new path when he married Pauline Trevelyan, the daughter of Sir Charles Trevelyan MP (champion of access to the mountains), and the niece

---

4 *Report of the National Park Committee*, Cmd. 3851, April 1931.
5 *Journal of the Royal Institute of British Architects*, vol. 55 (1947-48), pp. 38-9. Obituary by Prof William Holford.

of GM Trevelyan – both of them committed to protecting the beauty of Britain's landscape. In so doing, Dower married into a long-established aristocratic, but radical, family which offered him easy access to the corridors of power.

Like many of his generation, Dower deplored the suffering and waste of mass unemployment, and throughout the 1930s worked for the improvement of social and economic conditions by means of greater state planning. Rather than take to the streets, he chose to influence government more directly, working quietly in the background using his intellect, practical experience and a growing network of contacts. A newly-formed think-tank, Political and Economic Planning (PEP), proved to be an ideal platform from which to operate. There he wrote a number of influential papers – especially on agriculture – and made major contributions to the work of several countryside pressure groups like the Friends of the Lake District and the Council for the Protection of Rural England. In 1936 he became Honorary Drafting Secretary to the Standing Committee on National Parks, an umbrella organisation of several amenity groups fighting for the resurrection of the abandoned Addison Report. He set out an ambitious manifesto in 1938 in *The Case for National Parks in Great Britain*, 40,000 copies of which were distributed throughout Britain. In it he argued for a state-run National Park Commission with extensive powers:

> It should be the function and the right of the [proposed] National Park Commission(s) to examine in advance all such proposals which may seem likely to involve any interference with the landscape beauty or accessibility of potential National Park areas, to consult on an equal footing with the responsible bodies, to co-ordinate their activities, and – where necessary – to refer any matter in dispute for a considered decision by the Government as a whole. Only in extreme circumstances and with the specific sanction of Parliament should any substantial encroachment

by a Department or statutory body be permitted in an established National Park...

There is no need to justify the use of national resources for a purpose so obviously of vital service to the nation at large. The Treasury provides without comment more than £200,000 per year for the maintenance alone of London's Crown Parks, so surely it should be ready to provide at least as large an annual sum for the creation and maintenance of a system of National Parks distributed over the country...[6]

*

John Dower was a tenacious fighter in several senses of the word. This was quite literally true following his decision to join the Army at the age of thirty-nine, as events in Europe posed, in his words, 'a menace to all I valued'. As early as August 1937 he applied to join the Army Officers' Emergency Reserve, and he was enlisted as a Second Lieutenant in the Royal Engineers, less than three weeks after the outbreak of war. However, his military career was cut short after little more than a year following several severe bouts of what he thought was influenza. He believed this was due to working in the bitter weather of early 1940, and to the 'epidemic infection' affecting the thousands of troops passing through Dover harbour where he was billeted. In October 1940 an Army Medical Board declared him unfit for general duty, and refused to pay a disability allowance to tide him over while he looked for another job. It rejected Dower's contention that it was his military duties that were the major cause of his illness. His subsequent battle with the Army was to be rather different from the one he had enthusiastically anticipated.

The Army's loss was to be the countryside's gain. In August 1942 Dower took advantage of his contacts to join a small section of the Ministry of Works and Buildings,

---

6 Standing Committee on National Parks, *The Case for National Parks in Great Britain*, July 1938, pp.10-12.

charged with planning Britain's post-war reconstruction. Having been a leading figure in the pre-war voluntary movement, Dower could now work from the inside, where he became an influential and respected (temporary) civil servant. He was given oversight of rural policy, with a remit to carry out an enquiry into 'the practical needs in certain (national park) areas'.

So while German bombs were falling on Britain's cities, Dower quartered the countryside, identifying and surveying areas suitable to be given National Park status. He was convinced that National Parks should be a key element in post-war reconstruction, that they would offer the mass of the people opportunities for physical, mental and spiritual health and happiness – and more immediately provide war-weary citizens with something to look forward to. But to do this, he was obliged to fight on several fronts at once – including against those who might have been expected to be his supporters. The policies of almost every government department had some impact or other on the countryside, and all were reluctant to hand over their responsibilities to a small, *parvenu* ministry. And all the while Dower knew he had to act quickly, as month by month his health deteriorated, threatening his dream of National Parks. He knew he had to fight for it – now.

1. Foundations

John Gordon Dower was born on 2 September 1900, as the last few months of the long Victorian era crept briefly into the dawn of the twentieth century. On that day Queen Victoria travelled to Balmoral for what was to be her last visit to Scotland before her death four months later. Lord French's horsemen were making progress against the Boers in South Africa, while the residents of Mathieson Street in the Gorbals in Glasgow were terrified by an outbreak of bubonic plague among their neighbours.

This was the world that greeted baby John on that late summer Sunday. He was fortunate enough to be born into a comfortable, upper middle-class Victorian household, the first child of Robert Shillito Dower and his wife Mary (Millie) Hearnshaw. Their house – 'Willowdene' in King's Road – was located just beyond the centre of the small Yorkshire town of Ilkley, in what the local directory highlighted as one of the 'better-class streets'. From their windows the Dowers could see the huge Cow and Calf rocks dominating the skyline just over a mile away on the edge of the Ilkley Moor escarpment. The town sheltering below was described by one observer 'as a sort of Innsbruck in miniature... There is a freshness, an openness and vigour about Ilkley – a predominance of honest Yorkshire stone and a smell of heather. It is a ramblers' town, and on any Sunday morning the little main street is busy with rucksacks and boots.'[7]

In his spare time, Robert, too, was a rambler. He was also a man of considerable intelligence and culture, having gained a first class degree at St John's College Cambridge in Part 1 of the Moral Sciences Tripos – a combination of moral philosophy, economics, law, psychology and history. In his last year, his performance earned him a Foundation Scholarship, the Newcome prize for Moral Philosophy, and a college prize for an essay on the philosophy of Robert Browning. Among his university contemporaries and

---

7 Colin Speakman, Colin, *The Dales Way*, Dalesman Books, 1987.

friends was George Macaulay Trevelyan, the future Regius Professor of Modern History, who studied at Trinity College, next door to St John's.

After leaving Cambridge in 1895, Robert took over from his father as chairman of a steel merchants in Leeds – George Depledge & Co – from which he derived a comfortable living for the rest of his working life. But he kept one foot in academia and was for twenty years an extension lecturer at Leeds University, and at Oxford. He was also a Methodist lay preacher and a keen Rotarian.

As soon as young John was old enough, he was sent about a mile down the road to Ghyll Royd preparatory school, a former manor house set in wooded parkland bounded by a bend in the River Wharfe. The regime there was severe, designed 'to prepare the sons of gentlemen for entrance to the Royal Navy and to public schools'. Despite their tender years the boys were engaged in rifle drills, shooting, boxing and outdoor activities across the moors, like hunting and cross-country running.

Out of school, John soon began to explore the moors and dales on long rambles around Ilkley, sometimes with his father, but then more often with his brother Arthur, six years younger. Later, they went on walking holidays together, both in Britain and abroad, and the close contact with the landscape contributed significantly to John's knowledge of the English countryside (particularly in northern England) on which he could draw when he began his work on National Parks. Arthur, too was influenced by these youthful rambles: among his other achievements he was to become chairman of the Youth Hostels Association for ten years, and a member of the Yorkshire Dales National Park Committee.

At the age of thirteen, John followed his father's footsteps southwards to Cambridge, first to The Leys School, then to St John's College. He was at The Leys for less than a year before the outbreak of the First World War, which completely transformed Cambridge from a seat of learning into a military training camp. Most undergraduates joined the armed forces or took war-related jobs in London, so that the number of young men entering the University ('matriculating') dwindled from 1,200 in 1913-14 to just 280 in 1917-18. In the city, open spaces and college greens became tented army villages, with camp fires burning into the night, and war horses lining the streets. College tennis courts were taken over as drill halls for members of the University's Officer Training Corps (OTC). A hutted hospital was quickly constructed on a cricket field to treat the hundreds of wounded sent back from the mud and blood of the trenches.

Like most public schools then and since, The Leys had its own junior Officer Training Corps (OTC), which John joined in 1915, rising to the rank of sergeant. Later, he was accepted for the Royal Engineers' Officer Cadet Battalion, but this was shortly before the Armistice in November 1918, which narrowly spared him from being sent to the front.

Despite the diversions and excitement of the war, John thrived intellectually at The Leys, showing great aptitude in history and French, and a particular facility for writing lucid, concise and well-structured prose. He also showed considerable promise in drawing and painting. It was not altogether surprising, then, that in 1918 he passed the Cambridge entrance exam with flying colours, and was offered a Foundation Scholarship at St John's College, with effect from October 1919.

Dower chose to fill three months of his 'gap year' by taking up residence in northern France. The guns may have fallen silent by then, but he was confronted by life-threatening risks of a different kind. Tuberculosis was rife among the French soldiers returning home from the dirty and cramped trenches where the disease thrived – in 1917 an estimated 150,000 soldiers were discharged because of tubercular infections. So concerned were the Americans for the health of their own troops in Europe that the Rockefeller Foundation founded the Commission for the Prevention of Tuberculosis in France.[8] This provided dispensaries, hospitals, nurses, information, educational campaigns and organisational support for the French agencies, focusing

---

8 The Rockefeller Foundation, Annual Report 1918, pp. 20-31, (www.rockefellerfoundation.org/uploads/files).

particularly on the *département* of Eure-et-Loir south-west of Paris, and on the nineteenth *arrondissement* of the capital itself, which Dower might well have visited.

As if this were not enough, there was also the so-called 'Spanish 'flu' pandemic that ravaged Europe and the world in 1918-19. One-third of the world's population was infected and over fifty million people died – more than all the casualties in the First World War – and almost half a million of these were French. Unlike other influenza viruses, Spanish 'flu mostly killed young adults, primarily through secondary pneumonia.

Dower's visit in the spring of 1919 coincided with the final weeks of the epidemic, and he managed to escape infection. However, during his stay he lodged with a French *curé* who was apparently suffering from some form of respiratory disease, possibly either influenza or TB. Some members of the Dower family were later to trace the roots of the symptoms that John presented twenty years later to this otherwise innocent French holiday.

Back in England, as Dower walked through the gates of St John's, the city and University of Cambridge were still in the throes of post-war reconstruction. The streets were crowded with almost 2,500 new students, many of them more mature than normal as a result of their military service, and anxious to resume their postponed studies. Even though he was only nineteen, Dower was able to greet the older freshmen with some confidence. Over six foot four, lean, fit, and smoking the inevitable pipe, he struck an imposing figure and his familiarity with the college and the University gave him a certain social advantage among his peers, at least during the first few weeks of the term. And he was to prove a brilliant student, not only gaining a First in Part I of the Historical Tripos in 1921, but at the same time studying for an additional Ordinary BA in Architectural Construction and Architectural Studies, for which he was also awarded a First.

Dower's student notes on lectures and books were written in a tiny, neat script, perhaps an indication of his focused concentration. But his interests ranged far beyond just his studies. The entries in his occasional journals during this period include lists of books to buy, music to listen to, notes for short stories, epigrams extracted from other authors and reflections on the world about him.

The pressure of studying for two degrees while maintaining his extra-curricular interests inevitably took its toll, and in his final examinations in 1923 he gained an Upper Second Class in History, and a Second in the History of Art for the Ordinary degree. It was still, however, a considerable achievement.

*

Schools of architecture started later in Britain than in the US and mainland Europe. Before 1900, would-be architects learned their trade as articled pupils or assistants in offices, supplementing their knowledge with evening or day release classes. But the years before the First War saw moves in Britain to professionalise architecture by standardising training and qualifications, and establishing a proper system of architectural schools. Central to this development was the foundation in 1914 of the Town Planning Institute (TPI), which was distinguished from other architectural organisations by its emphasis on professional status rather than propagandist activism.[9] The leading figure in its development was George Pepler, who was appointed the TPI's Honorary Secretary and Honorary Treasurer from the beginning, becoming President in 1919. This was the same year in which he was appointed Chief Planning Inspector in the Ministry of Health, the government department then responsible for administering Britain's limited planning laws. Pepler introduced the TPI's first membership examinations in 1920, became an external examiner to most planning schools, and a dedicated supporter of the annual Town and Country Planning Summer Schools.

In Cambridge, a Department of Architecture was established in 1912, but did not fully get underway until

---

9 Gordon Cherry, *Pioneers in British Planning*, Architectural Press, 1981, p. 143.

after the hiatus of the war. It remained considerably smaller and less vocational than other urban schools, and was in effect a combined school of architecture and art history.[10] When Dower sat the special architecture examinations in 1922, the list of candidates numbered just sixteen.

It was Dower's architectural studies that set him on the path towards countryside planning. It was inevitable that such a small band of architectural students, working at a prestigious university like Cambridge, should develop strong links with the stars in Britain's architectural firmament. In particular, Pepler – also a Leys School alumnus – was to remain Dower's lifelong mentor and friend, and an important influence on the direction of his early architectural work. Later, in 1933, Pepler was to become godfather to Dower's first son, Michael.

Another key influence was Patrick Abercrombie, probably best known for his work during the Second World War on the Greater London Plan. In 1915, at the comparatively early age of thirty-six, Abercrombie became Britain's first Professor of Architecture at Liverpool University, a position he held for the next twenty years. Formerly a research fellow at the university, he was the founder editor (with Pepler) of the *Town Planning Review*, and subsequently his 'many activities helped to establish the department as a centre of planning activity more all-embracing than simply the conduct of professionally-oriented courses'.[11]

Abercrombie had a deep love of the British countryside, and was acutely aware of the damage being inflicted by what Cyril Joad was later to describe as the 'untutored townsman's invasion of the country'.[12] Increasing motor car ownership and cheap travel by buses and charabancs brought with them new road building, ribbon housing developments along arterial roads, weekend bungalows and huts, petrol

---

10 Andrew Saint, *The Cambridge School of Architecture: a Brief History* (www.arct.cam.uk/aboutthedepartment).

11 Cherry, *op. cit.*, p. 105.

12 CEM Joad, *The Untutored Townsman's Invasion of the Country*, Faber and Faber, 1946.

stations, noise and advertisement hoardings. Together with factory building, new satellite towns, afforestation, quarrying and the construction of reservoirs, there was in the 1920s a powerful assault on the traditional peace and beauty of the rural landscape.

In May 1926, Abercrombie published a 20,000-word essay 'The Preservation of Rural England', in which he wrote:

> We speak eloquently of the obligation that is on us to preserve and save from destruction the *ancient monuments* of this land, visible signs of our history... But we are apt to forget that the greatest historical monument that we possess, the most essential thing that is England, is the Countryside, the Market Town, the Village, the Hedgerow Trees, Lanes, the Copses, the Streams and the Farmsteads. To destroy these and leave a considerable number of archaeological specimens neatly docketed and securely fenced off from a wilderness of slag heaps or rubbish tips might satisfy the unadulterated antiquarian: but the plain man would lose his greatest possession – the country setting.[13]

Abercrombie was convinced that town and country needed to be planned together, on the basis of regional surveys and plans that would balance new urban and rural developments with conservation. The need was for strengthened legal powers for local and central government; greater co-ordination between statutory bodies; and improved awareness and education all round.

'The Preservation of Rural England' led directly to the formation of the Council for the Preservation of Rural England (CPRE). Although a wide range of rural societies and interest groups already existed, Abercrombie argued that a completely new organisation was necessary to co-ordinate these often overlapping bodies. A Joint Committee

---

13 Patrick Abercrombie, 'The Preservation of Rural England', in *Town Planning Review*, vol. 12, no. 1 (May 1926), Liverpool University Press, p. 6.

representing groups as various as the Town Planning Institute, the Royal Automobile Club (RAC) and the Country Gentlemen's Association was therefore established to oversee the new organisation, which was also given a strong regional structure to reflect the diversity of the English countryside.

CPRE's first annual report in 1928 emphasised that it was interested as much in preserving urban England as rural England. Its objectives were:

> (1) to preserve everything in the physical landscape of our country which we have inherited from our fathers and which is worth preserving; and (2) to ensure that modern building etc. developments do the minimum of damage to existing amenities and contribute, as far as may be, their share of grace, charm and dignity to our national inheritance...[14]

The report acknowledged the strong links between CPRE and the Royal Institute of British Architects (RIBA). All important CPRE meetings in the early years were held in RIBA's offices, while at regional level joint CPRE/RIBA expert Advisory Panels were set up to provide advice to local authorities and developers at regional level. Abercrombie himself became CPRE's Honorary Secretary and a member of the Executive Committee, while its Vice President, Guy Dawber, had been a past President of RIBA. JC Squire, who wrote the foreword to the 1928 report, was also the chair of the Press Committee of the Architecture Club.

Despite the dominance of architects in the new organisation, Abercrombie stressed that rural planning required a uniquely wide range of skills beyond those of architecture or local government. 'Rural planning, like Town Planning, is not a simple thing,' he wrote:

> It cannot be embarked upon casually by a country district with an understaffed and overworked surveyor and a quiescent Council "at ease reclin'd in

---

14 Council for the Preservation of Rural England, *Annual Report* 1928, p. 7.

rustic state". It requires, first, a general knowledge of rural affairs, combined with a prescience of external developments likely to affect them; a working acquaintance with geology; a sympathy for historic tradition and an appreciation of landscape beauty (a much more indefinable and unclassifiable thing than urban or suburban beauty). There must be a thorough knowledge of the trend and requirements of, and skill to aid, its smooth running but strength not to be hypnotised by it. A large measure of fair-mindedness is needed in balancing the rival claims of different people who use the country for their various purposes – always remembering that farming is our basic industry and that folk bred in our villages are the backbone of the nation. Finally, in the preparation and administration of any scheme, persuasive planning should accompany statutory power; there should be, after all, a light hand in compulsion but a heavy hand on outrage.[15]

This was written in 1926, three years after Dower had gone down from Cambridge. But he was already familiar with the future challenges of rural planning, through his engagement with the architectural community and his membership of the TPI. But he was not yet in a position to take on the challenge, for Cambridge was only the first stage in his training as a professional architect. To qualify as a RIBA Associate, he needed several more years' hands-on experience working as an assistant in an architectural practice, as well as success in the RIBA examinations.

*

In the autumn of 1923, Dower moved to London to join the practice of Herbert Baker (later Sir Herbert) in Barton Street, Westminster, within 'division bell' distance of the Houses of Parliament. Baker had had a distinguished career in South

---

15 Abercrombie, *op. cit.*, pp. 42-3.

Africa and India, where he collaborated with Edwin Lutyens on a long-term project designing government buildings in New Delhi. (The partnership, however, proved to be short-lived following an argument between the two men – which led to a long estrangement – over the levelling of the King's Way leading to Lutyens' Vice-Regal Lodge.) Dower made a significant contribution to the project as the only one of Baker's assistants whose maths was strong enough to work out the curvature and coffering of the central dome of the Legislative Building.

During his five years with the practice, Dower provided support to the teams designing and managing some of Baker's major projects, including the reconstruction of the Bank of England, the building of Rhodes House in Oxford and the construction of India House in Aldwych. After work, much of his free time was occupied in studying for the RIBA examinations, and he became a familiar visitor at RIBA's headquarters, then in Conduit Street, off Regent Street. Later, George Pepler helped secure Dower's appointment as secretary to a new RIBA Aerodromes Committee, of which Pepler was Acting Chair. These were early days in the history of aviation, and the committee was charged with considering the future land-use planning implications of a network of what were then described as 'landing fields'. Representatives of government, airlines, architects, the aviation industry and CPRE deliberated for eighteen months, after which Dower summarised their conclusions in an interim report published in March 1931. 'The day will be very soon,' he wrote, 'when it is recognised that a municipal aerodrome is something that every town must provide and equip, not merely for the needs of the moment, but for such future development of aviation as technically equipped and fully-empowered experts can foresee... The future comfort and prosperity of the people depends in no small degree on the extent to which this revolution can be controlled and assimilated by organic and deliberate planning.'[16]

---

16 'Town Planning and Aviation – The First (Interim) Report of the Aerodromes Committee', *RIBA Journal*, vol. 38, 1931, pp. 296-300.

Dower's report was perhaps a little too enthusiastic. 'The amenity of an aerodrome as an open space should not be forgotten,' he wrote. 'It may well have parks, playing fields, public golf courses and the like, laid out on the lands reserved for future extension or zoned to prevent obstructions around its perimeter.' But he can be forgiven for failing to foresee that what was then lowly Heston 'landing field' would one day expand into today's Heathrow airport...

Connections

Working in London was essential if Dower was to build his architectural career. For some years he lived with his younger sister Mary in the small Hertfordshire town of Tring, sheltering under the northern ridge of the Chiltern Hills. The attractiveness of the beech woods and the rolling landscape more than compensated for the daily commute of thirty miles each way into central London, and the consequent interference with his metropolitan social activities. Nevertheless, it was not enough to match the powerful pull of the fells and dales of his homeland. As often as he could during the 1920s, he would return there with friends for weekends and holidays of strenuous walking. And one such trip over the Whitsun weekend of 1925 proved to be particularly significant.

He was invited to join the annual Lakes Hunt, based at a remote farmhouse at the head of Borrowdale in the Lake District, six miles south of Keswick. This was no ordinary hunt with horses and hounds chasing foxes and hares, but a manhunt in which human hounds chased human hares, on foot, for three days across ten square miles of the Cumbrian mountains. It was generally referred to as the 'Trevelyan Manhunt', after one of its founders, GM Trevelyan (GMT). As a twenty-two-year-old undergraduate at Trinity College Cambridge, GMT and fellow student Geoffrey Winthrop Young were inspired by the account of the pursuit of Alan Breck Stewart in Stevenson's *Kidnapped*, and by the game of hare and hounds that Trevelyan had known as a schoolboy at Harrow. The Hunt started in 1898, the year that GMT became a Fellow of Trinity.

Robert Trevelyan, John Dower
(centre), James Wilkie in the
Trevelyan Hunt, 1927.

The first members were drawn mainly from their friends
at Trinity and a few other Cambridge colleges. They included
some of the outstanding figures of their generation, both
intellectually and athletically. Over the years, the Whitsun
Hunt at Seatoller House attracted a roll call of the great
and the good, the rich and the powerful. In addition to the
founders, they included many other Trevelyans, including Sir
Charles (Cabinet minister and for thirty-three years Master
of the Hunt) and Sir George (New Age guru and Master for
eighteen years), two Secretaries of State for India (Edwin
Montagu and Leo Amery), a Chancellor of the Exchequer
(Hugh Dalton) and a Home Secretary (Herbert Samuel), and
such formidable figures as William Beveridge, Hilton Young
(Lord Kennet), Admiral Herbert Richmond (the captain of
HMS *Dreadnought*), Archibald Nye (Vice Chief of the Imperial
General Staff during the Second World War), Professor Cyril
Joad (philosopher and member of the BBC's Brains Trust),
and mountaineer and explorer Freddie Spencer-Chapman.[17]
Most of the hunters were also prodigious walkers like GMT;
many were of a Liberal persuasion; and some were motivated
by a radical social conscience.

*

17 Edmund Gray, *100 Hunts: A Chronicle of the Trevelyan
Manhunt 1898-2007,* Stramongate Press, 2007.

19

On the evening of Thursday, 28 May 1925, Dower stepped for the first time over the threshold of Seatoller House and nervously opened the door to the library. Inside the small room, fifteen hunters, mostly standing, were enjoying a pre-dinner drink. The buzz of conversation lulled as Dower entered and made his way over towards GM Trevelyan.

Dower had already met GMT at a few social occasions. He and Dower's father Robert had known each other at Cambridge, and Robert had himself joined the Hunt before the First World War. Now fifty-four, he considered himself too old and unfit to take part – even though he was the same age as GMT's brother Charles, who was to be Master of the Hunt until 1933. It was probably Robert who encouraged his son John to take part, now that he had been freed from the constraints of Cambridge term times.

Almost exactly a year before, Charles Trevelyan had joined Ramsay MacDonald's first Labour government as President of the Board of Education. Now a Labour MP representing Central Newcastle, Charles had formerly been a Liberal. In 1908 he had tabled an Access to Mountains Bill in response to the growing demand among his (then) West Yorkshire constituents for the 'right to roam'. The Bill was successfully given a second reading, but was blocked during the committee stage and eventually buried by its influential opponents.

The dinner gong was about to sound, but Dower had just enough time to talk to Kenneth Spence. Spence was a radical socialist and, like Charles, a conscientious objector during the war. He was a founder member (with Abercrombie) of CPRE and active in a number of regional and national amenity groups. Spence told Dower of his passion for the Lakes and how it was currently threatened by the Forestry Commission's conifer plantations across Ennerdale and into the 'territory' of the Hunt. He revealed that in a few months' time he intended to move to Near Sawrey between Lake Windermere and Esthwaite Water (in a house next to Beatrix Potter), from where he could more effectively campaign against inappropriate afforestation. A few years later, in 1934, Spence was to found the radical campaigning group, the Friends of the Lake District.

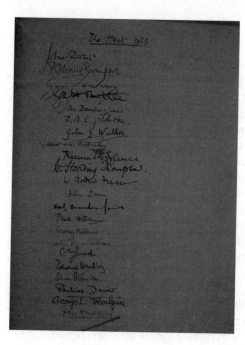

Signatures of John Dower, Master of the Hunt, 1935, and prominent fellow huntsmen.

*

The weekend proved to be a great success. With his wiry frame and long legs, Dower easily coped with running and scrambling across the steep fells. He managed to catch a 'hare' – the first of fifteen during his fourteen years of hunting. He was a hare himself on twelve occasions, avoiding capture on three of them. In 1935, at the age of thirty-four, Dower was to succeed Sir Charles as Master, introducing a rather more rigorous regime, marshalling the pack in a way not done before, and directing groups of hounds along different lines of attack. He balked, however, at the introduction of a hunting horn, which he considered 'ostentatious'.[18] Apart from the sport and the camaraderie, the Hunt provided Dower with a social network of unparalleled influence, with a significant effect on the direction of his career.

But it was a series of events during the autumn of 1929 that was to set the direction Dower's life, on a personal, professional and political level. On 3 September 1929 – the

---

18 *Ibid*, p. 38.

day after his twenty-ninth birthday – John was married to twenty-three-year-old Pauline Trevelyan, the oldest daughter of Sir Charles and Molly, Lady Trevelyan. Pauline was a remarkable young woman – intelligent, gifted and strong-minded. She was one of the very few women at that time to go to university, and one of the infinitesimally smaller number to study agriculture. Her agricultural studies at Reading followed a period at the Slade School of Art in London, where she became an accomplished artist, particularly in water colours and etching. She also rode a motorcycle, and was often seen clad in leathers and goggles travelling at reckless speed along the rough lanes of Northumberland.

As a Trevelyan, Pauline enjoyed a very privileged upbringing. Following the death of her grandfather George Otto Trevelyan, and a year before her marriage, the family had moved from Pauline's childhood home in Cambo to Wallington, a mile to the south. She was later to describe Wallington as 'a typical English country house'. But the estate was rather grander than that – 14,000 acres, including an estate village (Cambo), several smaller groups of cottages, one or two 'gentlemen's houses' and twenty-three farms (subsequently amalgamated into sixteen).[19] Her father Charles sought to reconcile his wealth with his socialism by offering his estate workers unusually generous terms and conditions, and by opening up the house and grounds of Wallington to the public, many of whom were his former constituents who travelled out from Newcastle by charabanc. Following extensive refurbishments, in April 1929 Charles invited all his tenants to a gathering in the Hall, ostensibly to celebrate his and Molly's silver wedding anniversary, but also to put on record what he felt about his privileged position. 'You are all aware that I am no friend of the system which by pure chance makes me rich and a thousand others poor for life,' he declared. 'I want you to know that I regard myself not as the owner of Wallington and the people of Wallington, but as a trustee of property which under wiser and humaner laws would belong to

---

19 Pauline Dower, *Living at Wallington*, Mid-Northumberland
    Arts Group, 1984, p. 10.

Sir Charles Trevelyan, John Dower's father-in-law and aristocratic socialist.

the community... I want you to feel that to come and see Wallington is on your part not an intrusion but a right... We would like to think that the pictures, the china, the books, the woods, the garden, are possessions for all the people around here to cherish or to use.'[20]

Twelve years later he took the dramatic step of signing over Wallington and its estate to the National Trust, with the major proviso that until his death he should remain on the estate as a life tenant. When asked what the justification was for delaying the Trust's takeover, he replied simply, 'Because I'm an illogical Englishman.'

As a small child, Pauline had already become familiar with the Hall and the surrounding fells, woods and rivers of the estate. The Trevelyans were great walkers, and she and the family would go on long hikes in all weathers, to Shaftoe, Steng Cross or Rothley Crags, or along the River Wansbeck. It was not altogether surprising therefore that she should join the Hunt, for the first time, over the 1928 Whitsun bank holiday. Wives and daughters were tolerated on these testosterone-fuelled occasions, but only as supporters and not

20 AJA Morris, *CP Trevelyan 1870-1958 – Portrait of a Radical.* Blackstaff Press, 1977, p. 171.

as participants. Pauline had other ideas. Her mother Molly wrote a song about the individual hunters, which began:

> Young hounds, old hounds, everybody come,
> Join Trevelyan's Man Hunt, and make yourselves at home,
> Take your pipes and baccy-pouch and sit upon the floor,
> And listen to some verses that you never heard before.

There followed poetic pen portraits of various male participants, to which she was later obliged to add this additional verse:

> Pauline was a daughter who had no right to come,
> But come she did and verily she made Seatoller hum,
> She singled out a hare who was straight and strong and tall,
> And she chased him and she caught him and she married him
> And all![21]

John and Pauline were pronounced man and wife in Holy Trinity Church, overlooking the Northumberland countryside, just a hundred yards from Pauline's recent home in Cambo House. Sir Charles gave away the bride, while John's brother Arthur looked after the ring as best man. It was a quiet and simple ceremony. Pauline had chosen to have no female attendants, and instead of a traditional wedding dress she wore her travelling frock and hat, ready for a rapid getaway to their honeymoon destination in the Austrian Tyrol.

The wedding breakfast at nearby Wallington was altogether a grander affair, with a large turnout of the Trevelyan and Dower families, together with local friends and neighbours. The third of September was Cromwell's Day, the anniversary of the death in 1658 of the Lord Protector. Pauline's uncle GMT – a strong Cromwellian – was asked to propose the health of the bride, but instead used the occasion to speak at length about the achievements

---

21 Gray, *op. cit.*, pp. 106-7. (In reality, in 1928 Dower remained uncaught physically – but clearly not romantically.)

John Dower at his wedding, 1929.

of his hero. Moreover, he had brought along his friend and colleague, the historian Arthur Bryant, who was to act as seconder, but he was a staunch Cavalier and chose to speak equally at length in favour of the Royalist cause – so in the end both of them had forgotten to propose the toast. Pauline was undismayed, however, and wrote that 'being a Cromwellian myself, I was delighted at the significance of the day being so well emphasised.'[22]

Sir Charles gave John not only the hand of his daughter, but also a wedding present of a fine Holland and Holland double-barrelled twelve-bore shotgun. This enabled him to take part in shooting parties both in the Wallington woods and fields, on the heather moors to the north, and on GMT's estates at Hallington and Housesteads on the Roman Wall. John enjoyed shooting, including on the grouse moors, and became convinced that with appropriate management grouse shooting and rambling were not incompatible, as so many landowners had argued. His experience was later to be reflected in his National Parks report of 1945.

There was, however, an additional and more subtle *quid pro quo* for becoming a Trevelyan son-in-law. Sir Charles and

22 Dower, *op. cit.*, p. 31

GMT in their different ways were both leading activists in the countryside movement – one in the campaign for greater public access to mountains and moorlands, the other in the protection of heritage and natural beauty. Moreover, Molly Trevelyan, Sir Charles' wife, was a founding member of CPRE and took a leading role in developing its public relations. She commissioned the architect Clough Williams-Ellis to edit his classic 1928 book, *England and the Octopus*, making sure it was distributed to 600 schools. Later, she devised a nationwide 'Save the Countryside' travelling exhibition, highlighting examples of positive solutions to ugly rural developments.

Against this background, it was inevitable that John would contribute his undoubted talents to the cause. His engagement with the Trevelyans, combined with his London contacts in the TPI, RIBA and CPRE, provided the impetus which led to his becoming a leading campaigner for National Parks in the 1930s.

John and Pauline set up their matrimonial home in Hampstead Garden Suburb, on the northern edge of London. Covering an area of some 800 acres stretching from Golders Green in the south to East Finchley in the north, it was an appropriate location for a young architect and a lover of the countryside. It was planned by Raymond Unwin – the principal designer of Britain's first garden city in Letchworth, with Edwin Lutyens as a consulting architect. Unwin had sought to realise the vision of Dame Henrietta Barnett, the moving force behind the suburb. She had dreamed of 'a community of all classes where the richer residents subsidised the rents of the poorer, and all lived in well-designed houses attractively grouped at low density and surrounded by gardens, bounded by hedges. There would be access to a variety of open spaces and the housing would be enhanced by the retention of significant areas of indigenous woodland, ancient hedgerows and mature oak trees. Allotment gardens would be included in the layout to enable residents to grow their own food...'[23]

---

23 Mervyn Miller, 'Raymond Unwin 1863-1949', in Cherry, Gordon, *Pioneers of British Planning*, The Architectural Press, 1981.

The Dowers' rented home at 66 Willifield Way stood at the corner of a triangle of roads, adjacent to a green and close to a cul-de-sac 'artisans' quarter' of allotments, tennis courts and communal gardens. Their first child, Susan, was born there in 1931, followed by Michael in 1933. Susan recalls that at weekends the house was often filled with 'muddy, wet-clothed men who played hockey', and that George Pepler, Cyril Joad and Cyril Pease were frequent visitors.

It was a brisk ten-minute walk to Golders Green tube station (often very brisk as Dower had a tendency to cut things fine in the mornings), from which John could travel down the Northern Line to his office. This was in a pleasant Georgian terrace in Gray's Inn Road overlooking a six-acre wooded park ('The Walks'), an oasis in the bustling heart of central London. After passing the RIBA examinations in 1930, Dower had set up his own practice with fellow Hunt member John Brandon-Jones in the offices of William Harding Thompson, a Fellow of RIBA and a future President of the Town Planning Institute. Thompson had close links with both CPRE and later the 'think-tank' Political and Economic Planning (PEP – see p. 35), and was instrumental in getting Dower work from both.

*

Both John and Pauline were independent-minded individuals with important external interests and commitments, which for some newly-weds might easily have led to friction and matrimonial disharmony. Soon after their tenth wedding anniversary, John was to reflect privately on what his marriage meant to him, and he copied down a number of passages from *Mrs. Miniver*, the best-selling wartime novel by Jan Struther. One of these passages sums up nicely the essential, but difficult, task of balancing matrimonial commitment with personal independence:

> … a certain degree of un-understanding (not mis-, but un-) is the only possible sanctuary which one human being can offer to another in the midst

Portrait of Pauline Dower, John
Dower's wife.

of the devastating intimacy of a happy marriage.
(Mrs Miniver) saw every relationship as a pair of
intersecting circles. The more they intersected, it
would seem at first glance, the better the relationship;
but this is not so. Beyond a certain point the law of
diminishing returns sets in, and there aren't enough
private resources left on each side to enrich the life
that is shared... Probably, perfection is reached
when the area of the two outer crescents, added
together, is exactly equal to that of the leaf-shaped
piece in the middle. On paper, there must be some
neat mathematical formula for arriving at this: in
life, none.[24]

Both John and Pauline were to demonstrate the strength
of their private inner resources – particularly Pauline, who
gave her husband crucial moral and practical support in
his work for National Parks, and went on after his death to
assume an important official role in their administration.

24 Jan Struther, *Mrs. Miniver*, Chatto and Windus, 1943, pp. 38-
41.

2. Commitment

On their wedding day, some 3,500 miles across the Atlantic the Dow Jones industrial share index peaked at over 381 points, a ten-fold increase since the end of the First World War. The boom in America during the 'Roaring Twenties' had been fuelled by speculators buying stocks and shares with money they didn't have, relying instead on easy credit. This high level of indebtedness was not sustainable, and by the end of October what became known as the Wall Street Crash saw the Dow Jones index fall to 230. Over the following months it was to slide much further, and on 8 July 1932 it closed at just over 41, its lowest level of the twentieth century. The 1929 Wall Street Crash was the catalyst that led to the global Great Depression during the 1930s, as investment and consumption fell in the US in response to the wipe-out of billions of dollars of wealth in just a few weeks.

The London Stock Exchange could not stay immune from the contagion. The loss of exports and tax receipts on top of cuts in government spending pushed the British economy into deep depression. Within a year, unemployment had more than doubled to two and a half million, some 20 per cent of the workforce. Hardest hit were the areas of heavy industry and coal mining in Wales, Scotland and the north-east of England. Just twenty miles east of Wallington, shipbuilding on the Tyne had fallen by 90 per cent by 1932, with knock-on effects on steel and coal production. In some north-eastern towns and cities, unemployment spiralled to over 70 per cent.

Against this background, the call to set up National Parks in Britain seemed to many an irrelevant diversion. But on 26 September 1929, the recently appointed Labour Prime Minister Ramsay MacDonald announced an official enquiry to investigate just this.

To John and Pauline, recently back from their honeymoon, this was a shaft of sunlight through the gathering economic gloom. MacDonald's initiative was the first occasion on which a government in Britain had officially raised the prospect of extending the role of the state to include the protection of natural beauty.

The government inquiry was to be chaired by the Parliamentary Secretary to the Minister of Agriculture, Dr Christopher Addison, a farmer's son with a lifelong love of the countryside. His terms of reference were:

> To consider and report if it is desirable and feasible to establish one or more National Parks in Great Britain, with a view to the preservation of the natural characteristics, including flora and fauna, and to the improvement of recreational facilities for the people, and advise generally, and in particular as to areas, if any, that are most suitable for the purpose.

Earlier in 1929, few in the countryside movement would have predicted this development. In January of that year GM Trevelyan had drawn attention to the government's continuing inaction and launched a public appeal for money on behalf of the National Trust. 'For persons desiring to secure the permanent safety of a beautiful place,' he wrote, 'the National Trust offers the *only* sure method in the present condition of society. The State, whether rightly or wrongly, declines to hold land for this purpose... the State, which remits death duty on pictures and art treasures of "national value", shows no such lenience for natural scenery, which is, forsooth, of no "national value" at all!'[25]

In much the same way, the Council for the Preservation of Rural England had to limit its role primarily to offering advice and good practice, rather than mounting political campaigns for state intervention. The chairman of CPRE's Thames Valley Branch, Viscount Astor, asked: 'What after all can we do, seeing that (we) have no statutory powers? Our belief is that the CPRE will, under wise management and a good organisation, rapidly become a recognised as permanent National Institution whose ideas will be accepted as of national importance, whose advice will be sought, and whose influence will be practical and great.'[26]

---

25 GM Trevelyan, *Must England's Beauty Perish? A Plea on behalf of the National Trust*, Faber and Gwyer Ltd, 1929, pp. 9-10.
26 Council for the Preservation of Rural England, *The Thames Valley from Cricklade to Staines*, University of London Press, 1929, p. 96.

Accordingly, in 1929, CPRE commissioned a series of regional surveys of sensitive geographical areas, aimed at highlighting threats to the countryside and opportunities for more positive and co-ordinated action by local statutory authorities and landowners. These surveys were undertaken by the architect and planner William Harding Thompson, who sub-contracted parts of the work to John Dower.[27]

Ramsay MacDonald was himself an enthusiastic rambler. He had hymned the praises of 'a pair of honest boots nailed like the oak door of an ancient keep, which of themselves direct one's way o'er moor and fell and bog and bypath away from the offence and clamour of cars and trains...'[28] Patrick Abercrombie regarded the advent of a rambling prime minister as a golden opportunity and on 2 August 1929 sent MacDonald a memo on behalf of CPRE calling for action on National Parks. His tone was tentative, however, and Abercrombie acknowledged the wide range of sometimes conflicting objectives that supporters of National Parks were demanding. 'At the present moment the CPRE confines itself to observing that the objectives are very varied and in some ways contradictory – recreation and repose, rambling, camping out, afforestation, nature study and the preservation of flora and fauna being the principal aims. It will be difficult to achieve all these objectives in a single area, and the Government is invited to take initial steps by making certain enquiries and preliminary surveys.'

It took less than two months for MacDonald to respond positively. Even though Dr Addison was not then a Cabinet minister – his committee comprised only civil servants, and its terms of reference provided much scope for interpretation – the establishment of the Addison Committee marked a

---

27 William Harding Thompson supervised surveys undertaken for CPRE branches of the following counties: Cornwall (University of London Press) 1930; Devon (A&C Black) 1932; Somerset (A&C Black 1934); The Devon Landscape (A&C Black 1934); The Surrey Landscape (A&C Black 1934); The Sussex Landscape (A&C Black) 1935; The Dorset Landscape (A&C Black) 1935.

28 JR MacDonald, *Wanderings and Excursions,* Jonathan Cape, 1925, p. 7.

crack in official obduracy which countryside campaigners hoped to widen as the 1930s unfolded.

The Addison Report was eventually published in April 1931, bearing the clear footprint of the countryside campaigners.[29] Abercrombie himself provided written and oral evidence on behalf of CPRE, alongside thirty-three other groups who gave evidence. John Dower contributed by drawing a number of the maps showing the boundaries of proposed National Park areas. Other key contributors included Dr Vaughan Cornish (for the Council for Preservation of Rural Wales, CPRW), Raymond Unwin (RIBA), George Pepler (TPI) and representatives of the Ramblers' and Pedestrians' Associations. Between them they proposed over fifty areas in England, Wales and Scotland as candidates for designation as either 'National Reserves' (i.e. National Parks) or 'Regional Reserves' – the latter being those within easy reach of industrial areas where freeing up access was to be the priority. The wish list ranged from the Lakes, Snowdonia and Dartmoor in the premier league, to Blenheim Park, the banks of the River Wye and Cheddar Gorge in the lower divisions.

Dower later reflected that the Committee had produced 'a favourable, though cautious Report', which assumed that the areas to be considered would certainly include the Lakes and Snowdonia – but also the coasts of Cornwall and Pembrokeshire, the Norfolk Broads, the South Downs and Dovedale.[30] But the Report failed to give a definitive answer to the key question as to whether National Parks in Britain were 'desirable and feasible'. It was a Green Paper rather than a firm statement of intent, a discussion document setting out the pros and cons and the views of interested parties.

'The measure of what … can be done and the methods to be employed must depend on the amount of money available for these purposes, and on this point we are not in a position to make any assumption,' the Report observed. 'It is not for us

---

29 *Report of the National Park Committee*, Cmd. 3851, April 1931.
30 John Dower, *A Brief Account of the National Parks Movement in England and Wales, September 1929 to December 1943*, December 1943, unpublished, in Dower Archives.

to say whether, and to what extent, the State can afford in the present difficult times to assist measures of this sort, neither can we gauge the amount of private contributions which might be forthcoming, though it is not unreasonable to hope that a well-conceived scheme for preserving the amenities of the more renowned areas in Great Britain might attract considerable offers of assistance from private sources.'[31]

Accordingly, the Committee put forward two options: (a) a *full* scheme, with the establishment of two executive National Park Commissions (one for England and Wales, and one for Scotland), estimated to require £100,000 a year; and (b) a *reduced* scheme run by the Ministry of Health and local authorities, with two advisory committees of 'laymen', estimated to require only £10,000 a year. The crucial difference between the two (apart from their respective budgets) was that in option (a) the proposed National Park Commissions would be at arms-length from the government and therefore could focus exclusively on the advancement and management of National Parks. Under option (b), protecting the countryside might well be sidelined in favour of other priorities set by central and local government.

Dower believed that this refusal to make a commitment 'seems to have been a last-minute adjustment in view of the economic crisis'.[32] This was undoubtedly true, and it reflected shifts in both national and departmental politics. Regardless of his personal commitment to National Parks, Ramsay MacDonald was severely weakened politically, and in April 1931 he was only a few months away from forming the Conservative-dominated National Government. Meanwhile Addison's political influence was waning after he had lined up in opposition to the Labour government's proposed dole cuts.

Into this vacuum stepped the Treasury. The responsibility for writing the draft final report was given to the Committee's Secretary, Mr Geoffrey Barnes, who just happened to be a Treasury official. And it was the Financial Secretary to the Treasury himself who on 23 April 1931 presented the report to Parliament.

---

31 *Report of the National Park Committee*, op. cit. para 65.
32 Dower, *op. cit.*

Despite the Conservative landslide in the October 1931 general election, Ramsay MacDonald remained Prime Minister, but of a National Government dominated by Conservative ministers. With Neville Chamberlain as the new Chancellor of the Exchequer, even option (b) of the Addison Report was deemed out of the question, let alone option (a). It was finally buried in February 1934, when the Minister of Health, Hilton Young, pronounced to the House of Commons its abandonment on the grounds of its 'low priority' in the face of the economic crisis.

Regrouping

Buried among Dower's papers is a yellowing, annotated copy of a short pamphlet written in June 1932 by the Conservative MP Harold Macmillan. *The Next Step: A Manifesto for a Planned Response to the Great Depression* was privately printed by Macmillan's own publishing company. It was a plea for the abandonment of *laissez-faire* in favour of radical state intervention to secure Britain's economic recovery. 'Whether we like it or not,' he wrote, 'we have entered a period in which planning – conscious direction, intelligent anticipation – is essential to national welfare and survival. Our task is to initiate a structure which will be responsive to these needs... A sufficient measure of centralisation and control must be achieved to enable the activities of separate industries to be brought into harmony with the objectives essential to national welfare and prosperity as a whole.'[33]

Five years earlier, in 1927, the thirty-three-year-old Macmillan and a few like-minded Tory MPs first set out their views on planning in a book entitled *Industry and the State: A Conservative View*. At that time its main focus was the need for *industrial* reform, but as the 1930s progressed Macmillan's views developed, so that by 1935 he was advocating a comprehensive approach to planning, based on varying levels of state intervention in economic, social,

---

33 Harold Macmillan, *The Next Step: A Manifesto for a Planned Response to the Great Depression,* Macmillan, 1932, p. 23.

environmental and international affairs.[34] Macmillan was in the vanguard of a broad cross-party and non-party movement whose supporters included JM Keynes, as well as bishops, intellectuals, the heads of Oxbridge colleges and trade union leaders, all demanding an end to government passivity in the face of mass unemployment and inequality.

One other key advocate of state planning was a twenty-six-year-old assistant editor of the *Weekend Review*, (Edward) Max Nicholson. In February 1931 he published a 20,000-word supplement to the *Review* entitled *A National Plan for Great Britain*. He followed this up with a dinner at The Ivy restaurant in London attended by a dozen influential figures from government, academia, finance and journalism. They jointly agreed to set up a new organisation to take responsibility for developing nothing less than a National Plan for Britain. At the end of March, the *Weekend Review* announced the formation of 'a Planning Society' (what today would be called a think-tank) to be called 'Political and Economic Planning' (PEP).[35] The first business of PEP, declared the *Review*, would be:

(a) to emphasise the need for National Planning, and
(b) to institute enquiry into selected aspects of the Plan by means of small study groups, covering:

• Reform of the machinery of government
• Self-government for industry
• Land-use and agriculture
• Town and regional planning
• Imperial and foreign trade relations
• Social services
• Finance

The results would be made public from time to time.

---

34 Harold Macmillan *et al, The Next Five Years: An Essay in Political Agreement*, Macmillan, 1935.
35 John Pinder, *Fifty Years of Political and Economic Planning: Looking Forward 1931-1981*, Heinemann, 1981, p. 6 ff.

At PEP's first general meeting on 29 June 1931, Sir Basil Blackett – an ex-Treasury official and a Director of the Bank of England – was appointed Chairman. Kenneth Lindsay, a social policy specialist and a future Labour – and subsequently, Independent – MP, was its first Secretary. Other members of the executive included Gerald Barry (editor of the *Weekend Review*); Sir Julian Huxley (biologist); Max Nicholson, and Leonard Elmhirst. Elmhirst was a millionaire (thanks to his American wife) and an agricultural economist who had set up the Dartington Trust to address economic and social problems in rural areas. The Trust provided considerable financial support to PEP over a number of years, and meetings of the PEP Executive were regularly held at Dartington Hall, Elmhirst's estate in South Devon.

In addition to his political talents, Nicholson was also a passionate and accomplished ornithologist. He had written *Birds in England* in 1926 while still an Oxford undergraduate, and while drafting his *National Plan for Great Britain,* he was also putting the finishing touches to a book entitled *The Art of Birdwatching.* Later, he helped found the World Wildlife Fund (WWF) and was to become the Director General of the future Nature Conservancy. His interest in natural history and the countryside married well with Elmhirst's rural concerns, and together they promoted a number of PEP studies and publications on agriculture, land management, forestry and food policy. Kenneth Lindsay observed that PEP's work in these areas 'preserved the balance of rural activity, with a largely London-based contingent'.[36]

During the 1930s, PEP published over 150 fortnightly issues of *Planning* (informally known as 'Broadsheets'), as well as fourteen longer reports. Each of the Broadsheets had a circulation of around 2,000 among an influential audience. Nicholson later observed that 'minds boggled at the acrobatic virtuosity with which (PEP) passed from one flying trapeze to another.'[37]

---

36 *Ibid,* p. 12.
37 EM Nicholson, *The System: The Mismanagement of Modern Britain,* Hodder and Stoughton, 1967, p. 49.

PEP had around 100 staff of 'working members' (paid and unpaid), as well as a network of some 300 leading figures in industry, government and the professions, many of whom contributed their knowledge and expertise 'off the record' as consultants (see Box 1). Around half of these were regular attendees to dinners and meetings in the PEP 'Club' at its headquarters at 16 Queen Anne's Gate in Westminster. Several were later recruited to government posts during the Second World War to work on plans for post-war reconstruction.

Box 1
Key Contributors to Work of PEP in the 1930s and 1940s[38]

- Leonard Elmhirst – Dartington Trust; Member of PEP Directorate; PEP Chair 1939
- Richard Fitter – Economist and naturalist, PEP staff 1936-40
- Arthur Greenwood – Member of War Cabinet, Minister without Portfolio 1940-42
- WG Holford – Professor of Town Planning, UCL, PEP Executive 1943-50
- Sir Julian Huxley – Founder Member, PEP Directorate
- Max Nicholson – Founder Member, PEP Directorate; Private Secretary to Deputy PM Herbert Morrison 1945-52.
- Lawrence Neal – Founder Member, PEP Directorate; Deputy Secretary Ministry of Town and Country Planning (MTCP) 1942-46
- Wyndham Raymond Portal – Minister of Works and Planning 1942-44
- Sir Stephen Tallents – Controller of Public Relations, BBC; Principal Assistant Secretary MTCP 1943-46
- Sir Geoffrey Whiskard – Member PEP Directorate and Executive; Permanent Secretary MTCP
  - John Dower (see below)

---

38 Pinder, *op. cit.*, pp. 201- 21.

Dower was understandably despondent following the government's lukewarm response to the Addison Report, but was determined to do something practical to advance the cause of rural planning in general, and National Parks in particular. PEP seemed to tick all the boxes: he was attracted by the land-use planning element in PEP's work programme; his analytical and writing skills and his attention to detail would be put to good use in drafting policy papers; he would be working with like-minded colleagues within a wider network of people with political influence; and the organisation was based in London.

From PEP's perspective, Dower could offer experience in several key areas of its work programme. As a qualified architect, he designed during the 1930s a number of working-class flats in Hackney, Shoreditch, King's Cross and Islington. He was critical of the way the Ministry of Health had approached the 'frontal attack' on slums and overcrowding, building blocks of flats that turned out to be 50 per cent more expensive than cottages of a similar size. At the same time, they were 'widely criticised as unpleasantly, sometimes intolerably, noisy; as unduly cramped in accommodation and limited in equipment; and thus in many material ways as less comfortable than cottages.' He designed improved 'demonstration' flats, and also called for the re-use of Georgian and Victorian terraces, moving away from multi-storey blocks to horizontally planned flats across three or four terraced houses.[39]

Dower designed several youth hostels in the Lakes, Northumberland and Yorkshire. He lectured in town planning in London at the Architectural Association and Regent Street Polytechnic, and at the University of Birmingham. He was also a consultant to planning authorities in Hertfordshire and Oxfordshire. On the basis of this experience, from 1933 to 1944 Dower wrote, or made a substantial contribution to, no fewer than sixteen issues of *Planning*, as well as a major report on housing in England

---

39 John Dower, 'Working Class Flats', in *Architect and Building News* (ABN), 24 September 1937, p. 361; and 'New Flats in Old Buildings', ABN, 5 November 1943, p. 87.

(see Box 2). Kenneth Lindsay described him as 'a devoted friend', and in recognition of his commitment and skills Dower was a made a member of PEP's Directorate as early as 1932.

Box 2 Towns and Industry
Dower's Contributions to PEP 'Broadsheets'

Date	Title	Edition
Town and Country Planning		
1933	Town and Country Planning	2
1935	Land and the Community	43
1938	The Planning of the Land	124
1938	Towns and Industry	125
1941	National Policy Towards the Land	181
Agriculture		
1933	Agriculture	8
1936	Grassland and Food Policy	77
1937	Agriculture's Part	97-99
Housing		
1934	Housing Survey	15
1934	Housing - Some Proposals	28
1934	Housing England	39
1937	Building and Housing Progress	107
1944	Old Houses	218
Recreation		
1942	Planning for Holidays	194

Support for farming and the farmer in Britain was top of Dower's list of personal priorities. Cheap imports of 'food, fodder and fertilizer' particularly from North and South America had depressed farm incomes in Britain, reduced investment in buildings and equipment, and in some areas led to land abandonment. In the spring of 1933 he drafted 'A Note on Agriculture', an outline of a proposed Broadsheet which he circulated to Leonard Elmhirst and other colleagues on the Directorate.[40] Dower's purpose was to:

- encourage 'land settlement' of unemployed urban workers in self-supporting smallholdings providing an adequate standard of living;
- help boost the production in Britain of food of improved quality, to meet the needs of an expanding population;
- ensure that good agricultural land was safeguarded from pressures from housing, industry, communications and the recreational needs of the non-agricultural population.

He believed that food from Britain's own resources would be of better quality than imported produce. It would also help address the balance of payments problem, while creating jobs for an estimated additional 300,000 agricultural workers. With dependents this could increase the rural population by around one million.

But Dower's concerns were as much spiritual as economic:

> Qualities born of agriculture and village life – the sense of land, of continuity and of inheritance, sympathy with nature and the slow marching seasons, craftsmanship, quietude, open-air health, and the moulding of living things – are more than ever essential in an age when the hurried, the mechanical, and the revolutionary are exploiting every human value and destroying every tradition in the industrialised life of the towns.

By September 1933 he had been made Secretary of the PEP Group on Land-Use Planning, in which capacity he drafted a proposal to set up a wider PEP Land Group. This

---

40 Pinder, *op. cit.*, p. 14.

had a broad and radical agenda. He suggested a number of subjects for study, including the limitations imposed on the Town and Country Planning system 'by the existing system of ownership etc; how far such limitations are damaging to present statutory planning – and would be to any desirable, more complete, planning system.'

Dower had already highlighted the weaknesses of the 1932 Town and Country Planning Act in a December 1932 memo 'Speeding up Town and Country Planning'.[41] This formed the basis of a PEP Broadsheet, 'Town and Country Planning', published in May 1933. It noted that the 1932 Act had made provision for the extension of local planning powers – including to potential National Park areas. The Ministry of Health (then the responsible government department) believed that these would be sufficient to achieve the objectives of National Parks policy – but without the administrative infrastructure proposed by Addison. 'In fact,' Dower wrote later, 'in the next three years and more, little or nothing was done by the local authorities concerned to justify the Ministry's hope: will and understanding were as deficient as resources and powers were inadequate.'[42] By 1 April 1933 the total acreage under government-approved rural planning schemes was just 1/250th of the total area of Britain. Dower calculated that it would take 400 years – until AD 2333 – before approved schemes would cover the whole country. 'Without wishing to belittle the efforts hitherto made,' he observed, sardonically, 'it is arguable that this rate of progress is not altogether satisfactory.'[43] He concluded:

> Recent history has shown that town and country planning in a *laissez faire* economy is an uphill task ... (it requires) a readiness to co-operate through common institutions if the bewildering number of separate interests – landowners, farmers, hikers, sportsmen, builders, residents, weekend visitors

---

41 PEP/PSI 12/73, 'Speeding up Town and Country Planning', 6 December 1932.
42 John Dower, *A Brief Account, op. cit.*
43 'Planning', *Town and Country Planning,* no. 2, 9 May 1933, PEP/PSI archives Section 17/1.

and so forth is to be reconciled by some middle course between anarchy on the one hand, or drastic negative restrictions on the other.

Dower had first-hand experience of the frustrations involved in trying to get local authorities to co-operate together to preserve the natural beauty of their shared regions. In 1931, before joining PEP, he had worked with Kenneth Spence and Patrick Abercrombie on a project to get the three Lakeland county councils – Lancashire, Cumberland and Westmorland – to draw up a joint regional plan for the Lakes. As a first step, separate surveys of each county and its problems were undertaken, highlighting the ways in which town and country planning could address them. Dower was responsible for covering the Furness Region of the southern Lakes in Lancashire, comprising the area bounded by the River Duddon, the Wrynose Pass, Windermere and the River Winster.[44]

However, the survey was only the first step. Far more difficult was getting the three councils to work together with CPRE and the Lake District National Reserve Committee (LDNRC) to establish a joint planning committee. Spence, like Dower, was impatient with the slowness of this 'bottom up' approach to regional planning. In the summer of 1931 in a bid to speed things up, he proposed to call a meeting of the three county councils to discuss setting up a single, regional planning committee. CPRE was lukewarm, however, arguing that local landowners would need to be involved as well – but first they had to be gently coached towards collaboration, not suddenly presented with a *fait accompli*. Already that year, the CPRE Executive had rejected Spence's call for a central organisation to campaign for National Parks and press for the implementation of the Addison Report.

Spence made clear his irritation at what he regarded as the procrastination of the more conservative CPRE. 'I

---

44 *The Lancashire Lake District: A Survey of the Furness Region with proposals for its Preservation and Development*, unpublished report in Friends of the Lake District Archive in Cumbria Records Office, Keswick – ref. WDSO 117/2/8/67.

am a little amused by your continual requests that you should not antagonise anyone,' he wrote to CPRE Secretary Herbert Griffin in October 1931. 'You must know that you and I both have our different methods, and what seems like antagonizing to you may only be getting on with the job to me, whereas getting on with the job to you may only seem like maintaining the *status quo* to a hard-bitten revolutionary like myself!'[45]

The delay in engaging with the county councils meant that they each began to develop their own separate plans, and they became increasingly reluctant to work together. After two more years of desultory meetings, it was clear that there would be no joint advisory committee bringing together the Lakeland county councils with CPRE and the LDRNC. All Dower's extensive work on the Lancashire Lakes seemed in vain. Spence was confirmed in his view that progress in the Lakes and other potential National Parks needed a 'top down' approach, supported by widespread public support and legislation. He considered that the LDNRC, with its membership confined to local and national *societies*, was not a suitable vehicle, and what was needed was a campaigning organisation based on *individual* membership, with the financial resources to make a difference. So in March 1934, plans were set in train to launch what was to become the Friends of the Lake District.[46]

---

45 Quoted in FR Sandbach, 'The Early Campaign for a National Park in the Lake District', in *Transactions of the Institute of British Geographers*, vol. 3, no. 4 (1978), p. 501.
46 John Cousins, *Friends of the Lake District: The Early Years*, Centre for North-West Regional Studies, Lancaster University, 2009, p. 30.

3. Activist

Beads of sweat were breaking on Dower's forehead as he lugged the large, heavy cardboard box through the hundreds of ramblers and their families picnicking in the hot June sunshine. He put the box down for a moment's pause, and with the River Greta behind him, looked north across the wide expanse of Fitz Park towards Skiddaw and Latrigg. How fortunate, he thought, for the residents of Keswick that fifty years ago these twenty-eight acres were saved by local philanthropists for the benefit of the town. And how appropriate that it should now host a gathering such as this. True, it was an urban rather than a National Park, but one that reflected a good piece of Lakeland's beauty.

With some effort he lifted the box again and made his way towards the makeshift stage where some of the speakers were already gathering. It was Sunday, 17 June 1934 – the hottest day of the summer so far – and hundreds of ramblers, youth hostellers and members of various amenity societies were gathering to celebrate the formal launch of the Friends of the Lake District (FLD). The event had been organised by Kenneth Spence, Secretary of the Lake District National Reserve Committee (LDNRC), together with the local Youth Hostels Association (YHA) and Ramblers' group.

Inside the cardboard box were 1,500 copies of a leaflet introducing the FLD, which Dower himself had helped draft and design. It was endorsed by an impressive list of signatories – a *Who's Who* of most of the key players in the countryside movement – GM Trevelyan and his brother Sir Charles, Patrick Abercrombie, the Revd. HH Symonds, Sir Norman Birkett, Professor RS Chorley (Hon. Secretary of CPRE), Lawrence Chubb (of the Commons, Open Spaces and Footpaths Society), TA Leonard (Chair of the National Council of Ramblers' Federations), and Evelyn Sharp (later to become Permanent Secretary of the Ministry of Town and Country Planning). Geoffrey Winthrop Young (joint founder with GM Trevelyan of the Lakes Hunt) and Gordon Wordsworth (a descendant of William) also expressed their support. Prime Minister Ramsay MacDonald had sent a letter of good wishes: 'Such gatherings are greatly to be commended,' he wrote. 'They encourage even larger numbers of people to seek out the loveliness of unspoilt country...' Lord Baden Powell, the founder of the Scout movement, was rather more prosaic in his note. 'You ramblers are lucky beggars. I wish I could be with you...' And as if to demonstrate the formidable sources of influence available to the FLD, an ecumenical service was conducted by the vicar of St John's Church, Keswick, alongside representatives of both the local Methodist and Congregational Churches.[47]

The leaflet spelled out the aims of the new organisation:

- to press for the implementation of the Addison Report, insofar as it concerned the Lake District – and in particular to demand a unified policy for the district as a whole;
- to campaign for the full use of those powers already existing in the 1932 Town and Country Planning Act;
- to create a fund for local authorities to provide compensation when otherwise valuable land needed to be preserved for agriculture, or as a public open space.

Spence was convinced that the LDNRC had been hampered by restricting its membership to local and national societies, when what was needed was a campaigning organisation with a mass membership of individuals to influence public opinion and raise money. Hence the minimum subscription was to be set at a modest two shillings and sixpence (12.5p) to encourage the widest national appeal, particularly among young people.

From the platform, Sir Charles Trevelyan acted as chair and introduced the speakers from among the signatories to the leaflet. He stressed the urgency of ensuring that the Lake District became Britain's first National Park. Just a few weeks before, three northern lakes – Buttermere, Crummock Water

---

47 *The Lake District Herald*, 23 June 1934, p. 6.

and Loweswater – had come up for sale. 'It would have been an awful thought,' Sir Charles told the crowd, 'that the loveliness of Buttermere might be changed to a shore dotted with red-roofed bungalows... You can never replace lost wildness, and you can only slowly recreate perished beauty.'[48] Fortunately, on this occasion the National Trust had been able to step in and buy them for the nation.

Notable by his absence at the rally was CPRE Secretary, Herbert Griffin. He opposed the creation of the Friends of the Lake District because of its close association with what he considered as the left-leaning youth movement, and the threat it presented to the leadership of the establishment-oriented CPRE. It was only two years before, in April 1932, that the mass trespass on Kinder Scout in the Derbyshire Peak District by 400 young ramblers had sparked an upsurge of direct action in the Peak and elsewhere. It had been organised by twenty-year-old Benny Rothman from the British Workers' Sports Federation, an appendage of the Communist Party. He and four others were jailed for between two and six months for incitement to cause a riotous assembly, and in one case for occasioning actual bodily harm to a gamekeeper.

In late June 1932, an estimated 10,000 ramblers had turned out at nearby Winnats Pass, demonstrating for an Access to the Mountains Bill. One of the principal speakers at the rally was writer, broadcaster and serial trespasser CEM (Cyril) Joad, who just a few weeks before had joined in the Hunt at Seatoller alongside his friends Dower and Spence. Although not directly encouraging ramblers to break the law, as a socialist he made it quite clear where his sympathies lay. He published the gist of his speech later in his book *A Charter for Ramblers*.[49]

> Our civilisation thinks it more important that rich men should have unhampered opportunities for the slaughter of birds than that its citizens should be given access to the heritage of natural

---

48 *Ibid.*
49 CEM Joad, *A Charter for Ramblers*, Hutchinson, 1934, p. 71.

loveliness which is theirs, and which is England;
more important that the 'rights' of its propertied
classes should be protected than that the spiritual
health of its citizens should be preserved… Grant
that country sights and sounds, moorland air, the
exercise of walking, the opportunity for occasional
solitude are goods; grant too that the welfare of its
workers is a matter of concern to the community for
which they labour, and the inference is inescapable
– they should be given access to the moors as their
playground…

Following Kinder Scout, two further mass trespasses
occurred in Derbyshire, the second of which was halted
by mounted police with Alsatian dogs. And in southern
England, fifty busloads of ramblers turned out for a protest
rally on Leith Hill in Surrey. 'This upsurge of direct action
in the Peak and elsewhere,' writes countryside historian
Marion Shoard, 'turned pent-up frustration into a significant
political force.'[50]

Yet many others in the countryside and access
movement distanced themselves from the mass trespass. The
Manchester and District Ramblers' Federation emphasised
publicly that it had 'no connection whatsoever with the
organisation of the rally'. Sir Lawrence Chubb wrote to the
Secretary of the National Council of Ramblers' Federations
complaining that 'it had been a peculiarly stupid and
mischievous business and those arrested should rightly face
the consequences of their foolhardiness.' Philip Daley, a
member of the Ramblers' Association's National Executive
(and later its chairman) wrote: 'Such access as we have gained
owes nothing whatsoever to the mass trespass organised by
the BWSF [British Workers' Sports Federation] (which was)
a positive hindrance and deterrent to the discussions and
negotiations to secure the freedom of the hills.'[51]

---

50 Marion Shoard, *A Right to Roam*, Oxford University Press,
    1999, p. 182.
51 Tom Stephenson, *Forbidden Land: The Struggle for Access to
    Mountain and Moorland*, Manchester University Press, 1989,
    pp. 162-3.

Despite such protestations, people like Herbert Griffin still considered that national campaigning and demonstrating to influence public opinion, as espoused by the FLD, was but a small step from lawlessness, and one which antagonised the landowners, politicians and government departments with whom CPRE was seeking to engage quietly behind closed doors. This fundamental difference of view – most marked between Griffin and Spence – was to lead to a complete breakdown in relations between the two organisations, which came to head over their respective responses to afforestation in the Lake District. John Dower had long-standing relationships with the leading figures in both organisations and sought to act as an honest broker between them. Living in Hampstead Garden Suburb, he was somewhat detached from Spence and Symonds 300 miles away in the Lakes, while at the same time near enough to meet Griffin face to face in central London. But it was still an uncomfortable position to be in, and his perspiration in Fitz Park at the launch of the FLD may not have been the result just of the heatwave alone.

Afforestation in the Lake District

Charles Trevelyan was right about the urgency of the situation. Just six months after his speech at the launch of the FLD, it was revealed that the Forestry Commission had bought the Hardknott Estate – some 7,240 acres in the valleys of Eskdale and Dunnerdale – with the intention of growing Sitka spruce on the 2,100 acres which it regarded as economically 'plantable'. Under the 1919 Forestry Act, it was the job of the Forestry Commission (FC) to boost supplies of home-grown timber. In 1932, a new Chairman of the FC was appointed. He was Sir Roy Robinson, an Australian and a former Rhodes scholar who was 'ambitious and energetic and ruthless in the prosecution of his task, which he saw primarily as the establishment of great new forests ... rapidly clothing huge areas of the hills of Britain...'[52] Robinson was encouraged by the fact that the FC

<hr>

52 John Gaze, *Figures in a Landscape: A History of the National Trust,* Barrie and Jenkins in association with the National Trust, 1987, pp. 118-9.

was given the additional task of creating jobs in Britain's most depressed 'Special Areas'. The government's Special Areas Commissioner had asked the Commission to plant an extra 200,000 acres in these areas, thus creating some 2,200 jobs. The Special Areas Commissioner had powers of compulsory purchase to secure land that he considered particularly suitable for afforestation. In north-west England, a grant of £100,000 per year for five years was made available for planting within a fifteen-mile radius of the depressed area of West Cumberland. Unfortunately, this took in about two-thirds of the entire Lake District.

The Forestry Commission already owned two large areas of Lakeland, in Ennerdale and the Whinlatter Pass. These had been planted taking little account of the beauty of the surrounding landscape, and in view of its record, the local CPRE and the Friends of the Lake District now demanded a halt to all afforestation in Eskdale and Dunnerdale. An offer by the Friends of the Lake District to buy the estate and preserve it for its existing beauty and uses was, however, turned down.

GM Trevelyan, chairman of the National Trust's Estates Committee and an owner and donor of thousands of acres of Lakeland, chose to embark on some private negotiations with Sir Roy, with a view to reaching a 'gentleman's agreement'. GMT's intervention was not entirely disinterested, for he wished to preserve the sanctity of the Langdale Valley. Here he owned a cottage, Robin Ghyll, where he could work and walk against one of the most glorious mountain backdrops in England. Even more important, it was close to where his beloved five-year-old son, Theo, had been buried almost a quarter of a century before, after his sudden death from appendicitis.

By the end of January 1935, GMT had secured an understanding that the Forestry Commission would refrain from planting an area of 100 square miles in the central Lakes, and would consult him before planting in Wasdale Head, or the wooded area between Ullswater and Windermere. In return, the National Trust would offer the Forestry Commission a relatively free hand on the fringes.[53]

---

53 *Ibid*, p. 119.

Trevelyan strongly recommended this agreement to the NT's Executive in mid-February 1935, but Professor Chorley – the Trust's representative on CPRE – insisted that there should be no decision without wider consultation, and subsequently lobbied Herbert Griffin of CPRE to become involved. The Forestry Commission wanted CPRE's support for public relations purposes, while CPRE saw itself playing the leading role nationally in addressing the increasing number of conflicts between the FC and local amenity interests. Robinson therefore agreed to the creation of a Joint Informal Committee of FC and CPRE representatives, chaired by Robinson himself, to deal with all matters relating to reconciling amenity with afforestation. The CPRE delegation on the Joint Committee included Sir Lawrence Chubb from the Commons, Open Spaces and Footpaths Society, as well as GM Trevelyan for the National Trust. The Friends of the Lake District, however, were excluded, and the FC was to discontinue all communication with what it regarded as 'a group of feckless and impossible romantics'.[54]

Despite the snub, Dower continued to work with CPRE behind the scenes, while Spence and Symonds made as much noise as possible about the affair in public. Dower was caught between his radical heart and the pillars of the Establishment to which he was now related. He did have some successes: when the Forestry Commission made some minor concessions, CPRE asked the Friends of the Lake District to prepare a report on their proposals. Dower's contribution was to draw up 'Red Line' maps demarcating the areas that *should* be preserved, and these were subsequently used in the Joint Committee as a basis for negotiations. In contrast to GM Trevelyan's 100-square-mile central exclusion zone, Dower proposed 520 square miles, with no planting at all in Eskdale or Dunnerdale. The Friends of the Lake District's report as a whole was uncompromising, with Spence threatening to issue a petition and raise the matter

---

54 HH Symonds, *Afforestation in the Lake District: A Reply to the Forestry Commission's White Paper of 26 August 1936*, JM Dent, 1936, p. 23.

in the House of Lords if the Forestry Commission failed to withdraw entirely from Eskdale.

It soon became clear to Dower and the Friends of the Lake District that CPRE and the other national organisations were willing to make damaging concessions. CPRE feared that all-out opposition to local planting in Eskdale would endanger a wider agreement in the Lake District and elsewhere. So on 18 July 1935 an impatient FLD carried out its threat and launched its petition. It read:

We, the undersigned, being some of us residents in the English Lake District, and all of us lovers of it and able to speak with knowledge of its beauty, wish to express our earnest hope that the Forestry Commission will reconsider its decision to proceed with the afforestation of Eskdale and Dunnerdale. We desire also to affirm our conviction that any further extension within the heart of the Lake District of afforestation such as that which has already taken place on the slopes of the Whinlatter Pass and in Ennerdale would do most serious damage to the landscape of a region unique in England and having unparalleled claims to be considered an inviolable national heritage.

The CPRE delegation on the Joint Committee refused to support the petition, and issued a joint press statement with the Forestry Commission to this effect. Thereafter, the relationship between CPRE and the FLD broke down completely. Griffin resigned from the FLD executive and tried to revive the moribund Lake District Safeguarding Society as a rival to it, and Spence was ousted as its (nominal) Secretary. In response, HH Symonds resigned from the Lancashire branch of CPRE.[55] Fortunately the polarisation was not total, for Dower and Chorley sought quietly to mediate between the two sides behind the scenes.

<hr>

55 *Ibid*, pp. xv-xxi. See also FR Sandbach, 'The Early Campaign for a National Park in the Lake District', in *Transactions of the Institute of British Geographers*, vol. 3, no. 4 (1978) pp. 498-514.

In October 1935, the petition – with no fewer than 13,000 signatures – was presented to the Forestry Commission, Prime Minister Ramsay MacDonald, and to a number of Cabinet Ministers. It was later described in the House of Lords as 'one of the most remarkable documents that can have been presented for many years to a Government department'.[56] The signatories were a roll-call of the great and the good, and included:

- The Archbishop of York and ten bishops;
- The Lords Lieutenant of Cumberland, Westmorland and Lancashire;
- Several Members of Parliament and members of the three county councils;
- The Vice Chancellors of six universities;
- Eight heads of Oxford and Cambridge colleges;
- Twenty-one professors and thirty-nine fellows of Oxbridge colleges (including John Maynard Keynes);
- The headmasters of fourteen leading public schools from all parts of Britain;
- The chairmen and officers of all of Britain's open air organisations.[57]

With such overwhelming support, it was not surprising that the conflict should reach the House of Lords. On 1 April 1936, a resolution in the name of Lord Howard of Penrith (the President of the Friends of the Lake District) called upon the government to set up a select committee of Lords to consider whether the Forestry Commission should be instructed to stop further purchases of land for afforestation within sensitive areas like the Lake District. In the meantime, it should suspend all further planting in Eskdale and Dunnerdale, except for those parts already covered by the current year's operations.

But Dower was uncomfortable with this confrontational approach, fearing it would drive a further wedge between the FLD and CPRE, and jeopardise last-chance talks with the

---

56 Lord Elton in House of Lords debate, 1 April 1936, *Hansard*, vol. 100, cols. 363-405.
57 Symonds, *op. cit.*, pp. 79-92.

Forestry Commission. He wrote to Lord Howard suggesting that the Lords' debate should be called off – but to no avail.

Bizarrely, it was the Secretary of State for India, the Marquis of Zetland, who replied to the debate for the government. As an arms-length agency, the Forestry Commission had no sponsoring Cabinet minister, and the Marquis, as a former Chairman of the National Trust, was considered the most appropriate individual to do the job. He was adamant that the government would not intervene, nor would it establish a Select Committee, since the matter would be best settled by continuing negotiations in the Joint Informal Committee. Already the Forestry Commission had agreed to plant 'with due consideration to the contours of the hillside'. He concluded: 'I think it is reasonable to say that the Forestry Commissioners have, so far as they can, met the demands of those who wish to preserve intact the amenities of the Eskdale Valley.' The chairman of CPRE, Lord Crawford, agreed with him and supported the Forestry Commission.

Throughout April 1936, many and weighty letters to *The Times* and other newspapers protested against the attitude of the Forestry Commission, and the government's inactivity. Buoyed by this demonstration of public support, and with its membership now exceeding 2,000 (twice that of CPRE), the Friends of the Lake District demanded a last-ditch summit meeting between the petitioners and the Forestry Commissioners. On 16 June 1936 a twenty-seven-strong deputation led by the Archbishop of York – including Dower, Spence and Symonds – gathered at the Commission's headquarters. They reaffirmed their demand that there should be no planting at all in Eskdale, and in Dunnerdale 'as much as possible' should be left unplanted. But in a bid to secure a compromise the FLD reduced its demands in relation to the central exclusion zone in the heart of Lakeland. Now they would accept a minimum area of 390 square miles, provided it was safeguarded by the state, and guaranteed as a protected area. This was a considerable reduction from its initial demand for 520 square miles, but at the same time such an initiative would have introduced national state planning to protect the countryside – a National Park by the back door.

Predictably, the Forestry Commission refused all three demands. The end of the battle was marked by the publication of a slim, five-page White Paper in late August 1936.[58] It set out the Commission's final decision – which had shifted hardly at all from its position of a year previously:

- In Eskdale, some 440 acres of otherwise plantable land would be excluded from the planting scheme, but only in return for compensation of £2 per acre;
- In the central Lake District, a block of 'about' 300 square miles would be excluded from afforestation (see colour map, p. ii). However, it was stressed this was only a *voluntary* restriction on acquiring land in this area. 'It is necessary to make the position clear because it has been suggested that something analogous to 'country planning' has been accomplished and that the rights of the owners of private property might be affected in some way';[59]
- The area south and south-west of this main block – the shaded area from the west bank of Windermere to include Coniston Water, Dunnerdale down to Ulpha, and Eskdale from Scafell to beyond Boot – would still be eligible for planting. The White Paper noted that 'the Commissioners cannot, without prejudicing the task set them by the Government, refrain from planting in this section if land becomes available.' However, the Commission would continue to consult with the Joint Informal Committee, and 'special attention' would be paid to amenity, through some planting of broadleaf woodlands.

The upshot was that the Forestry Commission would proceed with planting some 80 per cent of the plantable land in the Hardknott Estate, including much of Eskdale and all of Dunnerdale.

---

58 Forestry Commission, *Afforestation in the Lake District: Report by the Joint Informal Committee of the Forestry Commission and the Council for the Preservation of Rural England*, HMSO, 1936.
59 *Ibid*, p. 5.

As a matter of form, the CPRE representatives registered their 'disagreement' with the Forestry Commission's decision in regard to the 'shaded' areas in the south, but their opposition stopped well short of outright rejection. On the contrary, the White Paper reported that 'the CPRE are of the opinion that the arrangements are fair and reasonable as regards the whole of the west, north and east boundaries.'

The Friends of the Lake District may have lost the fight, but the smoke of the battle lingered on. At the end of September 1936, twelve members of the June FLD deputation – including Dower – signed a tart letter to *The Times* pointing out that the areas omitted from the central exclusion zone were 'among the most beautiful parts of the Lake District, and we cannot possibly accept as satisfactory a southern boundary for the protected area which does not include them.'[60] Moreover, the petitioners insisted that far from being 'fair and reasonable', the eastern boundary excluded the whole valley of Mardale and Haweswater, and 'the fine valley head of Long Sleddale'. The signatories also noted that there were alternative areas of plantable land available for job creation, much nearer to unemployment black spots than the Lake District.

GM Trevelyan was quick to defend CPRE's settlement. A brusque riposte in *The Times* on 1 October went to the heart of the conflict with the Friends of the Lake District. 'Never was the Lake District in such danger,' he wrote. 'The Forestry Commissioners could, by too rigid an interpretation of their instructions, have turned the greater part of the Lake District into a conifer forest like the shores of Thirlmere. But instead of using these powers so, the Commissioners have pledged themselves to leave the heart of the Lake District alone... The best way by which the interests of amenity can receive attention in this matter is the continuance of the present friendly co-operation between the Forestry Commission and the representatives of the CPRE on the Joint Committee...'[61]

---

60 *The Times*, 28 September 1936, p. 8.
61 *The Times*, 1 October 1936, p. 13.

The Standing Committee on National Parks

Conflict over planting in the Lake District was not the only *casus belli* between CPRE and the Friends of the Lake District. It also reflected fundamental rivalry over the wider issue of who should take the lead on National Parks policy in general.

On Saturday 30 November 1935, representatives of all the open air organisations who had given evidence to the Addison Committee gathered in Central Hall, Westminster to consider what further action could be taken to secure the establishment of National Parks. Crucially, the meeting of this new *ad hoc* Joint Committee of Open-Air Organisations was convened not by CPRE, but by Spence, Symonds and Dower. They were taking advantage of the strength of popular support reflected in the Friends of the Lake District's petition to advance their long-held objective of establishing a national, state organisation exclusively focused on identifying and managing National Parks.[62]

It was John Dower who drafted the keynote pamphlet – *National Parks: An Appeal* – which was widely distributed before the conference. Patrick Abercrombie gave the opening speech attacking the government's position that local councils – not a new national authority – should have responsibility for implementing schemes for countryside protection. He pointed out that they had neither the planning expertise, nor the money to pay compensation to affected landowners. Clough Williams-Ellis from the CPRW demanded a meeting with the new Prime Minister Stanley Baldwin – 'the Stanley Baldwin who is a keen supporter of the National Trust, not the one who refuses to find money to preserve the beauty of the countryside'. The Revd. HH Symonds proposed that the maintenance of National Parks could be paid for by part of the revenue of the Crown Lands. In the end, the conference voted unanimously to establish 'a National Parks Conference Standing Committee' to lobby for a National Parks Authority, and to secure the more ambitious of the two options set out in the Addison Report.

---

62 Sandbach, *op. cit.*, pp.510-11.

Both the Chairman and the Secretary of CPRE – Lord Crawford and HG Griffin – were adamantly opposed to the establishment of this new umbrella organisation. They feared it would lead to the break-up of CPRE – and anyway it was unnecessary since CPRE was 'satisfactorily dealing' with the National Parks issue. Griffin fired off a vituperative letter to Abercrombie for having participated in the conference – despite the fact that he was currently its Honorary Secretary, and had initiated the creation of CPRE in the first place.

Abercrombie replied more in sorrow than anger. He had participated in the Central Hall meeting 'in order to keep extremists within bounds'. It was not true, he insisted, that CPRE was the only body that could handle the National Parks issue – its Scottish and Welsh counterparts, the National Trust and the Commons and Open Spaces society would all demand a leading role, as well as the smaller open air organisations. So there was a need for co-ordinated action. 'I believe there is a very real danger that rival organisations may come into being which will immensely weaken the whole movement.' He concluded: 'I had better resign from the Hon. Sec. of the CPRE. I shall take no action … in future in rural preservation but apply myself to the equally urgent problem of urban reconstruction. It is a grief to me that … I should find myself thus forced to divide from you – but I have always tried to steer a middle course between extremists – you and Spence (as symbols!) – and the result is fatal.'[63] But behind the scenes Abercrombie and Dower continued to work together to avoid a complete rift. They offered the startling concession that CPRE should take over the administration of the new organisation – now called the 'Standing Committee on National Parks' (SCNP).

*

---

63 Letter from Abercrombie to Griffin, 18 December 1935, in CPRE archives CPRE C/1/78 no. 109, Museum of English Rural Life, University of Reading.

The SCNP brought together no fewer than twenty-one open air organisations under the chairmanship of distinguished lawyer and Ulverstone-born Sir Norman Birkett. At its formal launch on 26 May 1936, the SCNP's thirty-four-member Executive Committee included a disproportionately large representation – eight – from CPRE and CPRW. An Executive of this size was too cumbersome for day to day administration, so an inner cabinet of seven 'with executive powers' was created, comprising Sir Norman Birkett (Chairman); Patrick Abercrombie; John Dower (also the Hon. Drafting Secretary); HH Symonds; Kenneth Spence; Julian Huxley; and JA Southern. The balance had been more than redressed: four of the members of the inner cabinet held posts with the FLD, while Birkett was later to become the Friends of the Lake District's President.

Predictably, the issue of representation sparked off yet another ill-tempered spat between Spence and Griffin, this time on the related question of who should represent the FLD on CPRE. Spence had discovered that behind the scenes Griffin had tried to ensure that it wasn't him. Spence wrote on 4 June that 'it is only another of the many instances you have given lately, not only of antagonism with the objects and the efforts of the Friends of the Lake District, but of doing everything by fair means (and I do not think I would be far wrong in adding 'foul means') of belittling and stultifying our work... I have heard enough from different sources to make me utterly disgusted with what you are doing, and the way you are doing it.'

Two days later, Griffin replied:

Dear Spence

I received your strange letter this morning, and am inclined to pin it up in the office, so that it may be read with the contempt that it deserves...

For some time past, although the Friends of the Lake District is an affiliated body to the CPRE, you have ceased to keep me informed of action taken, or contemplated, by the Friends in matter(s) in which we are mutually interest(ed) – in fact, you appear to be a law unto yourself in these matters; when it suits you to make use of the machinery of the CPRE you do so just as any other local Branch or affiliated organisation; when it doesn't suit you, you assume the role of a national body, and take your own line. You do not seem to appreciate the difficulties to which such a procedure gives rise...

It is you, not I, who have ceased to be frank, and since plain speaking appears to be justified by your offensive remarks, it is high time someone told you, without any beating about the bush, that you have made yourself so amazingly unpopular that you are rapidly becoming a positive handicap to any organisation with which you are associated...

You won't like this letter any more than I liked yours, but you asked for it, and I am afraid that, regrettable as it may be, I am not made of the stuff that turns the other cheek with any good grace...

Yours faithfully...[64]

*

The campaign for National Parks in Britain moved up several gears with the launch of the Standing Committee. For the first time, there was a well-resourced, broad-based national pressure group dedicated to that single objective. Its twenty-one constituent bodies – ranging from the National Trust and CPRE, to the Pedestrians Association and the Wild Plants Conservation Board – represented thousands of people across Britain committed to the protection and enjoyment of the countryside.[65] And the new organisation was led by experienced campaigners under the efficient chairmanship of Sir Norman Birkett. From May 1936 to the outbreak of war in 1939 it ran a textbook campaign aimed at influencing public opinion, the press, MPs and government ministers.

---

64 Correspondence between HG Griffin and Kenneth Spence, CPRE, *op. cit.*, C/1/78 no. 109.
65 See Box 3, p. 60.

Box 3
Standing Committee on National Parks:
Constituent Bodies

Council for the Preservation of Rural England
Council for the Preservation of Rural Wales
National Trust
Commons, Open Spaces and Footpaths Society
Ramblers' Association
Pedestrians' Association
Cyclists' Touring Club
Royal Automobile Club
Automobile Association
Geographical Association
Alpine Club
Fell and Rock Climbing Club
Camping Club
Youth Hostels Association
Holiday Fellowship
Co-operative Holidays Association
Society for the Promotion of Nature Reserves
Wild Plants Conservation Board
Royal Society for the Protection of Birds
Zoological Society
Society for the Preservation of Fauna of the Empire

The SCNP's first milestone came in December 1936, when a sympathetic Liberal MP, Geoffrey Mander, introduced a motion in the House of Commons urging the government to implement the Addison Committee's full scheme. Remarkably, this was agreed without a division, but even so the Parliamentary Secretary to the Minister of Health, RS Hudson, stuck to the government's line that action by local authorities and voluntary bodies was sufficient, and there would be no specific machinery or extra finance available from the government. Subsequent face to face meetings with the Minister, and with the new Chancellor of the Exchequer Sir John Simon, drew the same response.

Dower had played a key role both in developing the SCNP's influencing strategy, and in drafting its campaign literature. In early 1937 he drew up a statement of National Parks requirements, backed by a considerable mass of evidence on damage and threats to potential National Park areas, and on the inadequacy of existing town and country planning to prevent them. In July 1938 he then wrote what was in effect a detailed manifesto for the Standing Committee – *The Case for National Parks in Great Britain* – of which 40,000 copies were distributed over the following twelve months.[66] This was a radical document going considerably further than the Addison Committee proposals, in particular in relation to the future powers of the National Park 'Commissions' (for England and Wales, and Scotland respectively) in relation to the policies and activities of other government departments and agencies.

'It should be the function and the right of the National Park Commissions,' he wrote, 'to examine in advance all such proposals which may seem likely to involve any interference with the landscape beauty or accessibility of potential National Park areas, to consult on an equal footing with the responsible bodies, to co-ordinate their activities, and – where necessary – to refer any matter in dispute for a considered decision by the Government as a whole... Only in extreme circumstances and with the specific sanction of Parliament should any substantial encroachment by a Department or statutory body be permitted in an established National Park.'[67]

On the vexed question of finance, he declared:

There is no need to justify the use of national resources for a purpose so obviously of vital service to the nation at large. The Treasury provides without comment more than £200,000 per year for the maintenance alone of London's Crown Parks; surely it should be ready to provide at least as large

---

66 Standing Committee on National Parks, *The Case for National Parks in Great Britain*, July 1938.

67 *Ibid*, p. 12.

an annual sum for the creation and maintenance of a system of National Parks distributed over the country.[68]

Widespread publicity continued during 1938, including exhibitions of National Parks photographs, and a National Parks film by CPRE entitled *Rural England: The Case for the Defence*. This was shown in more than 900 cinemas across the country, and was well reviewed by both the BBC and *The Sunday Times*. But any hope of early government action was dashed as the international situation darkened and rearmament moved to the top of the government's spending priorities. More in hope than expectation, Dower drafted a *Summary of Proposed Provisions for a National Parks Bill* in early 1939, and plans were made for a proposed House of Lords debate. However, in view of the progressive deterioration of international affairs it became impracticable to proceed with these or other parliamentary and public events, and there was to be no further significant activity by the SCNP until the summer of 1941.

---

68 *Ibid*, p. 10.

4. 'A Menace to All I Valued'

The mist was beginning to clear as they half-walked, half-jogged up the Simonside Hills towards the viewpoint at Ravensheugh. When they reached the rocky outcrop, 1,400 feet above sea level, Dower pulled off his small rucksack and settled back against the smoothest boulder he could find. He turned his back to the wind, and with some difficulty lit his pipe, and silently surveyed the familiar Northumberland landscape spread out before them – Rothbury and Coquetdale immediately below, with the Cheviot Hills just visible in the distance. From here, they would easily pick out the red sashes of the hares moving across the moors beneath.

The Whitsun Hunt in 1937 was the occasion for a special celebration. To mark its fortieth year, Charles Trevelyan had invited all previous 'hunters' to Wallington, and a record forty-two took part. After the greeting, feasting and speeches, the younger hunters were driven to the north of the estate to replicate in Simonside the usual annual chase through Lakeland. The five who had first hunted before 1903 were, understandably, excused.

Dower's companion, quietly eating a sandwich on an adjacent rock, was Archie Nye, a forty-two-year-old Lieutenant Colonel in the War Office. He was a modest man who had enlisted in the ranks in 1914, gained a commission and a Military Cross during the war, and was clearly destined for higher things.

'Do you think there's any way we can avoid a war, Archie?' Dower asked, suddenly, breaking the silence. Nye looked up from his reverie, startled, and paused before he answered.

'Well, Hitler certainly doesn't want to avoid one. In the past year or so we've had the German re-occupation of the Rhineland, German rearmament, his alliance with Mussolini, and the brutal interventions in the Spanish Civil War. And no-one doubts there's more to come.'

'I used to think,' answered Dower, 'that we could avoid

conflict provided Britain and France set about re-arming at once, on the largest scale, so that they could stand out unequivocally as champions of the next threatened country. Not anymore. The Tories have dawdled along with a completely inadequate rearmament programme, and seem bent only on postponing the evil day, no matter how much Hitler and Mussolini gain in the meantime.'

'Yes, and as for the Labour Party,' Nye responded, 'now they're demanding tough action on any and every front, conveniently forgetting our current military weakness, which they themselves have contributed to. It's only Churchill and a few others who have got any clear view of the dangers and what needs to be done, but they've got little prospect of power.'

Dower nodded, oblivious to the brief glimpse of a red sash moving swiftly down the mountain a hundred feet below. 'This is our fault – mine, as well as our friends and acquaintances. We've known what the situation is, but we've done little or nothing about it. We've been immersed in our peacetime jobs. I've been more and more absorbed in Britain's internal problems – housing, town and country planning, depressed areas, farmland improvement, open air recreation – giving less and less attention to foreign and military affairs.

'Archie, I've come to the point where I'm sure there will be a war – and I want to play my part. I've been wondering – has the War Office got any scheme for enrolling people like me against a future emergency, selecting in advance the square pegs for the square holes, as it were? With my architectural background, I could certainly help with – say – the building and repair of military bases, defences and airfields. What do you think?'

Nye looked at his friend with a mixture of admiration and concern. He knew that Dower meant what he said – after all, he had enrolled in the closing months of the First World War for the Officer Cadet Battalion of the Royal Engineers, but then the armistice had intervened before he could fire a shot. But now? He was thirty-seven, married with two small children and with poor eyesight. If he chose, he could avoid fighting in a future war altogether. Nye thought for a moment as he stood up. 'Well, as it happens I think there is a new scheme that's currently being developed. If the papers are ready I'll send them to you as soon as I get back to London. But we need to talk more about this.'

Later that afternoon Dower and Nye, weary and hot, were making their way down to the Crown and Thistle at Forestburn Gate when they caught up with fellow hunter, Cyril Joad. Joad was short, rather portly and tweedy, and Britain's best known 'radio philosopher'.[69] He had been attending the Hunt since 1922, but now at the age of forty-six his powers as a runner had declined in inverse proportion to the expansion of his waistband. Rather like Longpast in his semi-autobiographical book *Folly Farm*, he 'had been in his later years particularly addicted to "soliquots" (quotas of solitude), alleging that a day's solitude in grand scenery followed by a hearty social evening passed with a score of beer-drinking, chorus-singing men, wedged together in a little parlour at the back of a hotel, was a way of passing the time as near perfection as man was entitled to wish for in his life.'[70] Joad was a *bon viveur* and wit, and also a dedicated socialist, rambler and pacifist. He was Chairman of the National Peace Campaign, the co-ordinating body for all the peace and pacifist groups in Britain.

'Ah Cyril – had a good day's hunting?' Dower asked, with more than a touch of good-natured sarcasm. 'Let me introduce Archie Nye – I don't think you've met before.' This was true, but both men knew all about each other's CV.

'We've been up there on Simonside talking about the future of the world – or more precisely, whether a war against the dictators is unavoidable,' said Nye. Joad's smile faded as he began to rehearse the speech he had made dozens of times before:

'Well, my case is that:
• prodigious armaments are not a means of safety in the future, and do not form a hopeful basis for negotiations

---

69 Tony Judge, *Radio Philosopher: The Radical Life of Cyril Joad*, Alpha House, 2012.
70 CEM Joad, *Folly Farm*, Faber & Faber, 1954, p. 108.

with Germany in the present;
- war is not something that is inevitable, but the result of
certain man-made circumstances; and man who made
the circumstances in which wars flourish, can abolish
them, as he abolished the circumstances in which
plagues flourished;
- man is a reasonable being, and that, if arguments of
sufficient weight are brought to bear upon him, and
brought with sufficient frequency, then he can be
induced to abolish war.'

Dower said nothing, and was not convinced. He rather
suspected that neither was Joad.

*

Back in Hampstead a few days later, Dower signed the
declaration at the bottom of the application forms, just
a few hours after he had received them. 'I hereby give an
honourable undertaking,' he pledged, 'that I will accept
service under the War Department on or after general
mobilization, if called upon to do so.' His was among the
very early – if not the first – batch of volunteers for the
Officers' Emergency Reserve, and he offered himself for 'any
position for which my qualifications seem suitable'. These
included his training as an army cadet; experience in the
design and construction of houses and civilian aerodromes
(including those in Germany); and a good knowledge of
French. There was little doubt that he would be accepted,
for it was Lt. Col. Nye himself who was responsible for the
final selection.

During the next twelve months Dower was convinced
by developments in Europe that his decision had been the
right one. He wrote in his journal: 'My expectation – *our*
expectation, for Pauline had reached in her own way the
same view – of war in a year or two increased from month
to month. If it came, we must expect that I should be quickly
called up to service in some unpredictable place away from
home. In such case there would be no reason whatsoever

for Pauline and the children to continue to live in London, where they would be subject to maximum risks of air attack, and whence they might be compulsorily and very uncomfortably evacuated.'[71]

For some time they had toyed with the idea of renting a *pied-à-terre* somewhere in the Lakes or Pennines. They could use this for holidays, as a base for Dower's monthly visits to supervise the building of youth hostels in Malham and Eskdale, and to attend committee meetings of the Friends of the Lake District. The likelihood of war, together with Pauline's pregnancy (the birth was expected in October 1938), gave more urgency to the project. When and if war came, the family could move to the new house for the duration, while Dower could use it in weekend snatches.

Dower was quietly excited by the prospect of loosening his ties with London, and he spent many hours during the spring evenings of 1938 poring over one-inch Ordnance Survey maps. His desiderata were (a) proximity to a mainline station for trips to and from the south, and (b) closeness to friends and family. So the first search was to be in the Craven District of the Southern Yorkshire Dales, with Skipton or Hellifield as rail centres. 'Here was the walking country of my Ilkley boyhood,' he explained, 'and here my father & mother & brother and a number of other good friends and acquaintances, old and new, would be fairly near neighbours.' Alternative sites were gradually crossed off the list. Lancaster and Carnforth were 'unknown and friendless', while the North Riding, Durham and Northumberland (despite proximity to the Trevelyans) were 'all too far from suitable rail centres'.

The Lake District was an attractive option, but was more problematic. 'It was the home of one close friend [i.e. Kenneth Spence] and numerous acquaintances,' he wrote. 'I knew no pleasure greater than walking its fells; I was – and shall ever be – devoted to the preservation of its peerless landscape beauty, so richly and harmoniously varied, so wild and yet so delicate.' But moving there would mean a longer and less convenient rail journey to London, and

---

71 John Dower, Unpublished fragment of autobiography, n.d.

suffering 'the rainy and rather relaxing climate, especially during summer holiday time'. There was something about the mystery of the place. 'Some instinct told me,' he wrote, 'when it came to the point, that the Lakes should be kept as a place to *visit*, not to live in: a vintage wine reserved for occasional and special refreshment of body, mind and soul, not used as an everyday beverage.' To Pauline, too, the disadvantages of the Lakes (such as distance from her parents) outweighed all attractions.

It was in late June 1938 that they stumbled across The Rookery. As they drove, hood down, through the Aire Valley in their stylish, light blue Vauxhall 20 Wingham Cabriolet to view a house in Malham, Dower chanced to notice from the car a much more attractive house in Kirkby Malham, the next village down the valley. It was curtainless and apparently empty, save for a packing case or two in one of the ground floor windows. 'We could not then see inside the house. But all we could see from outside charmed us. It was just the right size, with a pleasant sheltered southward prospect from its main rooms and sturdy stone walls and a stone-slate roof of indefinite age – ample outhouses, a walled back-garden, and a croft [paddock] of perhaps an acre and a half, with a small stream and a group of tall trees beyond that. Rooks' nests in the tree explained the house's name – 'The Rookery'.[72] Coincidentally, the house was just a few hundred yards from what was to be the route of the future Pennine Way.

With 'amazing rapidity', Pauline subsequently tracked down the owner and learned that the house had just been vacated. It had been 'half-promised to another tenant who was not altogether to the landlord's liking. If he could be got rid of, we could have first refusal... We had fallen in love with the place at first sight, and were determined to have it; and, after rather prolonged negotiations about minor details, we got it, on a three years' lease at £45 a year.' A few alterations – including wiring for electric light, which had only recently become available to the village – and considerable redecoration were needed. This would be

---

72 *Ibid.*

done during the autumn, and the house would be used for the first time either during the Christmas or Easter holidays, as soon as the baby was old enough to be moved.

They finally moved into The Rookery in March 1939.

*

War was declared six months later, on 3 September. It was John and Pauline's tenth wedding anniversary, and a day after his thirty-ninth birthday. Dower knew he would be called up imminently, but there was just enough time to tie up some loose ends. Arrangements to let the London house in Haverstock Hill had to be put in hand, while his architectural work on two youth camps near Henley he handed over to a colleague. His client, the National Camps Corporation, was not best pleased with the abruptness of his departure. Then there was his work for CPRE. On 12 September, he attended a meeting of the Executive Committee in London to discuss how it was to operate during wartime. HG Griffin's report noted that it would have fewer resources as staff were called up or moved away from London, but there was no question of closing it down for the duration. On the contrary, he declared, 'the importance of safeguarding the English countryside would be, if anything, increased rather than diminished in time of war, and the work of the CPRE would be of increasing importance. Quite apart from any damage due to enemy action, irreparable havoc may be done needlessly while thoughts are preoccupied by other cares.'[73]

Dower was appointed to a small, eleven-man War Emergency Committee to administer CPRE's affairs, and 'take whatever steps were deemed necessary to continue its work and to handle any emergency duties that might be assigned to the Council.' Meetings were to be summoned as necessary by the President and Chairman – the first of which was fixed for 24 October. Dower must have assumed that

---

73 Council for the Preservation of Rural England, Secretary's Report, October 1939.

he would be close enough to London and given sufficient flexibility by the Army to attend this 'War Cabinet'. But when on 22 September the inevitable letter arrived, he had to revise his plans. Second Lieutenant JG Dower (no. 100602) was given just one week to join the No. 1 Training Battalion, Royal Engineers, at Shorncliffe Barracks in Dover.

His first day there was filled with inevitable administrative tasks, settling in and meeting the other new recruits. Later, in a rare moment of quiet during the evening, he suddenly felt lonely, and for the first time rather powerless as a very junior officer. He was also a little guilty at having left Pauline behind with three young children to look after. Although she had accepted his decision to join the Emergency Reserve, she had been taken aback that John's posting was about as far away from Kirkby Malham as you could get within the UK.

His first letter home sought to offer some reassurance – possibly as much for his benefit as for Pauline's. 'The instruction course at Shorncliffe is, of course, a preliminary, and I've no doubt that the War Office intend in a month or two to employ me on some technical job that uses my capacities,' he wrote. 'The RE is the obvious branch for me to be in. But I am not leaving it to the W.O to do as they will. Yesterday, I telephoned Pat Abercrombie (who is in close contact with the senior 'Works and Fortifications' people at the W.O.) and found him very ready to take any opportunity of putting my name forward for work on the selection and/ or vetting of sites for camps: he agrees with me that this is the work I could be most useful in.'

Dower also reported that he had been passed medically fit – but for Home Service only. 'I was not passed for general service (i.e. covering service abroad) purely on the ground of my short sight – otherwise I'm A1,' he wrote, adding (possibly unwisely), 'the doctor indicated that I could probably get passed for general service later, if it proved desirable.'

But there was also note of pride in his letter, particularly in relation to the fitting of his new uniform. Dower's vertical dimensions could not easily be accommodated by the Army's standard-issue clothing. 'My tailors are making a special effort and have every hope of equipping me with the full service-dress uniform by Friday, and I shall be able through them to collect other necessary equipment.' And he added, unaware then of its significance: 'Greatcoats can't be got, so I am getting a good quality Burberry of army pattern. My present mac is too thin and worn-out.'

*

If Dower was hoping for a swift posting further north, he was to be disappointed. He was indeed allocated to the maintenance and strengthening of 'Works and Fortifications' – but there, in Dover, just twenty miles from the future battle front across the Channel. His job was to design and supervise improvements to Dover Harbour. The work was exhausting, wet, and intensely cold. During much of January, February and March 1940, heavy snow fell on Kent and across much of the rest of Britain. January was the coldest recorded for over one hundred years. In the middle of that month, the temperature in Kent remained around -10°C for several days, made worse by freezing easterly and northerly gales. 'The good quality Burberry of army pattern' was hardly sufficient against temperatures such as these, and this, together with his unaccustomed close contact with hundreds of soldiers and refugees at Shorncliffe (many of whom were suffering from a variety of illnesses) meant that Dower was laid low on several occasions with influenza and associated chest infections.

There was occasionally some respite through the frozen gloom of that winter. On the weekend of 17-18 February 1940, he was given leave to attend the Garden Cities Annual Meeting in London, with a special dinner in honour of its Chairman, the press baron Lord Harmsworth. It was a welcome reminder of his former life. Dower's major contributions to the National Parks campaign was acknowledged when he was invited to propose the health of the retiring Chairman, George Pepler, who – Dower reminded his audience – was not only godfather to his son Michael 'but also of the whole Garden Cities and town planning movement'. On the Sunday morning he went with William Harding Thompson in the snow to visit the office in Verulam Buildings 'to see how it was looking', before being pressed to take the chair at another conference later that morning on the report of the Royal Commission on the location of Industry (the Barlow Commission). Then it was back to the Garden Cities conference, and dinner with Patrick Abercrombie and his wife.

Meanwhile, Pauline had become increasingly concerned about her husband's health and pressed him to contact Nye once more to see if there was an alternative posting which was less arduous and exposed -- and if possible nearer the family. It seemed to pay off, for in early April 1940 a letter arrived from the War Office requesting him to report for duty to No. 3 Training Battalion, Royal Engineers, in Ripon – just thirty miles from Kirkby Malham.

Dower was fortunate that he moved when he did. Six weeks after leaving Shorncliffe, over 180,000 Dunkirk evacuees landed in Dover over the course of ten days. On just one day – 31 May – no fewer than 35,000 troops – many of them with wounds of every description -- were disembarked from 130 warships and small vessels. In the thick of it were the local sappers, themselves weak from lack of sleep and exhaustion.[74] Then a few weeks later, Dover was a prime target of the German Luftwaffe in the initial skirmishes of the Battle of Britain. On 19 July, five German bombers were brought down as they approached the town, at the cost of ten RAF fighters and their crews.

Examining the 'what ifs' of history is a fascinating, but ultimately fruitless, pastime. Nevertheless, it is the case that had Dower stayed in Shorncliffe, he would have been subject to great and possibly fatal dangers. Had he been killed in 1940, it would almost certainly have set back the struggle for National Parks in Britain in subsequent years, or at least pushed it in a different direction.

As events turned out, he was safe in Ripon, some 250 miles from the German bombing. But on 19 July he was

---

74 Robert Jackson, *Dunkirk: The British Evacuation*, 1940, Cassell, 1976, p. 176 ff.

suddenly confronted with a peril of a different kind. A fierce temperature which lasted for a week led to his admission to the military hospital at Catterick. He was subsequently diagnosed as having pneumonia, and his symptoms fluctuated over the following month while medical tests were undertaken. He remained weak, and in mid-August he was transferred to lighter duties with the Royal Engineers' Officer Cadet Training Unit.

But by September 1940 it was apparent that Dower's illness was not improving, and on 25 October a Medical Board pronounced him permanently unfit for general duty. He was told to relinquish his commission with effect from 11 December 1940. The Army also concluded that his illness was 'not attributable to military service'. This came as a great blow, which Dower considered groundless and unfair. At that stage there may have been suspicions that he was suffering from tuberculosis, but his discharge letter spoke only of 'ill-health' as the reason for terminating his commission. Moreover, as late as May 1941, he was to write to Pauline from London with the news that his doctor could find 'no indication by sounding my lungs of any TB activity, and is fairly sure that the trouble is some slight non-TB infection in the windpipe' (although he was advised 'to go rather carefully for a week or two' and to avoid overwork).[75]

Dower was dismayed by the Army's refusal to accept any responsibility for his condition. It meant that he could not receive a disability allowance to cover the period during which he would be unable, on doctor's orders, to take up civilian employment. So on the day before his discharge, he wrote a terse letter to the War Office in Cheltenham:

I do not agree with the assumption that my illness is not attributable to military service. I have always enjoyed good health up to the time of joining the Army, and there was no symptom of any such illness till at least five months after I began military service, during which period I was twice medically examined and passed as perfectly fit, and worked, played

75 Letter from Dower to Pauline, 4 May 1941.

73

hockey etc most vigorously and tirelessly. I was, however, in the course of my military duties during the early months of this year exceptionally exposed to epidemic infection and to severe weather conditions simultaneously. In consequence, I had several attacks of influenza, and, in my opinion, picked up the germs of my subsequent illness while my resistance was weakened by these. Such conditions would not have arisen had I continued in civilian life...[76]

This, however, was a losing battle, for even if TB had been diagnosed with certainty, the precise source would have been impossible to pinpoint, since the infection can lie dormant in a patient for many years. Dower may have been right, later, in suspecting his Army driver to be the carrier, but equally it might have been the French *curé* with whom he had stayed twenty years before.

Outgunned, he returned to Kirkby Malham to convalesce and consider his future.

---

76 Letter from Dower to the Under-Secretary of State, War Office, Cheltenham, 10 December 1940.

5. Reconstruction

The crackling log fire and the warm glow of the Christmas tree lights immediately raised the festive spirit of the guests entering Wallington's central hall, leaving the winter gloom outside. But for Dower, Christmas 1940 was a sombre affair. He had felt physically well enough to drive up from Kirkby Malham with Pauline and the family a few days before, despite the insistence of his doctor that he needed as much bed rest as possible. It was more the nagging feeling of failure and disorientation pressing down on him that made joining in the family fun such an effort.

For days he had been pondering what he should do with his life. He had wound down his architectural work on being called up, and getting new commissions amid the bombing and destruction was highly unlikely. The National Parks campaign had been mothballed on the outbreak of war, and his opportunity to contribute directly to the war effort had been prematurely snatched away by an illness that he still didn't fully comprehend. He needed to rebuild his life, but so far he had no plan.

There was a glimmer of hope, however. In the week before Christmas, his friends at the Town Planning Institute had sent Dower a draft of a paper – *Reconstruction of Town and Country* – written for the War Cabinet by Sir John (later Lord) Reith, the newly appointed Minister of Works and Buildings.[77] The first Director-General of the BBC, Reith was a technocrat rather than a politician, a dour Calvinist Scot who was impatient to get things done. He was six feet four tall and looked down – both literally and metaphorically – on all his ministerial colleagues and officials, including the Prime Minister, Winston Churchill. 'To Churchill, Reith was an unfathomable creature, towering over him in puritanical zeal as well as physical stature,' wrote one historian. 'Once, when Reith had departed after a difficult interview, Churchill remarked: "Thank God, we have seen the last of

---

77 War Cabinet WP (G) 321, November 1940.

that Wuthering Height".[78]

Reith's paper underlined the urgency of planning for the peace, notwithstanding the nation's current preoccupation with winning the war. The case was put eloquently a few weeks later by the former Liberal leader Viscount Samuel in a House of Lords debate:

> Some of our towns have been largely destroyed and they will be eager to proceed with the work of reconstruction. Hundreds of thousands of families who have been evacuated from their ordinary homes, often scattered, will wish to reunite, but will find that their old homes have been destroyed. There is already much overcrowding, and there will be at least two years of normal building to be made good. At the same time there will be millions of men demobilised from the Armed Forces, and hundreds of thousands, perhaps millions, of men and women released from the work of making munitions. Their wages will have stopped, and they must at once find other employment; perhaps in many cases their old employment will not still be available.
>
> If, beforehand, there have been no plans made for meeting that situation then all the evils which have been seen in this country for many years will be repeated, and perhaps emphasised. Industries will again be located haphazard; the countryside will again be invaded and often spoiled; building will again take place wherever it can be done easiest and quickest, and that will be along the main roads. Ribbon development, which has not been stopped – the ribbons have been made somewhat broader but they have not been made shorter – will be given a fresh impetus. It is the most inconvenient of all ways of housing the people, giving them fewer social facilities and amenities and increasing most, the dangers of the highways; nevertheless, if there are no

---

78 Paul Addison, *The Road to 1945: British Politics and the Second World War,* Jonathan Cape, 1975, p. 176.

plans, it will be reverted to because it is the cheapest form of building, and the evils which have been deplored will be repeated. The work of the Royal Commission on the Distribution of the Industrial Population will be ignored, the effort of bodies such as the Council for the Preservation of Rural England will be defeated, and just as we condemn now the failure of the citizens of London after the Great Fire to adopt the great planning schemes proposed by Sir Christopher Wren, so we in our turn will be condemned by posterity for having failed to seize a great occasion...[79]

Reith's paper to the War Cabinet was a little more prosaic, but it pulled no punches in setting out what needed to be done. Controls should be put in place to secure the best use of land – the safeguarding of fertile farmland through restrictions on urban growth; the redevelopment of congested areas; and the co-ordination of those government sectoral policies with an impact on the use of land, such as housing, transport, recreation, and the preservation of places of national and historic interest. To do all this, he argued, a Central Authority was needed to draw up and execute a national land-use plan. Later in the House of Lords, Reith made it abundantly clear that it was his job 'to exercise the functions of central planning and co-ordination, to initiate the work and to give general guidance and supervision to it. By arrangement with colleagues, I propose to utilize the resources of other Departments and to ask for the collaboration of professional and technical associations...'[80]

As Dower leafed through Reith's memorandum, he reflected that he could well have written it himself – which was not altogether surprising, since a number of his own friends and colleagues in the planning profession had provided a significant input to it. As an outsider who had originally

---

79 House of Lords debate, *Hansard*, 26 February 1941, vol. 118, cols. 485-516.
80 *Ibid.*

been brought into government as Minister of Information by Neville Chamberlain, Reith had little understanding or sympathy with politicians and departmental officials, and now, as a Minister, sought expertise and support from elsewhere. In the first weeks of 1941, he set up a consultative group on physical planning and reconstruction of around 'twenty individuals who have special experience in this field to assist me and to be associated with this work from the beginning'. He also announced his intention to select a small staff of outside experts to work with him directly 'at the centre'. Harold G Vincent, a senior civil servant who had been Private Secretary to Prime Ministers Ramsay MacDonald and Baldwin, was given the task of finding and bringing them together, reporting directly to Reith.[81]

Unsurprisingly, Reith's claim – after only a few months as Minister of Works – to be the chief co-ordinator of the work of all government departments made him many enemies. There was already a Cabinet Committee on Reconstruction Problems chaired by the Minister without Portfolio, Arthur Greenwood, which claimed primary responsibility in this area. Meanwhile, the Minister of Agriculture, RS Hudson, was particularly aggrieved and wrote a personal letter to Churchill accusing Lord Reith of setting up a 'Ministry of Cranks' which would 'concoct all sorts of schemes and when the war is over and we have the job of putting a sane agriculture policy into operation, we shall be faced with a whole series of theoretical plans and vested interests which will make our task quite impossible.' Later, he sent a further memo to Churchill, warning of the 'dangers of one sector of government setting priorities in the planning field which inevitably encroached on the sectoral interests of other ministries' and insisting that the use of land was purely a matter for his Ministry.[82]

The general ministerial unease at Reith's ambitions led to the establishment of an Interdepartmental Committee

---

81 JCW Reith, *Into the Wind*, Hodder & Stoughton, 1949, p. 428.
82 J Sheail, 'The Concept of National Parks in Great Britain, 1900-1950', *Proceedings of the Institute of British Geographers*, 1975.

on Reconstruction to 'advise' the Ministry of Works. It consisted of senior officials from a wide range of interested departments – the Treasury, the Board of Trade, the Ministries respectively of Health, Transport and Agriculture, the Scottish Home, Agriculture and Health departments, and a representative of the Minister without Portfolio. But the prospect of slow death by committee led Reith to insist it should be chaired by his own man, Vincent, whose experience at managing such committees would help to redress the balance a little.[83]

Vincent had a clear idea of his role in the Ministry of Works. In early April 1941, he drafted a memo to Reith which was ostensibly about staffing needs, but went much further in setting out a radical strategy for the Department. 'We are seeking to introduce a strengthening of the planning system immediately, and a stimulation of physical planning all over the country. For this we say that the Central Authority should be formed now. I understand that this is your view. Accordingly, I look upon our organisation ... as the nucleus of the Authority. It will be reforming a system and not just carrying on an existing system; and reconstruction planning will be beyond any planning yet done in this country.' He concluded, conspiratorially: 'I do not consider that in its nature planning properly falls to the Ministry of Works as part of its functions. I regard the planning staff as a separate attachment under your Ministerial responsibility – in fact, that is how it has worked hitherto...'[84]

So Vincent regarded the existing Ministry of Works simply as a chrysalis from which would emerge, butterfly-like, the new Central Planning Authority. The nucleus of this new department would be the small staff of outside experts that Vincent was busy assembling – as Reith described it, 'small in numbers, great in experience and in enthusiasm'.[85]

83 JB Cullingworth, *Environmental Planning 1939-1969 Vol 1. Reconstruction and Land Use Planning 1939-47*, HMSO, 1975, p. 57.
84 Memo from Vincent to Lord Reith, 4 April 1941, HLG 124/5 91649/14.
85 Reith, *op. cit.*

But Vincent urgently needed someone on his small staff who understood the complexities of town and country planning; had experience of communicating the need for protection of the countryside; was familiar with the labyrinthine working of Whitehall departments and committees – and, crucially, in view of the war, was available.

In short, he needed Dower. So on 4 March 1941, Dower walked across Lambeth Bridge to Albert Embankment to join the Ministry of Works as a Temporary Assistant Secretary, working directly with Vincent.

*

John and Pauline's house on Haverstock Hill had been let with the move to Kirkby Malham, so for the first few weeks in London Dower was obliged to stay at a guesthouse in nearby Keats Grove on the edge of Hampstead Heath. Apart from the landlord, the other residents were refugees – a Czech couple, and a German Jewish woman and her daughter-in-law. It was quite comfortable, but too cramped to accommodate a desk and all his books and papers, so Cyril Joad – now his near neighbour – recommended somewhere more spacious in Christchurch Hill. Dower wrote to Pauline that Mrs Mabbit, the landlady, offered 'a good furnished sitting room and adequate bedroom adjoining each other on the ground floor, with all meals including lunch at weekends, and full service for two guineas a week, which seems reasonable.'

If he had to live in London, then Hampstead was the ideal place. He was surrounded by attractive Georgian and Victorian houses with well-kept gardens set back from the hilly streets and lanes, and was within a few hundred yards of the Heath, where he would go for long walks. These had a noticeably beneficial effect on his health. He wrote to Pauline, reassuringly: 'My two five or six mile walks to and from the house, with rucksack, were a great success – they finally cleared away the slight indigestion I'd had earlier in the week, didn't tire me at all or even make me stiff, and left me feeling really fit and ready for anything.'[86] And in addition, Parliament Hill was at a relatively safe distance from which to survey the blackened and still-smouldering bomb sites in the City and the East End, spread out below.

Meanwhile, at the Ministry he was surrounded by old friends, most of whom, like him, had been recruited from outside the civil service – William Holford, Professor of Town Planning at Liverpool; HC Bradshaw from the Royal Fine Art Commission; Thomas Sharp, town planner, and George Pepler from the TPI, seconded from his post as Chief Town Planning Officer at the Ministry of Health. His working regime was not too arduous. 'I spend 10 to 1.15 and from 2.30 to 6.30 or thereabouts at the office each day, nearly all the time either writing or reading or talking at a fairly high mental pressure ... all very interesting and right at the heart of the subject – for the main thing thrown at me is "what is the best practicable system for national, regional and local planning after the war"?'[87] Most days he would walk across the river to Westminster and then Queen Anne's Gate for a 'longish lunch' at PEP, where he would meet 'lots of old friends and quite a bunch of new acquaintances'.

A week after his arrival, Dower had his 'first good talk with Reith, and was favourably impressed'. With both of them standing at nearly six foot six inches, they met eye to eye in more senses than one. 'I think he was satisfied with me – anyway, he listened to me, which he doesn't do to everyone!' A few weeks later, he organised a lunchtime meeting at PEP where Reith gave a speech – drafted by Dower – to a crowded and enthusiastic gathering on 'Our Planning and Reconstruction Objectives'.

He soon established a close working relationship with Vincent. 'More than half the talking is with Vincent, with whom I get on splendidly,' he wrote. 'He relies increasingly on my accumulated knowledge and experience of the whole subject and of the people concerned in it (or who think they ought to be concerned!)' Vincent was aware of Dower's medical history, and encouraged him to go home for the

---

86 Letter from Dower to Pauline, 17 April 1941.
87 Letter from Dower to Pauline, 23 March 1941.

weekend to see the family 'every month or so' since 'it would not do either of us any good to be too lonely in London for too long a stretch.' But it soon became apparent that visits to Pauline and the family in Kirkby Malham would be infrequent and fleeting. A circular from the Treasury to all civil servants decreed that because of staff shortages leave would be restricted during the following six months – to just one week.

*

On the night of Wednesday, 16 April, the Luftwaffe launched the heaviest air raid on London of the war so far, in reprisal for British air attacks the previous week on residential and cultural centres in Berlin. The attack began soon after dark and continued until shortly before dawn. The first set of Junkers Ju 88 bombers dropped great numbers of flares, followed by more than 100,000 incendiaries which caused extensive fires across London. *The Times* reported that early next morning 'the whole of the capital was covered with a lurid red glow, which was so vivid that the barrage balloons stood out clearly.' In central London, eight hospitals were hit, together with several churches, hotels, two department stores, a theatre, a music hall and two cinemas. There were heavy casualties and thousands were made homeless. At St Paul's cathedral, a large bomb pierced the roof of the north transept, destroying the saucer dome and bringing down heavy masonry, which in turn caused the floor of the building to collapse into the crypt. Every stained glass window was lost.

The following morning Dower added a hasty postscript to the letter to Pauline he had written but not posted the previous evening. 'Safe and sound this morning, but it was a very noisy night – all clear not till 5am, but I slept from 3.30 am. Some bombs but not near.' On Sunday 20 April he wrote again conceding that the blitz had been a lot worse than he had realised. 'The damage was widespread rather than intense at any one point: traffic that morning was hopelessly disorganised and congested – I had to walk from Leicester

Square to the office, where I found water, electricity and gas temporarily cut off.' Crossing Lambeth Bridge, he came across large quantities of unexploded incendiaries, at least half a dozen of which had been smothered with sandbags. Not so in the yard at the back of the office, where he discovered a 1,000-kg unexploded bomb. It was to remain there for a week before being removed. Dower evacuated his room for a safer one nearby, and noted coolly that it would have made 'a bit of a mess if it had (a) hit the building and not the yard and (b) gone off!'

Another heavy raid the night before had caused widespread damage and heavy casualties. But Dower once more reassured Pauline that 'no bombs fell anywhere near us.' The nearest during the first raid were a landmine to the south-west of Belsize Park, and several high explosives about a quarter of a mile from his house, one of which was unexploded 'and went off, noisily, at breakfast time on Friday.'

Dower was acutely aware of the personal costs of his new life in London. Pauline was bearing more than her fair share – not just looking after, now, three small children and the house in Kirkby Malham – eighty miles away from her family – but more importantly enduring the constant anxiety for his safety while London was being blitzed. They had talked about the possibility that the Ministry might be moved to a temporary location in Cambridge, and he had mentioned to Vincent that there might be space in Trinity College. But there was no immediate prospect of this, and besides, he was convinced it would compromise his primary objective. 'While we're fighting our policy through the Departments, and getting ready to fight it through the Cabinet and Parliament, we must be in London,' he wrote.[88] After just three months at the Ministry, the nature of the opposition had become clear. 'The vice I christened 'compartmentalism' is still rampant. Government is an old-fashioned railway coach with entirely separate carriages, not even a corridor, still less an open saloon car. If contact between the compartments is necessary, you must pull the

88 Letter from Dower to Pauline, 23 April 1941.

emergency cord, stop the train and have an argument on the permanent way...'[89]

But he tried to raise Pauline's spirits by reminding her of the sights and smells of springtime in London. The weather had been 'much sunnier and warmer with fleecy clouds sailing across pale blue skies and fine sunsets: the best sort of London weather... all the almond trees are in full bloom: I am surprised, as I am every spring, what a lot of almond trees there are in various parts of London – when they've dropped their flowers one never notices them (as such) again until the next Spring...'

---

89 Letter from Dower to Pauline, 8 June 1941.

6. The Upturned Hourglass

A few days later, a small dark cloud no bigger than a man's hand cast a shadow over the almond trees in the Maytime sun. 'A slight bronchial irritation' had returned, and when Dower coughed he noticed small flecks of blood on his handkerchief. He wrote to Pauline that 'a slight indigestion attack' had laid him low for a couple of days, which had made him 'a bit below par'. A visit to Dr Rollins, his former doctor in Golders Green, provided some reassurance. 'He could find no indication by sounding my lungs of any TB activity and is fairly sure that the trouble is some slight non-TB infection in the windpipe,' he wrote. 'At the same time he wants me to watch out for any other signs (eg temperature) and go rather carefully (sleep and eat as much as possible and avoid over-work) for a week or two. I have as a matter of fact been taking my temperature for several days and it's never been above normal ... but I took yesterday and am taking today very quietly with two 10 hour nights in bed; and have quite thrown off the indigestion and am feeling very fit.' And he was not losing weight: 'just under 12 stone in my clothes against eleven and three-quarter stone a few days ago'.[90]

He would not normally have troubled Pauline with such details, except that at home ten-year old Susan and three-year-old Robin had contracted whooping cough. Dower had never had whooping cough, and despite his reassurance, Dr Rollins had made it quite clear that it would be 'foolishly risky for me to come to the Rookery while S & R are having whooping cough – so that's that.' He would have to postpone a visit to the Rookery until Whitsun at the end of the month, but he wondered whether in the meantime he and Pauline could meet elsewhere for a weekend. 'I can come anywhere within reason,' he wrote. 'Could you come as far as Cambridge or Oxford – or would you like us both to go to Kenneth Spence's near Monmouth? He's been pressing me to go soon and I'm sure would be delighted to have us both...'

---

90 Letter from Dower to Pauline, 4 May 1941.

In the event, Pauline arranged for the children to be looked after elsewhere in the village, allowing Dower to return earlier to The Rookery for 'a good weekend holiday at home'. On his return to London, he wrote to her reassuringly: 'It's not so much that I feel better for it (though I do) as that it has convinced me that I am completely well.' But two weeks later he sent a postcard asking her to fix up an X-ray with his local doctor when he returned to The Rookery at Whitsun.

The result of the X-ray and other tests indicated that he had a small patch of active infection at the apex of his right lung. What the prognosis was, however, was less clear. Diagnosing tuberculosis at that time was not straightforward, for the symptoms were common to a number of other disorders, and GPs were often reluctant to give a firm diagnosis because of the implications for the patient's future employment. Dower did not feel unwell, and felt he had the energy and determination to see through his struggle for National Parks. He made himself believe that he would be cured.

But for the time being he was obliged to take sick leave from the Ministry. On 23 July 1941, he wrote to his colleague and mentor, George Pepler, who was covering for Vincent while on leave. 'My doctor ... has ordered me to bed for a month, though I am not feeling at all unwell. The more thorough the physical rest, the quicker the cure! Both he and I hope that the month will do the trick: but I expect in any case he'll want to keep me in the country for a while after it. Let's call it a Long Vacation, and hope I can return in three months' time or so. Meantime, I can be as mentally active as I like, and I am most anxious to do all I can to keep in touch with developments over the whole field, and to give all possible help to the cause and to the Ministry ... by reading, drafting and correspondence.' He wanted to be treated as a sort of 'branch office', and so asked Pepler and other colleagues to send him copies of all relevant papers.[91]

Dower's expectation that he would soon be back at his London desk proved to be wildly optimistic. By October

---

91 Letter from Dower to George Pepler, 23 July 1941.

1941 it was clear that he was not recovering, and he was admitted to Oakwood Hall Sanatorium in Rotherham, where a further X-ray and sputum test confirmed that the patch in his right lung was still active. He finally had to accept he had TB.

It was not until 1943 that the antibiotic Streptomycin was to be discovered in the United States, and in Britain it would not be widely available until 1947. In conjunction with other drugs, Streptomycin proved to be a very effective and relatively rapid cure. Before then, however, the traditional treatment was extended bed rest lasting for months, good food and fresh air, and, often, 'collapse therapy' to rest the infected lung by putting it out of action. This was done by paralysing the diaphragm by interrupting the phrenic nerve which supplies and activates that muscle. In a relatively simple operation the nerve can be reached by a small incision in the neck, just above the collar bone. In Dower's case, the healthy left lung would do all the work while (hopefully) the inactive right lung would heal and the 'crushed' nerve grow again.

But the operation was postponed for several weeks while the staff monitored his progress. Meanwhile, Dower was confined to his bed for no less than twenty-two hours a day – hugely frustrating for someone normally so active. From his bed he was able to read and write, and he was quick to inform Pauline that he was (astonishingly) 'allowed to smoke and will expect you to provide tobacco at intervals...' What he could not have, however, was any contact with his children. While back in May it was *he* who had to be protected from *them*, now, with the confirmation of TB, both Dower and the children had to be protected from one another. Looking back, his oldest son, Michael, regretted that his father's periods of quarantine combined with his absences in London meant that he barely saw him for seven years.[92]

By mid-November he could write to Pauline that his doctor was 'most satisfied' with his general health and that he was 'promoted' to three hours out of bed. At the end of

---

92 Personal communication with author.

the month he was transferred to the Middleton Sanatorium in his home town of Ilkley, in preparation for his operation. The hospital was barely a mile from his childhood home, and he had 'a splendid view out from my bed straight across the town to the highest point of Ilkley Moor, with my old haunts – White Wells, Cow and Calf, Rocky Valley – all in the picture'. It brought back joyful memories of his long, youthful walks across the moors thirty years before with his brother Arthur – but they were mixed with a nagging anxiety that his rambling days might now be gone forever. He put this to the back of his mind by engaging in another of his favourite occupations – making lists, this time of those many friends, relatives and colleagues to be sent Christmas cards. Meticulous as ever, he ticked those whose addresses he knew and wrote envelopes for them, leaving Pauline to see to the rest.

His proposed operation was a more serious affair than the relatively minor 'phrenic crush' he had expected. He wrote to Pauline in early December explaining that his doctors had now recommended a permanent cut instead of the short-term crush '(a) because they don't expect the healing to be complete for six months or more (b) because the lung will want all the rest it can get for 12 months from now and (c) because it will be all to the good to "soft pedal" that lung for the rest of my life. I shall not notice any difference after the first 3 days or so: and it won't make me short of breath.'

*

'It all went off swimmingly – has quite certainly done me no harm – and there is every reason to suppose it has done the intended good,' Dower wrote to Pauline on the day after the operation, lying flat on his bed for the forty-eight hours he had been prescribed. Predictably, he was reassuringly upbeat, describing the operation as 'a very interesting experience with no more pain than an average visit to the dentist's'. He had felt drowsy afterwards for an hour or two 'because they had given me a dope injection, but I ate a good tea and a good supper, and I slept quite well without needing to call for any sleeping-draught. Today, apart from a tickle or two from the wound in my neck I feel quite normal … and as far as breathing is concerned I'm not conscious of any difference.' He was passing the time reading Trollope, solving the *Yorkshire Post* crossword, and looking forward to coming home for Christmas at The Rookery.[93] (The children, however, would be sent to Wallington.)

Dower had been told that his convalescence would take at least a further six months, and for some time after that he would have to avoid continuous living and working in London to avoid metropolitan stress and the frequent smogs. But the prognostication was not discouraging. A similar TB sanatorium on the south coast reported that of 500 patients who had undergone treatment similar to Dower's, after five years 50 per cent remained well and working; 25 per cent were well, but not working; 15 per cent were unwell and undergoing further treatment; and 9 per cent had died.[94]

But once again Dower was uncertain and anxious about his professional and financial future. He was disappointed to miss a meeting early in the New Year (1942) between Lord Reith and a deputation from the Standing Committee on National Parks, particularly since his own pamphlet, *The Case for National Parks*, had been circulated by the Standing Committee to Reith and his officials in advance. Vincent afterwards reported to him that Reith had agreed entirely with the principle of establishing National Parks, and also with the Standing Committee's three main objectives for them – natural recreation for the public; the preservation of flora and fauna; and the continuation of agricultural use. However, there were many detailed points to consider, and it was agreed that Professor Abercrombie, the Revd. Symonds and Mr W Platts (from the County Councils Association) should meet together informally with Vincent and Pepler to address them.[95]

---

93 Letter from Dower to Pauline, 12 December 1941.
94 EF Laidlaw, *The Story of the Royal National Hospital, Ventnor, 1990*, p. 89.
95 National Archives HLG 92/46, note by Vincent of meeting with Standing Committee, 13 May 1942.

Dower was deeply disappointed – on several levels – to hear a few weeks later that Reith had been sacked. After the fall of Singapore and other disasters, Churchill needed to re-shuffle his government for public relations purposes – and Reith was particularly vulnerable. He was not a Conservative and had no party to support him, and neither had he been sufficiently 'clubbable' and assiduous in nurturing political support among his fellow-Ministers.

Dower had admired Reith's determination and his achievements in his short period of office. Firstly, he had quickly established the Uthwatt Committee to investigate the highly abstruse problems of compensation and betterment – that is, paying compensation to landowners when planning decisions imposed restrictions on what they could do with their land; or on the other hand, taxing the gain in the value of land resulting from the grant by local authorities of planning permission for development. The issue of compensation and betterment needed to be addressed before an effective system of land-use planning – and the establishment of National Parks – could be achieved.

Secondly, in July 1941 Reith had managed to secure a government statement which spelled out his leading role in planning post-war reconstruction. It read in part:

> Within the framework of the general study of post-war problems which is being undertaken by the Minister without Portfolio (i.e. Arthur Greenwood), Lord Reith retains special responsibility for long-term planning policy in the sphere of physical reconstruction. Lord Reith will be in charge of this work, not in his capacity as Minister of Works, but in pursuance of *the special responsibility assigned to him personally* for the guidance and supervision of the preparatory work of formulating the methods and machinery required for physical reconstruction of town and country after the war. (Author's italics)

This went some way towards strengthening Reith's position in relation to Arthur Greenwood's committee and other rival government departments, and a further advance came on 9 February 1942 when the War Cabinet finally agreed that town and country planning should be taken from the Ministry of Health and transferred to the Ministry of Works and Buildings, henceforth to be re-named the Ministry of Works and Planning. The new Ministry would lay down the general principles of town and country planning in England and Wales, and would ensure that planning schemes produced by local authorities reflected these principles. However, the War Cabinet decided that the new Ministry would be overseen by other government departments in an inter-departmental Committee of Officials.

The title of Reith's autobiography *Into the Wind* reflected the frustrations and setbacks he was to experience in dealing with other departments.

Reith enjoyed this partial promotion for just ten days. On 19 February he received a telegram delivered unceremoniously by a motor cycle courier announcing that he was sacked. If there was any consolation, three days later his regular sparring partner, Arthur Greenwood, resigned as Minister without Portfolio, reflecting his less than dynamic performance as chairman of the Reconstruction Committee.

*

Another of Reith's achievements that Dower admired was to set up the Scott Committee on Land Utilisation in Rural Areas. The initiative was intended to produce independent evidence of the need for a central planning authority to co-ordinate the reconstruction of the countryside. The Committee's rather tortuous terms of reference were:

> To consider the conditions which should govern building and other constructional development in country areas consistently with the maintenance of agriculture, and in particular the factors affecting the location of industry, having regard to economic operation, part-time and seasonal employment, the well-being of rural communities and the preservation of rural amenities.

The choice of Lord Justice Leslie Scott as the Committee's Chairman was carefully considered. He was a founder member of CPRE, Chairman of its Berkshire branch, and a member of its National Executive. As early as 1936 he was writing papers calling for 'a carefully designed constitutional step in the direction of co-ordination and central control as regards rural planning'.[96] Arthur Greenwood's rival Reconstruction Committee, predictably, had opposed the establishment of the Scott Enquiry, as did the Minister of Agriculture, RS Hudson. As a result, Reith was obliged to appoint the Committee 'in consultation' with Hudson, and the convoluted terms of reference were a reflection of Hudson's influence.

In the event, Scott's final report did everything that Reith had intended. Published in August 1942, it called for an 'immediate five-year plan of work' as part of a long-term rural planning policy, and emphasised that 'the establishment of National Parks in Britain is long overdue... We recommend that the delimitation of the parks be undertaken nationally and we recommend the setting up of a body to control National Parks under the Central Planning Authority, or other appropriate Central Authority.'[97]

Behind the scenes, Dower himself had exercised a major influence on Scott's report. Even before the Committee had been formally appointed, Dower and Vincent were briefing him on the path they wished to follow. In a letter to Pauline at the end of April 1941, Dower wrote that they had had a 'good talk' with Scott, and added in parenthesis: 'Our campaign to get ourselves made into a real central planning authority at an early date is going well at present, but there are many difficulties to overcome yet – and will have anyway to bide our time till the war situation becomes less critical and preoccupying before coming into the open about it – this for your private ear.'[98]

---

96 Council for the Preservation of Rural England (Hampshire Branch) *An Address delivered by The Rt Hon Lord Justice Scott*, Winchester, 25 April 1936.
97 Ministry of Works and Planning, *Report of the Committee on Land Utilisation in Rural Areas*, August 1942, para. 178.
98 Letter from Dower to Pauline, 2 May 1941.

The release of Scott's final report coincided with the publication of what amounted to a manifesto on rural reconstruction, written by Dower as he convalesced at home in The Rookery. *Reconstruction in the Yorkshire Dales* was a 15,000-word statement of Dower's approach to rural planning, and it was to provide the foundation of his own major report on National Parks, published three years later. The articles had a particular focus on his homeland, the Yorkshire Dales, and were therefore published, appropriately, in *The Yorkshire Dalesman* – 'A Monthly Magazine of Dales' Life and Industry' – in six sections from June to November 1942.[99] The style was informal and committed, suggesting that Dower was considering a possible new career in journalism.

An editorial in the August edition of the magazine noted that the Scott Report 'will have special interest for our readers, because of the similarity of many of its proposals to those put forward in these pages in recent months by Mr John Dower'.[100] This was not at all surprising since it is almost certain that Dower had made available a draft of the articles to Scott to inform his final report.

The first instalment of Dower's 'manifesto' set out a daunting range of problems to be addressed in achieving 'reconstruction'. The approach should be *forward-looking*, he argued, embodying 'the hope and vision and purpose of the happier and fuller lives, in a juster, better-ordered and better-equipped country and world, which we may make for ourselves and our children and our children's children after the victory of freedom has been secured.' Millions of new houses would need to be built; the persistent unemployment, waste and dereliction of the 'distressed areas' would have to be tackled through carefully located new industries; and high-quality farmland protected against building development. The problems of ever-increasing traffic – the rising toll of accidents, congestion and ribbon development along main highways – would need to be

---

99 John Dower, 'Reconstruction in the Yorkshire Dales', *The Yorkshire Dalesman*, vol. 4, nos. 3-8, June-November 1942.
100 *Ibid*, p. 102.

managed and reduced. As regards open-air recreation and the preservation of our 'green and pleasant land', Dower pointed out that there was, regrettably, little to show for the effort expended so far. 'Every gain – a beauty spot preserved, a park or group of playing-fields provided, a Youth Hostel built – more than offset by new disfigurements, by further inroads on our beautiful countrysides of ugly and ill-placed buildings, advertisement hoardings and other incongruous urban features...'[101] 'Place, Work, Folk' should be the three pillars on which post-war planning should be built, argued Dower, borrowing the *leitmotiv* from the father of modern town planning, Patrick Geddes. Anticipating by some fifty years the contemporary debate on 'sustainable development', Dower insisted that:

> Place, work and folk must all advance together, and in tune and balance with each other. No development of the land – new or improved villages, farms, roads, open spaces etc – will be successful unless it corresponds to the needs, tastes and occupations of the people, both residents and visitors. No changes in agriculture or industry will stand much chance unless they are suited to the dominant characteristic of the Dales country and its inhabitants. No attempt to enrich the social life of the Dalesfolk ...will get very far unless it takes full account of their physical and economic environment. We have, then, to see the Dales as a whole and living thing – place *and* work *and* folk...[102]

Running through all six articles was a conviction that the *laissez-faire* of the 1930s would have to give way to far greater state intervention. He called for 'large and progressive transfers of land, or of controlling rights over land, to public ownership – a selective nationalisation which could readily be developed into general nationalisation later, if experience showed this to be desirable.' Markets for agricultural products should be managed, for otherwise

---

101 *Ibid*, p. 45.
102 *Ibid*, p. 46.

'there can in my view be no worthwhile "reconstruction" of farming in the Dales, nor indeed throughout the hill grazing country, which comprises about a third of Great Britain.' A comprehensive state agricultural service should provide low-interest capital, make available specialist machinery, labour, information and advice. And 'it should be the business of the state to see that every farm can have a telephone, without special installation charges; that electric light and power are available to the whole rural population at the same rates as in the towns (if this can't be done without general nationalisation of the country's electric services, then the sooner they are nationalised the better!); that every village has a satisfactory water supply, sewage disposal and refuse collection, and that no community, however remote, is without its village hall and library and playing field.'[103]

On housing, Dower insisted that 'we must strive to eliminate the "snob values" which have led to the segregation, in separate estates, of municipal housing from the higher-rented (but often no larger or better) speculative builders' housing, and of both from the "bespoke" housing of the car-owning middle class. I don't think class distinctions are going to have much meaning after the war, anyway: but if classes survive at all let us try to keep them well mixed!'

All this might suggest that Dower had a strong commitment to socialism – like his wife Pauline, as well as her father Sir Charles Trevelyan.[104] But the centre ground in British politics had markedly shifted to the left in the 1930s, and more rapidly with the outbreak of war. Dower's views on the role of the state were in fact no more radical than those the future Conservative Prime Minister Harold Macmillan had espoused since the mid-1920s.[105]

The third instalment of his *Yorkshire Dalesman* articles was entitled 'The Open Air', and so Dower returned to a familiar theme. He demanded 'the preservation of the

---

103 *Ibid*, pp. 64-7.
104 See for example letter from Sir Charles Trevelyan to Pauline, 28 January 1944.
105 See Harold Macmillan *et al*, *The Next Five Years: An Essay in Political Agreement*, Macmillan, 1935.

landscape (and of the farming on which it depends), freedom and facilities for open air recreation, and protection of wildlife in the best of Britain's larger stretches of beautiful, wilder country' through the creation of National Parks, 'which the people so widely desire, and which government at last seems to regard with favour as an element in post-war reconstruction.' National Parks would require 'a real central planning authority with the clear duty of making national plans, and with effective power to direct the land-using activities not only of local authorities, and through them, of the people at large, but also of Government departments and statutory undertakings.'

Finally, he reminded his fellow Dalesmen that the people 'always get the governments they deserve', and therefore 'we must be jealous watchdogs over all that is good and lovely, showers-up of the bad and the ugly, propagandists for new worth and beauty. It is, in fact, up to us.'

*

Following the establishment of the Ministry of Works and Planning, eighteen staff in the Planning Division of the Ministry of Health were transferred to the Reconstruction Group in the new Ministry to form a new Planning Division. These new arrangements were to come into effect on 1 July 1942, and a big increase in the staff of the Planning Division was foreseen, particularly if the scope of town and country planning were to be extended. For Dower this was all good news, and it significantly increased his chances of returning to a job in government. He was in good spirits when on 14 May he wrote an optimistic note to his former PEP colleague, Leonard Elmhirst. 'As for me, my doctor vetted and X-rayed me a few days ago and was most satisfied. I expect to get back into Ministry of [Works and] Planning service in about two months' time, but on some job which permits me to spend most of my time in the country, with perhaps 3 or 4 days in London each month... Meanwhile, I am most happily rusticated here, dividing my time between reading and writing and cultivating my vegetable garden –

a fascinating job which I have never before had a chance to tackle systematically.'[106]

Two weeks later, over the Whitsun bank holiday, Dower was once again in the Lakes at Ulverston, walking with his friend the Revd. HH Symonds, and Mrs Chorley. From there he travelled south for a few days' break at the holiday home of Kenneth Spence in the Welsh borders, where they were soon joined by Cyril Joad and 'Maud' (described by Dower as Cyril's 'friend and occasional mistress'). 'It is good to feel plenty of energy again for a full-length day like yesterday,' he wrote to Pauline, 'even if not a very active day physically – and to be moving about the world again.'[107]

Cwmcarvan Court was a beautiful, stone-built Regency house sequestered in the crumpled landscape a few miles south-west of Monmouth. Dower's walks with Spence and Joad around the thirty-acre estate and out into the hills beyond helped clear his mind about the next steps in their shared campaign. There was no doubt that Reith's departure had been a major setback. His successor Lord Wyndham Portal – in stark contrast to Reith – was a Conservative millionaire, one of Churchill's intimates, and quite uninterested in the challenges of post-war rural and urban planning. A leading historian of the period later observed that 'Portal pursued a policy of masterful procrastination at the Ministry of Works and Planning until, to his great relief, the town and country planning responsibilities were hived off into a separate ministry.'[108]

A further barrier to progress was the new Chairman of the War Cabinet's Reconstruction Committee. Sir William Jowett was even more adamant in his opposition to a central planning authority than Greenwood had been, as he explained to his Committee a few weeks after his appointment:

---

106 Letter from Dower to Leonard Elmhirst, 14 May 1942, in Elmhirst Papers, Devon County Archives, LK/NP/5/B.
107 Letter from Dower to Pauline, 1 June 1942.
108 Paul Addison, *The Road to 1945: British Politics and the Second World War*, Jonathan Cape, 1975, p. 177.

Detailed examination shows that such a solution would cut across the whole existing organisation of government, with the new department absorbing important and indeed essential parts of many existing departments, and even then failing to bring in the most important element of finance – because the Treasury of all departments must remain undivided...[109]

The Chancellor, of course, agreed. On 1 May Sir Kingsley Wood wrote to Jowett opposing the establishment of a National Park authority at that time, and indicating that National Parks 'would not take a very high place in the queue for national funds'.

Although his energy for the fight was seemingly restored, Dower, his family and friends suspected that the sand was now trickling through the hourglass. He had to work quickly to recover lost ground, and remembered that he had encouraged his neighbours in the Dales that it was 'up to us' to champion 'new worth and beauty'. Now, he was convinced it was up to *him*.

---

109 JB Cullingworth, *Environmental Planning 1939-1969, Vol. 1 Reconstruction and Land-Use Planning 1939-1947*, HMSO, 1975, p. 67.

7. Preparing to Face the Music

Dower had already drawn up a detailed work plan on National Parks for the new Planning Division in the Ministry, several weeks before his holiday conversations with fellow campaigners. The 1,000-word document was closely typed on three foolscap pages, was as logical and analytical as might be expected from Dower – and was hugely ambitious. This was even before he had been offered a job.[110]

The paper started from first principles. He asked: Was there a government commitment to National Parks, and was there agreement that they should be established by *national* action at *national* cost as an essential element of a *national* plan? He assumed from Ministerial speeches and responses to deputations that the answer was 'yes'. Therefore, he argued, there should be a carefully worded statement to this effect from the War Cabinet. This would 'ensure a firm foundation' and 'ought to be made public at the first suitable opportunity – a considerable public opinion would be cheered and satisfied thereby.'

He proposed that the first practical step should be a systematic study of *all* the issues involved in setting up National Parks. This would include:

- A preliminary survey of the whole of England and Wales to determine the location and extent of all potential National Park areas;
- Visits to a sample of these, to investigate their special conditions, problems and requirements, and to consult informally with local authorities and stakeholders. Dower proposed six 'pilot' areas that he considered were likely to be top of the list. These were: the Lake

---

110 *National Parks: England and Wales – Suggestions for Preparatory Work by the Planning Division, Ministry of Works & Buildings*, National Archives, HLG 92/46, 12 May 1942.

District; the Peak District and Dovedale; Snowdonia, the Pembrokeshire coast, Dartmoor and the North Cornwall coast;

- An analysis of the impact of likely post-war government policies on planning, agriculture, forestry, transport and water catchment, and the recommendations of government commissions, such as the Barlow, Uthwatt and Scott Reports;
- Lessons from National Park systems in the United States, Canada and other countries.

Next, the powers and administrative machinery needed to run National Parks should be 'thrashed out' *within* the Ministry. He accepted that negotiations with other government departments would be essential at some stage, but during the first six months of preparatory work, 'the issue should not be complicated by formal consultation by other Departments, local authorities and outside interests, with a consequent heavy and distracting programme of inter-departmental and other committee meetings...' He concluded his paper with a warning: 'Be thoroughly well prepared before you face the music!'

Vincent discussed Dower's memo with George Pepler as soon as he received it. Lawrence Neal, the new Head of the Planning Department, had already stressed to Vincent the importance of gathering concrete evidence as soon as possible on the feasibility of National Parks, in case other, less sympathetic, government departments or committees were to seize the initiative first. In these circumstances, Neal considered Dower's rational, step-by-step approach to policy making far too ambitious and protracted. And even Vincent himself had reservations about Dower's choice of the pilot areas.

'Would you be content to start with the Lakes, Snowdon, Exmoor-Dartmoor?' he asked Pepler. 'I am not anxious to start in the Peak which I regard as to some extent of *regional* [rather than national] importance – rather irregular and artificial in boundary rather than compact, only patchily wild, and complicated by minerals...' He was also sceptical about 'launching into Pembrokeshire', for which he believed there was little public support.

Vincent also raised a number of questions about how the survey work would be done. Should one man be appointed for each area? Should Dower superintend the team, or be allocated the Lakes, which he could survey first as a learning exercise for the others? And was Dower's reputation sufficiently impartial for him to act officially for the Ministry? Pepler agreed that it was 'a little unfortunate that he has been fairly closely identified with the Friends of the Lake District – but I think that with tact, he could get this forgotten.'[111]

A few days later Vincent wrote an optimistic note to Neal recommending Dower for the job. 'He has studied the subject in his connection with the CPRE, more than anybody else in the country. He has recovered from his illness and can now do part-time work. In 1-2 months' time, he will be able to do full-time work – but not in London. He will be able to pay 3-4 day visits to London for committees etc.' He considered that Dower should be given two planning assistants and an Assistant Principal in London to work with him.[112]

*

On 10 July 1942, Dower returned to Lambeth Bridge House for the first time in over a year. 'It was a great delight to be back at the office in the thick of things again, if only for one day, and to find you and all the others in good form,' he wrote to Vincent. His contract was settled a few days later – but with several major changes from what he had initially proposed. Dower's proposal to kick-off with a major preliminary report was dropped, in order to speed up work on what were now to be four area reports (the Peak District now being reinstated). Each would address six key issues:

- The appropriate boundaries, possible alternatives to them, and where particular districts within the boundary should be excluded;

---

111 Memo from Vincent to Pepler. 13 May 1942, and Pepler to Vincent, 19 May 1942, in HLG 92/46.
112 Memo from Vincent to Neal, 19 May 1942, HLG 92/46.

- The main characteristics of the area – such as places of special scenic, historical, architectural, geological, zoological and botanical interest, and opportunities for public access and enjoyment;
- Existing and potential uses of the land likely to affect the preservation of the landscape, wildlife protection and public access;
- Any consequential requirements for areas *adjoining* the National Park;
- The activities of the National Trust and other voluntary bodies, and their potential contribution to maintenance and the provision of campsites etc.

Neal wanted the first report on the Lake District within two months, whereas Dower had asked for three to enable work on all four reports to be undertaken simultaneously. This would allow him to take advantage of the longer, drier days of summer and early autumn for all the surveys, and so be able to finish within six months. Vincent, too, had doubts about Neal's demands – and, indeed, about his judgement generally. Neal was not a professional civil servant, and indeed had been in post as Deputy Secretary for only a few months. He was a retailer, the Chairman and Managing Director of a children's outfitter, Daniel Neal and Son. The nearest he had come to government was in 1941 when he was appointed a member of the Retail Trade Committee of the Board of Trade. Largely through the influence of Kenneth Lindsay, he had been a founder member of PEP, where, according to one of its subsequent Directors, 'he represented more what is sometimes called the 'Greats' type of mind – a Socratic acuteness of questioning, thesis, and reasoned argument', but he was not a 'people person' who could show empathy towards his staff and colleagues.[113]

Vincent, on the other hand, had enjoyed a distinguished civil service career working directly to Ministers and Prime Ministers, and now he was being given instructions by a shopkeeper four years his junior who had little experience

---

113 John Pinder, *Fifty Years of Political and Economic Planning: Looking Forward 1931-1981*, Heinemann, 1981, p. 6 ff.

of land-use planning, or of working with planning professionals. That this rankled somewhat was evident from Vincent's re-draft of Dower's letter of appointment. 'I do not think it is possible to specify definite times for the several reports,' he remarked, 'but *it is expected* that the report on the Lake District will be presented within two months, and the remaining Reports within *approximately* six months. The work, including the desirability of extension to other areas, will be *subject to review* before the expiration of the six month period.' (Author's italics)

Neil was rather more accommodating in relation to Dower's place of work. Given that his home was 200 miles away in Kirkby Malham and the work involved considerable travel, Dower was to be available in the London office for only two to three days a month. He was to be paid £900 a year as a Principal (later re-titled 'Research Officer') – approximately £40,000 at today's prices. But in the event of illness, he was to inform Headquarters, and 'payment of salary would not be made during suspension of work'.[114]

What was omitted from the contract was any reference to the three assistants to support Dower in what would inevitably be a heavy programme of work. He would have to find help wherever he could.

*

Although Dower had done the journey many times before, his excitement mounted as the train steamed towards the Ribblehead Viaduct. Saturday 19 September 1942 was a day of sun, wind and white clouds dappling the fells with small fleeting shadows. From his vantage point on the viaduct the views of Pen-y-ghent, Ingleborough and Whernside were glorious. A young Army officer sharing Dower's compartment did his best to make polite conversation, but Dower's attention was focused outside, on the panorama of the Yorkshire Dales, and the prospect of the Lakes to come.

---

114 Vincent to Dower, 15 July 1942, HLG 92/46.

This was his second official survey trip to the Lakes, and this time he had managed to secure some help. Dudley Stamp was an eminent geographer and adviser to the Ministry of Agriculture. He was waiting for Dower in his car at Carlisle station, accompanied by his wife, and Mr Engholm, a driver from the Ministry. From here – as he wrote to Pauline – 'we did a most enjoyable motor tour of the Western Lake District, taking tea at Seatoller (Mrs Honey, in good form, sends her greetings to you and all at Wallington) – then over Honister, at the top of which we had a short walk, and then from the foot of Ennerdale to a good dinner and comfortable bed at Seascale.'

Seascale was just a mile south of the small rural community of Sellafield on the Irish Sea coast, where the War Ministry had recently begun to construct a Royal Ordnance factory. The 300-foot tower topped with its famous 'cardinal's hat' had yet to be constructed, as part of the infrastructure for producing plutonium for Britain's nuclear weapons programme. The social and environmental impacts on the area threatened to upset the balance of 'Place, Work and Folk' that Dower had recently espoused for the reconstruction of the Yorkshire Dales.[115]

Lying awake in the Seascale Hotel, Dower reflected that there were limits to what could be learned from these surveys. The practical difficulties soon became apparent on the following day as the party drove up Wasdale to Wasdale Head. 'Stamp and Engholm have walked off (against my advice) to "see the heart of the Lake District from the top of Styhead",' he wrote to Pauline. 'They will see nothing, for the clouds are down – and they will get back very wet, for it is raining most of the time! (Anyway Styhead is a poor viewpoint.)'

Dower himself was already familiar with this part of the Lake District from his work with Kenneth Spence on the forestry issue, and an unfocused sightseeing tour such as this was not going to add very much to his knowledge. In order to investigate the areas and problems that *he* wanted to, he would have to have control of his own transport – but this required a driver and adequate petrol coupons. He wrote to

---

115 See p. 94.

Vincent early in October: 'It seems to me of major importance for my work on Snowdonia & Dartmoor & the Peak (which I know far less well than the Lakes) that I should be able to see for myself their boundaries and problem areas... and it's really quite impractical to do this within the time I can spare for it, except by car. Clough Williams-Ellis is ready and keen to drive me around Snowdonia, but he also has no petrol to spare for the purpose.' Dudley Stamp, by contrast, had been provided with 'ample' petrol coupons for his official survey work for the Ministry of Agriculture. Dower calculated that three day-long runs of about eighty miles each in his rather thirsty Vauxhall 20 (at sixteen miles to the gallon) would require fifteen gallons, 'plus a contingency of an extra 20 gallons to cover any underestimation of distances'. He also asked for 'suitable written authority covering the use of a car for my survey work, in the event of police enquiry'.[116]

*

The Snowdonia survey was provisionally scheduled for the week beginning 19 October, and Dower had proposed to come down to London beforehand to visit the Ministry on the 12th. But in the event, he kept neither appointment. On 23 October he wrote to Vincent that he had been 'rather off colour – nothing serious my doctor says, and anyway I'm now basically cured, but I've thought it best to take things rather easily for a few days.'[117] But only for a few days – for he was proposing to do a survey of the Peak District at the end of the month. Pauline was concerned that he was overworking, a view confirmed by a note from her father, Sir Charles Trevelyan, who wrote from Wallington expressing his 'deep sorrow' that his son-in-law was unwell again. 'I cannot say I am surprised. And I fear that until he begins to treat himself rigorously as an invalid, no true recovery is likely to be possible...'[118]

---

116 Dower to Vincent 8 October 1942, HLG 92/46.
117 Dower to Vincent, 23 October 1942, HLG 92/46.
118 Letter from Charles Trevelyan to Pauline, 20 October 1943.

But the visit to the Peak District was difficult to postpone, since he had been invited to attend a meeting in Sheffield on the possible boundaries of the National Park. This was a contentious issue, for there was some local support for a National Park for Dovedale, separate from the Peak moorland areas. In addition, he was to be hosted on the tour by the formidable Mrs Ethel Haythornthwaite, the Secretary of the Joint Committee for the Peak District National Park, and Honorary Secretary of the local CPRE branch. Realising that this was likely to be a somewhat stressful few days, Pauline stepped in and volunteered to accompany her husband, and to act as his driver. As well as sharing some of the burden, this would have the additional benefit of allowing Dower to take notes during the tour.

With the canvas hood of his convertible Vauxhall firmly tightened down against the cold and mist of November, Dower spent three days inspecting the northern and western parts of the Peaks. 'This was very useful and enjoyable,' he later wrote to Vincent, 'though mists at times obscured the

Ethel Haythornthwaite,
Peak District campaigner.
(CPRE)

views which I had gone to see.' In Buxton, he interviewed a Mr FA Holmes, the leading protagonist of the proposed Dovedale National Park. 'I did my best with him,' he reported to Vincent, 'but he's a thorough one-track mind, and may prove a nuisance later on (unless we adopt his ideas verbatim – which would be a mistake!'[119] Reflecting on the tour a few weeks later, he concluded that 'the area is far more problematic in every way' than either the Lakes or Snowdonia, and without the assistants he had expected, an early survey report on the Peaks 'would be mainly a statement of the problems'.[120]

The tour of Snowdonia, rescheduled for the last week of November, was agreeably more comfortable and sociable for being hosted by Clough Williams-Ellis. Plas Brondanw, his sixteenth-century home some eight miles south of Snowdon, near the Traeth Bach estuary, was 'a most diverting mixture of primitive Welsh and Cloughish baroque,' Dower wrote to Pauline. 'Outhouses, small village, gardens, a mock-ruined tower etc – all complete and magnificently situated with superb views.'

'Clough' had met him off the train at Shrewsbury and they had driven via Corwen, Bala and Trawsfynydd. The weather improved as they travelled westwards, with, finally, 'a brilliant golden sunset with purple mountains, and fox-red oak trees'. The following day, Sunday, they set off towards the Lleyn Peninsula. Dower should have been accompanied on the tour by Patrick Abercrombie and Kenneth Spence, but in the event Abercrombie had to cancel and Spence was delayed by a day. Nevertheless, the trip proved no less sociable, with a generous lunch *en route* with Clough's brother, and then tea with a Mr Helm of the Welsh Ancient Monuments Commission on the way back, near Criccieth.[121] In view of the social aspects of the trip it was not altogether surprising that he should write to Vincent explaining that he needed another visit before reporting. Once again, without more assistance from the Ministry, his itinerary and

---

119 Letter from Dower to Vincent, 20 November 1942.
120 Dower to Vincent, February 1943.
121 Letter from Dower to Pauline, 22 November 1942.

timetable had been dependent on the generosity of others –
and the mixture of work and friendship was not altogether
conducive to maximum efficiency.

*

Meanwhile, back at the Ministry in London, Neal had begun
to panic. Where, he asked Vincent, was Dower's report
on the Lakes, which should have been delivered in mid-
November? His anxiety mounted as November gave way to
December and the government announced – at last – that
the new Ministry of Town and Country Planning (MTCP)
would be established as the central planning authority for
England and Wales. Its new Minister WS Morrison (then
Postmaster-General) would take over the reins in early
February 1943. Dower had an hour's conversation with
Morrison soon after his appointment, and found him 'a
most ready, intelligent and charming person: very good on
National Parks – a good planning job all round!'[122]
   The pressure was on for the new Ministry to hit the
ground running – to show leadership to other, mainly
hostile, government departments, and to make clear to
the public that it had a vital role to play in reconstructing
England's war-shattered towns and countryside. Yet so far
the outgoing Ministry of Works and Planning had little to
show in terms of legislation or new policy initiatives. From
this perspective, Dower's work on National Parks was crucial,
even more so following the publication of the timetable for
implementing the recommendations of the Scott Report.
Moreover, by February 1942 morale in Britain had sunk to a
new low following the fall of Singapore – one of the greatest
defeats in the history of Britain's armed forces. Against this
background, a carefully-focused public relations strategy by
the Ministry was regarded as a 'win-win' initiative benefiting
both the department, and the war effort as a whole.
   On 4 August 1942, a bright young Principal, Miss Ann
Jenkins, handed over to her superiors a key paper she had

_____

122 Letter from Dower to Pauline, 16 December 1942.

drafted entitled *Public Relations in the Planning Department.*
It was forthright in declaring that 'the prime justification for
the existence of a Ministry of Planning during the war is one
of morale'. It went on:

> Its success or failure (looked at in the short term)
> must be largely measured by whether it is making
> people more hopeful of the future and thereby
> more willing to endure the present. The best way
> of achieving this is by producing visible results i.e.
> legislation. When this is impossible, the next best
> way is to explain why the results are not immediately
> forthcoming and to give assurance that everything
> possible is being done to produce them and that
> they will in fact be produced by the time they are
> really needed... The publication of the Scott and
> Uthwatt reports will call for a good deal of work
> on the explanatory, as well as the legislative, side
> during the next three months...

At the bottom of the document, Ernest Hill noted in his
scrawling handwriting that he 'should myself put as the
prime reason [for the existence of the Ministry] the urgent
need to have at least provisional plans ready at the end of
the war. I agree, however, that from the point of view of
the reaction of the general public, the psychological factor
is immensely important.'[123] So important indeed that on
the launch of the Ministry of Town and Country Planning
in February 1943, a new Head of Public Relations was
appointed – a distinguished former Controller of Public
Relations at the BBC and Head of its Overseas Services,
Sir Stephen Tallents. His Press Officer was to be Tom
Stephenson, a Yorkshireman, prominent rambler, former
journalist on the *Daily Herald* and future founder of the
Pennine Way. He had been jailed during the First World
War as a conscientious objector, and afterwards became
active in the Labour Party. Stephenson and Dower were to
become good friends, despite their contrasting social and

---

123 *Public Relations in the Planning Department*, 4 August 1942,
HLG 71/1253.

professional backgrounds. He described Dower as 'my only kindred spirit' in a Ministry otherwise staffed by grey civil servants.[124]

There was much discussion within the Ministry of Morrison's inaugural press conference which was expected to be a big event attended by 125 journalists from local and national newspapers and magazines. In the absence of any concrete policy initiatives, Tallents proposed a 'big picture' speech highlighting five key challenges and opportunities that the MTCP would tackle. The first two were 'National Parks' and 'Protection of the Coastline'.[125] When eventually Morrison delivered the speech at the end of May 1943, he concluded by saying: 'We must recognise that healthy and rapidly growing enthusiasm of townspeople for the pleasures of the country. That will mean planning for adequate protection of natural beauty, and for provision of access to National Parks, the coasts and other parts of the country... there is a great amount of preparatory work to be done, many difficulties to be overcome, innumerable details to be worked into an ordered scheme, and much legislation to be drafted, so that when at last we turn from war to peace, we may begin the building at once.'

The 'great amount of preparatory work' was exactly what Neal had been worrying about for several months. In late January 1943, he had written to Vincent once more asking where was Dower's report on the Lakes, and whether the six month deadline for all the work would be respected. Vincent knew the answer: the delay was caused by an increased workload, insufficient practical support for Dower and his periods of ill-health. And anyway Vincent challenged Neal's rigid interpretation of Dower's contract. 'I did not... intend his [terms of] reference to have such rigidity, but rather to be a guide, and that the run of work would be arranged concurrently and in accordance with our needs... It has been my intention to make a further recommendation as to the use

---

124 Tom Stephenson, 'Fifty Years of Fellowship', in *Making Tracks: A Celebration of 50 years of the Ramblers Association*, ed. Ann Holt, Ramblers' Association, 1985.

125 Minister's Press Conference, HLG 71/1255.

of Dower's services, but in the first instance to get from him up-to-date-information on his health once he returns.'[126] He reported that Dower had intended to come to London that week, but had been delayed 'by influenza' and could not come to the office until 8 February.

Back at The Rookery, Dower hastily scribbled a note on progress, on the basis of which Vincent, rather wearily, penned a memo to Neal. He pointed out that the advance report on the Lakes was originally requested to provide information to a potential government committee on the whole question of National Parks. This had not materialised, and so he had agreed with Dower that the Lakes report could be forwarded later, with the others. Then, following the appearance of the Scott Report schedule, and the prospect of early consultations with other departments, there was a need to accelerate work on the 'big picture' policy issues – the 'general report' which had originally been given lesser priority. Neither of these changes to Dower's terms of reference had been put in writing, but Vincent had understood that Dower had spoken to Neal and that both changes were agreed.[127]

In fact, by mid-February Dower had already written 11,000 of an estimated 15,000 words for the general report, which he told Vincent could be completed in a further week. As regards the individual survey reports, he had amassed a great deal of factual information on most of them, but had not yet had the opportunity of visiting Dartmoor 'and would prefer not to report at all till I have done so'. Dower summarised the position thus: 'In sum, partly due to an underestimate of the amount of work involved (in which it has not proved practicable to get assistant help) and partly owing to the decision to prepare a general report first, the original programme is behindhand.' Not surprisingly, he made no mention of his health.

A face-to-face meeting with Dower in London temporarily helped allay Neal's anxieties, and a new timetable was agreed:

---

126 Vincent to Neal, 2 February 1943, HLG 92/46.
127 Memo from Vincent to Neal, 13 February 1943, HLG 92/46.

- Dower was to complete the general report 'in the next week or two', supplemented by a short document giving broad conclusions as to the administrative machinery required for National Parks;
- The detailed reports on the Lakes, Snowdonia and the Peak District were to be completed within a maximum of three months;
- The Dartmoor visit and report was to be postponed until the first three reports had been completed;
- Two additional surveys and reports on the coasts of North Cornwall and Pembrokeshire would follow Dartmoor.[128]

This represented something of a climbdown by Neal, and was roughly in accordance with what Dower himself had suggested to Vincent weeks before. But to save face, Neal sent a headmasterly reprimand to Vincent pointing out that 'it is desirable that if any important changes are contemplated or made in a programme of work that has been submitted to the [Permanent] Secretary, a written record should be made and the Secretary should be minuted.' This was endorsed by Sir Geoffrey Whiskard, the Permanent Secretary. It was a further nail in the coffin of the Vincent–Neal relationship, and within a year Vincent was to be moved to a post in Washington.

128 Memo from Neal to Vincent, 15 February 1943, HLG 92/46.

8. 'A One-Man White Paper'

Dower missed the deadline for submitting his report by almost a month. It was not until 20 March 1943 that Vincent finally received part one of the document, containing the meat of his conclusions, while the much shorter part two on administrative arrangements was delayed until mid-June. The additional, detailed survey reports on the Lakes, Snowdonia and the Peak District – due for submission by mid-May – were also put on the backburner while Dower finished the main report.

In response to Neal's rising agitation about the delay, Dower pointed out that his draft was considerably longer and fuller than expected – over twice the size of the 15,000-word document originally foreseen. Vincent gave him additional support by explaining to Neal that staff shortages in the Ministry had required Dower to undertake extra missions. These included the inspection of quarrying on the Roman Wall, leading to a report and a conference; the surveys with Steers of the coasts of Pembrokeshire and Snowdonia; and an extra visit to London to assist in the organisation of further survey work.[129]

As it turned out, these were just one in a series of delays that postponed by two years the eventual publication of Dower's report in May 1945. It had to await the completion of detailed negotiations with a wide range of other interested government departments, as well as the further development of Britain's planning legislation – including on the crucial issues of compensation and betterment (see p. 146). Later, in a light-hearted review of his work, Dower reported wryly that he had drafted 'the whole Report myself, with my own pen – most of it several times over...'

*

129 Unless otherwise referenced, documents relating to the first draft of Dower's report can be found in National Archives (NA) HLG 95/55.

Dower made clear from the beginning that although the broad principle of National Parks had been accepted by the government, 'all the details remain to be filled in – the choice of areas, the controls to be imposed, the facilities to be provided, the machinery, powers and technique required, and the necessary co-ordination with other purposes of planning, and with the policies and activities of other Departments.'

Therefore, his report – fifty-three densely written foolscap pages – set out 'a general consideration' rather than offering a detailed blueprint. It was not at all a conventional civil service document. Despite its length, it was written in a clear, accessible style, with frequent use of the word 'I' – a personal rather than a departmental review of the issues.

Dower defined a National Park, in the British context, as

an extensive area of beautiful and relatively wild country in which, for the benefit and by appropriate national decision and action, (a) the characteristic landscape beauty is strictly preserved, (b) access and facilities for public open-air enjoyment are amply provided, (c) wildlife and buildings and places of architectural and historic interest are suitably protected, while (d) established farming use is effectively maintained. The several requirements and qualifications of this definition are all important...

Britain's National Parks would therefore differ fundamentally from those in North America or Africa, where they had been established mainly in virgin country, in high mountains, forests or jungle. As a small and heavily populated country, Britain had no such extensive stretches of pristine land, even in the Scottish Highlands. The process of designating and managing National Parks in Britain would therefore be more complicated, involving difficult trade-offs between competing uses.

The report covered England and Wales only. The Addison Committee in 1931 had recommended separate consideration of Scotland on a number of grounds, including its far smaller population, less pressure on the countryside, and *de facto* public access to much Scottish hill and mountain country. In addition, a number of powerful landowners with extensive Highland estates were opposed to the imposition of any further planning restrictions. Accordingly, a separate but parallel enquiry to Dower's was set up in January 1944, chaired by Sir Douglas Ramsay, which reported in 1945.[130]

Dower was not altogether reconciled to this arrangement. As early as 1935 he had proposed a list of possible National Parks for Great Britain which included the North-West Highlands and Islands, the Central Highlands, the Argyll Highlands and Islands and the Southern Uplands – in effect, most of Scotland. His draft report was slightly less ambitious than this, but its title – *Preliminary Report on National Parks and Associated Matters* – made no reference to its restriction to England and Wales. Indeed, he wrote that it was:

> exceedingly important – and may perhaps be assumed – that national parks should be established, and areas for further national parks reserved, in Scotland *pari passu* with England and Wales, and at a rate of not less than one [Scottish] to three [English and Welsh]. The mountain masses of the Highlands, with their glens and lochs, are far larger and more continuously wild than any corresponding areas south of the border; and (in my opinion) at least two selected Highland National Parks – one preferably beyond and the other this side of the Great Glen – should be created simultaneously with the first batch of English and Wales.

Although Dower was the sole author of his report, he acknowledged his debt to the Addison Committee for its 'valuable assembly of facts and opinions', and also to the publications of the Standing Committee on National Parks. This was slightly disingenuous, since it was Dower himself who had drafted the keynote paper – *National Parks: An*

---

130 See Gordon Cherry, *Environmental Planning Vol II, National Parks and Recreation in the Countryside*, HMSO, 1975, chapter 4.

Appeal – for the meeting in November 1935 of the Joint Committee of Open Air Organisations which had led to the foundation of the Standing Committee in the first place.[131] And subsequently, as its Honorary Drafting Secretary, Dower had written *The Case for National Parks in Great Britain* in 1938, and a draft National Parks Bill in 1939. Even so, he recognised that his knowledge of a number of British regions was incomplete, and he was reliant on the expertise of other members of the Standing Committee to fill the gaps.

In March 1942, a year before Dower was to submit the first draft of his report, the Revd. HH Symonds on behalf of the Standing Committee had drawn up for the then Ministry of Works and Buildings a list of fifteen possible National Parks. These were selected so as to secure a roughly equal distribution of parks as between the North of England (marked 'N' in the Box below), the South of England (S), and Wales and the Welsh borders (W). Symonds wrote to his Committee that 'the method adopted in the list has its advantages. It secures a better geographical distribution of the areas over the country, and also a better distribution of them among the different types of landscape. It is likely to appeal to general judgement as fair to the population as now distributed.'[132]

Box 4: Standing Committee on National Parks: Selection of Proposed Parks (1942)

First Priorities (Minimum)		
1	Lake District	N
2	Dartmoor	S

131 *National Parks: An Appeal*, November 1935, in Standing Committee on National Parks archive, Box 36, Museum of Rural Life, University of Reading.
132 Standing Committee on National Parks, *Suggested Priority Selection of National Parks, England & Wales*, 18 March 1942, HLG 92/51.

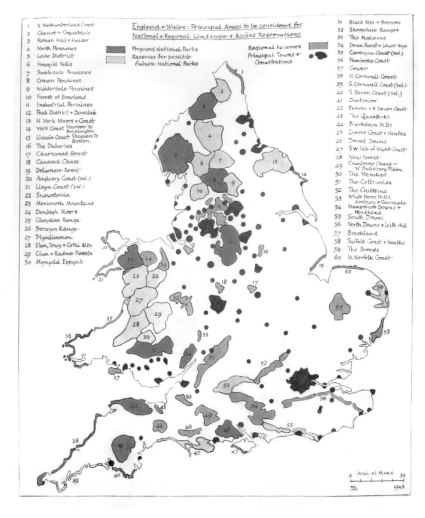

John Dower set out bold initial proposals in June 1943 for the areas to be considered by the government, either as immediate or future National Parks, and 'Regional Reserves' (later Areas of Outstanding Natural Beauty). (John Dower)

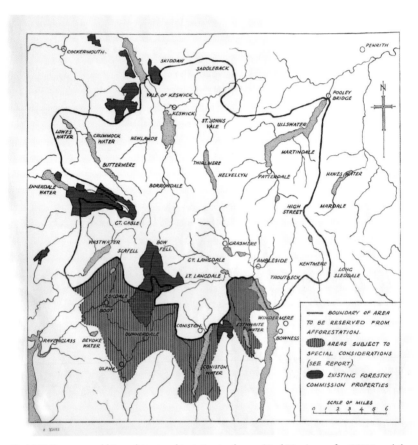

In 1935 Dower used his architectural training to draw a 'Red Line' map for CPRE and the Forestry Commission identifying proposed limits to afforestation in the Lake District. He proposed an ambitious 520-square-mile exclusion zone – which was reduced through later negotiations. (John Dower)

The Peak District was Britain's first National Park, designated in 1951 at the end of thirty years of long and winding negotiations. (Lukasz Pajor/Shutterstock)

The Peak District is uniquely bounded on all sides by current and former industries, providing a convenient source of recreation for a very large population. (Steve Horsley/Shutterstock)

The feet of thousands of ramblers in the Peaks cause serious erosion, offset by long sections of paved pathways. (Next level Shots/Shutterstock)

The Lake District is the most popular of all the National Parks, with over 16 million visitors a year. The beauty of mountains like Causey Pike, Robinson and Cat Bells explains why. (Kevin Eaves/Shutterstock)

Vintage steamers on Lake Windermere provide a more relaxing way to enjoy the National Park. (David Young/Shutterstock)

More adventurous fell-walkers in Snowdonia can't resist the dangerous challenge of tackling the knife-edge ridge of Crib Goch, with a drop of 900 metres. (Hill2K/Shutterstock)

Snowdonia was the first Welsh National Park, with an area only a few square miles less than that of the Lake District. At sunset in winter its snow-covered mountains take on a special beauty. (Valdis Skudre/Shutterstock)

Dartmoor's unique attraction derives from the dramatic uprising of its high, bare hills and rocky granite tors. Here, on the western edge of the park near Brentor, the church of St Michael of the Rock is a landmark for miles around. (Julian Gazzard/Shutterstock)

Pembrokeshire hosts Britain's only exclusively coastal National Park – 168 miles of cliffs, sandy bays, offshore islands, and deeply indented valleys. Tenby Harbour, with its sandy beaches and Georgian architecture, lies at its far eastern end. (Michael R Evans/Shutterstock)

As autumn approaches, the North York Moors are ablaze with heather and ling – a purple carpet right across the forty miles from the Vale of York to the sea. Half way along its southern flank is Helmsley, one of the few market towns in the 550 square miles of the Park. (Johnbraid/Shutterstock)

Malham Cove in the Yorkshire Dales lies just two miles north of the limestone village of Kirkby Malham, where John Dower wrote much of his seminal report *National Parks in England and Wales*, published at the end of the war in May 1945. (Albonini/Shutterstock)

A few miles east of Dower's house lies Grassington, a small town surrounded by rolling sheep pastures, and dappled light and shadow on miles of dry-stone walls. (Albonini/ Shutterstock)

Wild Exmoor ponies in an early morning mist over Porlock Common and the Bristol Channel in Exmoor National Park. (Stephen Clarke/Shutterstock)

Sailing, wind surfing, camping, birdwatching and fly fishing at Wimbleball Lake in the south-east corner of Exmoor National Park. (Mike Charles/Shutterstock)

Northumberland National Park: a spring sunset at Sycamore Gap on Hadrian's Wall near Housesteads Roman Fort, once owned by historian and National Park campaigner, GM Trevelyan. (Matt Gibson/Shutterstock)

The bare, rolling hills of Northumberland are the least populated of Britain's National Parks (with just 2,200 residents). After the death of John Dower, Pauline, his widow, campaigned successfully to double the size of what would otherwise have been a small Roman Wall National Park. (Duncan Andison/Shutterstock)

The Brecon Beacons became the third Welsh National Park in 1957. Stretching from Abergavenny in the east to Llandeilo in the west, the National Park has provided an accessible playground for people in the industrial cities of South Wales. (Stocker 1970/Shutterstock)

After a long gap of 32 years, the Broads in Norfolk became Britain's tenth National Park in 1989, with an emphasis on wildlife and water-based recreation. Thurne Mill on the River Bure is visible for miles in the flat Broadland landscape. (Richard Bowden/Shutterstock)

Millions of residents along Britain's south coast were deprived of an easily accessible National Park until 2005, when the New Forest was so designated. The landscape of purple heather and broom on Rockford and Ibsley Commons in Hampshire is typical throughout the hundreds of square miles of parkland. (Helen Hoston/Shutterstock)

The most recent and most populated (120,000) of Britain's National Parks are the South Downs, stretching over seventy miles from Winchester to Eastbourne. They meet the sea at the famous Seven Sisters chalk cliffs. (Paul Daniels/Shutterstock)

A winter landscape of the rolling South Downs between Lewes and Brighton in East Sussex. The inclusion of the South Downs as a National Park was recommended by the Hobhouse Commitee in 1947. It took 63 years - until 2010 - for the government finally to overcome the opposition of sceptical local authorities and powerful landowners. (SimonPRBenson/Shutterstock)

John Dower unsuccessfully championed the Dorset coast and heaths as a potential National Park, since much of it was commandeered by the Army and Navy. The Man O War cove on the Jurassic coast was therefore appropriately named. (Matt Gibson/Shutterstock)

The Wheal Coates tin mine near St. Agnes on the North Cornish coast. Despite strong support among some members of the Hobhouse Committee for a National Park right around the coast of Cornwall, administrative practicalities stood in the way. (Helen Hotson/Shutterstock)

Despite the undulating beauty of the North Wessex Downs, the expansion of wartime farming and several new airfields ruled out National Park status – despite its relative proximity to London. (Skyearth/Shutterstock)

The Broads National Park provides a special habitat for the beautiful, but rare, Swallowtail butterfly. (Ibrahim Kavus/Shutterstock)

Red Grouse hide and thrive among the heather moorlands of the North York Moors National Park. (Tony Mills/Shutterstock)

Some National Parks attract rather more visitors and walkers than can be comfortably absorbed. The Pennine Way near Edale in the Peak District National Park has had to be paved in places to hold back serious erosion along the trail. (Ian Francis/Shutterstock)

During summer weekends, walkers wishing to climb to the summit of Mount Snowdon suffer long and slow queues all the way to the top. (DMP Images/Shutterstock)

The Rookery, Kirkby Malham. With the inevitable approach of war in 1939, John Dower moved the family away from London to a former stone farmhouse in Kirkby Malham in the Yorkshire Dales, where they lived until February 1945. Much of Dower's work on National Parks took place here. (David Wilkinson)

As his health deteriorated, John Dower and the family moved to the village of Cambo, just a mile north from the home of the Trevelyans in Wallington Hall, Northumberland. The nineteenth-century Holy Trinity Church was where John and Pauline were married in 1929. (Peter Barham)

John Dower's ashes were scattered in November 1947 at Woodhouse Crag on Ilkley Moor, a favourite boyhood walk with his brother Arthur. (David Wilkinson)

3	Snowdonia	W
4	Peak District	N
5	South Downs	S
6	Pembroke Coast	W
Addition 1		
7	Craven Pennines	N
8	North Cornish Coast	N
9	Black Mountains	W
Addition 2		
10	Roman Wall	N
11	Exmoor	S
12	Brecon Beacons	W
Addition 3		
13	Cheviots	N
14	White Horse Hills (Wiltshire)	S
15	Plynlimon	W

But this geographically 'balanced' criterion posed several difficulties. It took no account of the wide variation in population as between the North, the South, and Wales; gave little consideration to the comparative quality of their respective landscapes; and completely neglected potential candidates in east and south-east England. Symonds acknowledged that his list 'might be arranged on another principle', and asked his colleagues: 'Which six (or more) areas (irrespective of their being in this or that part of England and Wales) would you yourself name, in an order of choice, as the *best* national parks?'

Symonds had discussed his selection with Dower, who added the approximate areas of each proposed park, and some explanatory notes. A year later Dower's own draft report looked very different. He estimated that in England and Wales there were about 8,000 square miles – some

14 per cent of the total – of suitably wild, beautiful and extensive country where National Parks and other protected areas might be designated. But not all of this land would be required for National Parks, so clear criteria needed to be established to guide the process of selection. He identified almost five times as many areas as Symonds – a total of sixty, arranged in three groups according to their importance and the *kind* of park they would be.

- **Group A** consisted of twelve potential National Parks, selected in order of importance rather than for their geographical location (see colour map, p. i). Omitted from this priority group were the South Downs, the White Horse Hills, and Plynlimon (all of which Symonds had proposed), but included were the New Forest and the Forest of Dean. The first six in this list were the 'jewels in the crown' (the Lakes, Snowdonia, Dartmoor, the Peaks and Dovedale, the Pembrokeshire Coast and the North Cornwall Coast). The Craven Pennines (later the Yorkshire Dales), the Black Mountains, Exmoor and the North Devon coast were proposed for the second (but early) instalment, while the remaining three (the Roman Wall and Kielder Forest; the Forest of Dean and Lower Wye, and the New Forest) Dower proposed as special types of National Park, to be established in consultation and collaboration with the Forestry Commission – and in the case of the Roman Wall, additionally with the Ancient Monuments Department of the Ministry of Works.

- **Group B** comprised a further eighteen areas to be reserved for *future* National Parks. Dower regarded the first nine of these as 'probables', and the rest as 'possibles'. Again, collaboration with the Forestry Commission and the Ancient Monuments Department would be required in relation to the White Horse Hills (with Avebury and Savernake), while the Norfolk Broads would be a unique 'waterway park' requiring special consultation and management.

- **Group C** – the longest list – comprised thirty more
  areas described by Dower as 'Regional Reserves'. These
  were the 'also rans', unlikely to be found suitable or
  important enough to be designated as future National
  Parks. They were to be regarded as amenity areas
  where local authorities or other agencies would be
  expected to take the leading role in their selection
  and management. (Later, most of these were to be
  designated as Areas of Outstanding Natural Beauty –
  AONBs.)

An important feature of Dower's initial list of sixty was the
prominence of coastal areas – eighteen in total, and three
in the priority Group A. Much of the south-west peninsula
along the seaboards of Devon, Cornwall and Dorset he
considered important enough to be given either priority, or
reserve, National Park status. The emphasis on preserving
large lengths of the coast doubtless reflected the intensive
advocacy and survey work undertaken for the Ministry by
Britain's leading geomorphologist, Alfred Steers, during the
first six months of 1943.[133] However, such narrow, elongated
parks posed a range of practical and administrative
difficulties.

There were a number of anomalies in Dower's suggested
designations. He relegated the South Downs and the White
Horse Hills in southern England from priority National
Park status (as proposed by Symonds) to the 'reserved'
category in Group B. But at the same time, the Chilterns, the
Cotswolds and the Mendips – with similar topography and
recreational attractions to the South Downs - were proposed
only as 'regional reserves' in Group C, unlikely ever to merit
National Park status. He later explained:

> It may be thought that some of the areas in the
> South and East, here included in Group C, should
> be promoted to balance the high proportion (in

---

133 JA Steers, *The Coastline of England and Wales*, Cambridge, 1946.

Groups A and B) of areas in the North, West and South-West. The answer is that the wild country most suitable for National Parks *is* preponderantly in the north, west and south-west. Nevertheless, I should have included several southern or eastern areas in Groups A or B, if I had not been reasonably sure that they are likely to be dealt with satisfactorily by other agencies, notably the South Downs (by the county and local authorities) and the New Forest (by the Forestry Commission).

In fact, these proposals were met with strong opposition by the affected authorities, and Dower could produce no further evidence to support this optimism.

*

Only around a quarter of Dower's draft report was devoted to the selection of National Park areas. The rest addressed a wide range of other countryside issues, including the role of farming; rambling and access to National Parks; recreation; cars and roads; visitor accommodation; and the conservation of wildlife.

As regards protecting the beauty of the landscape, Dower pulled no punches in detailing a range of misuses and disfigurements, many of them caused by the government's own departments and agencies. The problem was not just ill-placed and ugly building developments, for

damage, no less widespread and enduring, has come and may come from quarrying and mining, with their trail of waste-heaps and polluted streams, and in some cases of associated industrial plants; from large scale afforestation, blanketing the varied colours and subtle moulding of the hillsides with monotonous sharp-edged conifer plantations; from ill-considered felling of woodlands or hedgerow timber of 'amenity' value; from the dams and other works of water supply and hydro-electric undertakings, particularly where these convert natural lakes into artificial reservoirs with large rise and fall and consequently unsightly margins; from the poles and pylons of electricity distribution; from the cruder forms of draining and embanking operations; from military occupation, especially in permanent artillery, tank and bombing ranges; and from unnecessary or unsuitable road 'improvements' in wide variety – new routes, widenings, bridge-works, car parks and discordant urban types of surfacing, fencing, signposts and other 'furniture'...

It is not a question of prohibiting such uses of land anywhere and everywhere. But it matters enormously *where* and *how*... They must be made subject to a control no less effective than that applied to ordinary building development; and, if continuance of uses and works already established must usually be accepted, any new exploitation – or major extension of an existing one – should be permitted only on clear proof that it is required in the national interest and that no satisfactory alternative site, *not* in a national park area, can be found. Such cases should be rare.

Traffic congestion and road building were also major threats requiring comprehensive regulation. Dower focused on the increasing volume of cars, coaches and lorries that he argued should be funnelled away from National Parks by providing new or improved routes for through traffic *outside* the park area. *Within* the parks, the principal problem was the unrestricted freedom of motor tourists to use major roads to enjoy the scenery, expecting 'endless widening and improvement of all such roads to enable them to travel everywhere at high speeds, regardless of "the view", and without risk of congestion, however many of them may take simultaneously the same Sunday outing. Trying to "beat the band" – more traffic, more improvements; more improvements, more traffic *ad infinitum* – is palpably absurd.'

As for the more minor roads – those which were narrow,

steep or winding, or rough mountain and moorland cart tracks – Dower proposed selective restriction and segregation of traffic. There should be a 'share-out' of these subsidiary and rough routes between motorists and non-motorists. 'Bearing in mind that walkers constitute by far the most important section of the public for whom the parks are provided', they should have a generous share, including almost all the 'green lanes', drove roads and mountain and moorland cart tracks, and many of the by-roads with no through-route value, or where there were better alternative routes. Dower supported the Scott Committee's recommendation that a national policy should be framed to determine the future status of all roads, and proposed 'close and continuous consultation' between the National Parks Authority, the Ministry of Transport, the Traffic Commissioners and county and other councils. Crucially, he argued that any disputes should be referred to an unspecified 'appropriate higher authority' – a move that was sure to set a collision course with other Ministries and councils.

The protection of wildlife was one of four major objectives for National Parks set out in the opening paragraphs of Dower's report. As well as an accomplished architect and rural planner, Dower was a very competent botanist, who during his later years became increasingly interested in the developing discipline of ecology. He looked forward to a 'wildlife conservation policy... as an integral part of a comprehensive programme for conservation and development of our national resources. We have not yet got in this country *any* national policy for the conservation of wildlife,' he wrote. 'All controllable human activities likely to have a material effect on the distribution and density of the immense variety of the country's flora and fauna are relevant material' for this policy. It would need to encompass not only the protection of species and habitats generally, but also the establishment of a range of state-funded nature reserves. A key question was: who should manage such nature reserves, both within and outside National Parks? This was to give rise to a prolonged 'turf war' between rural planners on the one hand, and nature conservationists on the other.

A group of eminent zoologists, botanists and ecologists

had established the Nature Reserves Investigation Committee (NRIC) in June 1942 to champion the cause of nature conservation in the National Parks debate. Their concern was that the various objectives set for National Parks could be incompatible: greater access and more facilities for the public in the countryside, and the development of farming, could potentially be damaging to wildlife. In addition, the need to protect species and habitats was not confined just to National Parks. The proposed National Parks Authority, declared the NRIC, 'must deal with a range of interests different from, and wider than, those of nature reserves, and a specific Nature Reserves Authority would provide an invaluable centre of scientific knowledge and opinion...' The Committee proposed a new Authority – provisionally named The Wildlife Conservation Council – which should have full executive responsibility for the selection, acquisition, control and management of all nature reserves, including those within National Parks. It did, however, concede that reserves of less than national importance in the parks could be the responsibility of the National Parks Authority.[134]

Dower's report rejected all the NRIC's arguments, apart from the establishment of a Wildlife Conservation Council – provided this was only an advisory rather than an executive body.

> It is – in my view – both practicable and desirable that the National Parks Authority *should* administer National Nature Reserves, certainly those which fall within National Parks, and preferably those outside as well. For the latter, it is a matter of practical convenience, in simplification and in economy of 'overhead' costs by using one executive authority rather than two; but for the former it seems to me essential. Wildlife conservation is an integral part of National Parks policy; and I do not see how a proper balance and inter-relation between it and

---

134 Peter Ayres, *Shaping Ecology: The Life of Arthur Tansley*, Wiley-Blackwell, 2012, p.161ff.

the other main objects – landscape preservation, protection and improvement of farming, and development of access and recreational facilities – can be secured and maintained, unless the National Parks Authority is responsible for the provision of Nature Reserves.

The National Parks Authority would require expert guidance both in the management of nature reserves and in all other measures for wildlife conservation. The Wildlife Conservation Council would fulfil this training role, Dower argued, through a small joint standing committee.

The stand-off between nature conservationists on the one hand, and campaigners for preservation and access to the countryside on the other was to be a major feature of the debate over Dower's report, and was not reconciled for over sixty years – until the establishment of Natural England in 2006.

*

Dower proposed one major exemption from planning control in the countryside: farming. 'It is above all else to farming ... that the landscapes of all our potential national parks owe the man-made element in their character; and it is to the farming communities that we must look for continuance not only of the scenic setting but of the drama itself – the rural life and work, "the mild continuous epic of the soil", the endless battle between man and nature – without which the finest of English or Welsh scenery would lack an essential part of its charm and recreational value... Efficient farming is a key requirement in National Park areas [and] agriculture, landscape preservation and recreational provisions must march together. There should be no substantial difficulty in working out the necessary practical arrangements, for in all major matters there is community and harmony of purpose.'

Such faith in farming and farmers was to prove short-sighted, in view of the extensive damage and pollution inflicted on landscapes, water courses and habitats by post-war advances in agricultural technology and production incentives. However, Dower's encouragement of farming should be seen alongside his proposals for greater state involvement in agriculture. 'It should ... remain the right and duty of the National Parks Authority,' he wrote, 'to consult and collaborate with the Ministry of Agriculture and its subordinate bodies, and with farmers and farm-owners, individually and collectively, in many matters of common concern... In return for protection against loss of land or interference through building and other forms of non-agricultural development, farmers and owners should accept, ungrudgingly, the planning control of the siting and appearance of new or altered farm buildings [as recommended by the Scott Report]... Farmers and owners should also be ready to accept a general control – not prohibition – of timber felling, and consultation about any major "improvement" schemes, with possible adjustments of detail to prevent needlessly harsh or discordant landscape effects.'

On the question of greater provision for open-air recreation in the countryside, Dower's view was that 'between rambling and farming there is no major conflict of interest, nor in practice any serious amount of trouble.' Opening up the countryside was justified on egalitarian grounds: access should be 'amply provided' for the public at large, not just for privileged sections of the community. At the same time, however, he was surprisingly forthright – even snobbish – in drawing attention to a significant section of society who did not enjoy 'the beauty and quietude of unspoilt country'. There was a danger, he argued, that National Park authorities would be pressurised into providing not so much a 'full-blown lido, or fun-fair', but more modest intrusions – 'here a garden-pleasure ground (small bar attached), there a simple bathing enclosure (with old-world café)', particularly where they adjoined a major road. He observed:

It is not just a question of custom or of education, or the lack of it. Many people of all classes are, by taste and temperament, far better satisfied by town than by country as a holiday setting. How very many, and how well most of them know what they want, are sufficiently testified by the size and popularity of Blackpool and Brighton and a hundred other coastal and inland 'resorts'. For all who want to spend their holidays in a noisy crowd, to parade their best clothes, to sit and listen to the band or watch a county cricket match, to be entertained at cinema or music-hall, to dance in large dance-halls or bathe in large bathing-pools, National Parks are not the place. They had far better keep away, and (some of them, perhaps, after an unsuccessful experiment or two) they pretty certainly will keep away. On one condition: that no provision is made for them...

*

The second part of Dower's draft report – on the administrative machinery for the establishment and management of National Parks – was finally delivered three months after the first, on 16 June 1943. It was short, at only 3,000 words, and bore the marks of being written by a man under pressure. 'I have, thank God, finished my Report,' he wrote to Vincent from Wallington, 'though I've not got time before today's post to complete the fair-copying of the last two paragraphs, which I will send tomorrow...'

Part two reiterated the point that National Parks must be nationally selected, and therefore 'provided and supervised' by a 'National Authority'. Much of this section was concerned with setting out Dower's controversial proposals for distributing power between, respectively, the Authority, central government ministries and local councils. The autonomy of the Authority, he argued, would be ensured by establishing it as a separate Commission – what would now be called a 'quango' – rather than as a sub-department within the Ministry of Town and Country Planning. This would only open the way to controlling the Authority's budget, and the day-to-day interference by the Ministry in local planning decisions.

The proposed new National Parks Commission would consist of a Chairman and six other Commissioners, appointed by the Minister. It would have powers to make regulations *inter alia* to preserve landscape beauty and wildlife, establish public rights of way, and close highways. Each National Park (with the addition of its fringes) would be a single area administered by one joint planning committee comprising representatives of the Commission and of the local authorities. Any point on which the Commission's representatives were outvoted could be referred for decision to the Minister, and the Commission would be entitled to take over any or all provisions of planning schemes in National Park areas. As regards relations with other government departments or statutory undertakers, their proposed development proposals affecting National Parks could also come under the direct control of the Commission, subject to reference to the Minister or a Ministerial committee. Dower concluded his report with details of the day-to-day operation of the Commission, its budget and staffing, and the work of individual National Park committees. It was so technical that it was eventually omitted from the final version.

Jumping the First Hurdle

Within the Ministry of Town and Country Planning, Dower's report was received with some relief, as well as acclaim. The new Permanent Secretary, Sir Geoffrey Whiskard, and the head of the Plans Division, George Pepler, both described it as 'masterly'. Even Lawrence Neal went so far as to praise 'so fine an effort'. However, it was the work of one man only, and its widespread political and administrative implications would need to be considered, negotiated and endorsed first within the Ministry; then among the numerous other central government departments and agencies whose activities would be directly or indirectly affected; then externally among local authorities and relevant voluntary organisations like the Standing Committee and the National

Trust.

The immediate response in the Ministry focused on the presentation of the report, and how this would affect its external reception. Neal stressed the overriding importance of cultivating the goodwill of other departments, and wanted the document to be 'critically reviewed' with this in mind. 'At times Mr Dower hits out unnecessarily, at other times unwisely, when he assails a number of interests... It would be a pity if so fine an effort were to be handicapped through a certain lack of restraint here and there. References to Forestry in other places may also create antagonism... Some other pruning could be considered, as the writing is a little overloaded at times... Would Mr Dower please use his blue pencil in this regard...?'[135] Even Harold Vincent remarked that 'Others might put some of it a trifle differently.' He proposed a number of cuts to the report – in particular, references to financial requirements. 'I don't want to start by asking for a limit of money available, particularly as we cannot yet present any estimates.'[136]

Vincent's main criticism focused on how such an ambitious programme of National Parks would overlap with the developing policies of the new Ministry. 'There is too specific a policy of safeguarding areas of wild country, which are not in the first instalment, as reserves for future National Parks,' he wrote. 'I think the emphasis gives N.P.s too much weight in the general scheme of land utilisation.' This was an early indication of the inherent tension between the new Ministry and a future National Parks Authority over their respective roles in developing rural planning.

George Pepler expressed his general agreement with most of Dower's report, but listed a number of practical difficulties in the operation of joint planning committees in each National Park:

(a) A [National Parks] Commission of seven will have its hands very full if it is to be represented on 12 joint

---

135 Neal to Vincent, 29 March 1943.
136 Vincent to Neal, 20 March 1943.

committees to start with, with another 18 in prospect;
(b) The respective duties of the joint committee and the Commission would need very careful adjustment so as to avoid overlapping administration…;
(c) I doubt whether the suggestion that the Commission might become the responsible authority for carrying out all the provisions of a planning scheme would work…;
(d) I agree that more than a National Park area should be planned as a unit, as the control of the fringe land outside and of the approaches will be very important;
(e) But it will not be at all easy to carve out these joint committee areas as they will disturb some existing joint committee areas.

Pepler drew attention to the situation in the Lakes, where each of the three counties (Cumberland, Westmorland and Lancashire) was very hostile to having its part of the Lake District 'cut off' from the rest of the county. He also doubted whether the proposed coastal National Parks could form practicable joint planning committee areas. And as regards the first twelve National Parks in Group A, 'time was of great importance', since their designation would mean disturbing existing collaborative arrangements and negotiations 'when we are nursing authorities along under very difficult circumstances and short staffs'. He concluded: 'Prolonged and difficult negotiations will be required which cannot be entered into until we know for certain that the Government will accept financial responsibility for National Parks and the form of body has been definitely agreed.'[137]

*

With the many political sensitivities it aroused, plus the fact that it was a personal expression of one man's opinion written in an informal style, Dower's report might well

137 Pepler to Neal, 1 July 1943.

have been consigned permanently to a dusty and forgotten shelf in the basement of the Ministry. But it soon became apparent to both Vincent and Neal that what appeared to be weaknesses were in fact strengths. Vincent noted:

> The Report represents Dower's opinion. I think it will be of advantage in opening discussions with Departments to present a conception of national parks in this personal form. Officially, it would be more difficult to show the errors of the past, of the Departments and different undertakers; it might be dangerous to put so strongly the case for control of industry or military enclosures; it might be presumptuous to suggest so specifically the functions of roads. But I should like Departments to see this background, which is best given in personal opinion.[138]

In addition to its circulation among relevant Ministries, wider publication of the report – beyond Whitehall – also offered a number of advantages. Sir Stephen Tallents, the head of the Ministry's Public Relations department, thought that 'much of the Report seems to me admirably suited for publication... for the sake of informing the public about, and stimulating public discussion of, a problem of great importance and interest...' A document of over 30,000 words, however, was too long 'for a popular purpose', and a shorter version – or even part of the report – would be more appropriate.[139] Neal also saw benefits for the status of the new Ministry. 'During a period when we have to keep silent on so many topics, we might well give evidence of vitality on this one. The [Permanent] Secretary is most favourably disposed to the idea, subject to proper timing and to vetting... I am fully aware that it will require careful handling from several angles, administrative and editorial.'[140]

The form in which Dower's report was to be published presented some difficulties. It was described later by Dower's colleague, William Holford, as 'a one-man White

---

138 Vincent to Neal, 20 March 1943.
139 Tallents to Neal, 3 September 1943.
140 Neal to Vincent, 10 August 1943.

Paper',[141] but White Papers were statements of official government policy, and Dower's report was more akin to what would be described today as a Green Paper, setting out options as part of the process of policy development. It was, however, eventually to be published in May 1945 as a Command Paper, 'A Report by John Dower... Presented by the Ministry of Town and Country Planning to Parliament by Command of His Majesty'. With the exception of Sir William Beveridge's 1944 Report on Employment Policy, this was to be the only official Command Paper ever to acknowledge its author.[142]

*

Dower's draft was examined on 15 and 20 September 1943 in two 'Secretary's Meetings' chaired by the Ministry's Permanent Secretary, Sir Geoffrey Whiskard.[143] He had few concerns that its principal recommendations would be endorsed, following the conversations he had already had with senior colleagues. These included Neal, Vincent, Pepler, Professor Holford and Ernest Hill (Head of the Legislation Division). Tom Stephenson (standing in for the Head of Public Relations, Sir Stephen Tallents) was one of six less senior officials to be invited. Dower was reassured by the fact that the Minister himself, just twenty-four hours before the first Secretary's Meeting, had confirmed that he had no differences of principle with the report.

Accordingly, the meetings endorsed in principle Dower's list of proposed National Parks, and it was agreed that a National Parks Authority should be established as a Commission responsible to the Ministry of Town and Country Planning, rather than as a less influential department within the Ministry. But Dower's proposal

---

141 John Dower obituary, *Journal of the Royal Institute of British Architects*, vol. 55 (1947-8), pp. 38-9.
142 White Paper on Employment Policy, Cmd. 6527, HMSO, May 1944.
143 Secretary's Meetings: Minutes of the 20th and 21st meetings held on 6 and 15 September 1943.

that the Commission should act as 'advocate and defender' of all potential National Park areas was not approved, on the grounds of the workload this would involve. Further discussion on these and other administrative details would be taken forward by an Interim Committee rather than an Interim Commission. Although this sounds like mere semantics, it was important since establishing a Commission would require time-consuming special legislation. Dower stressed that the change should not be construed as downgrading its authority, emphasising that the Committee should have sufficient status 'to stimulate public opinion and give the National Parks project a suitable public send off'. (The Committee was later established in 1945 as the Hobhouse Committee – see Chapter 11.)

Despite Pepler's reservations, the meeting agreed that each National Park should be administered by a Joint Committee comprising representatives from the local authorities involved, plus one or more members of the National Parks Commission. Should the latter be outvoted on sensitive planning issues, the Minister would have the power under existing legislation to have the matter referred to him for decision.

Some doubts were expressed about open access to ramblers to all areas in a National Park. Different parts of the parks required different forms of access, depending on the kind of land-use involved, and it was agreed that further detailed consideration of the issue would be necessary. Sir Geoffrey also foresaw difficulties with the Treasury over grouse-shooting disputes, since access to these areas might require buying out grouse moors and shooting rights. Ernest Hill was also concerned about opening access to water catchment areas. Dower's report, he argued, 'would inevitably create a hostile attitude towards the Report in the Ministry of Health'. Dower insisted, however, that some reference to water catchment areas was essential, but he would revise the existing paragraphs with Hill's point in mind. Finally, it was agreed that the section on the financial implications of National Parks should be dropped. Instead, it was decided that a detailed Appendix on the costs of acquisition and administration of the first six National Parks should be added as a basis for discussion with the Treasury alone.

9. Engaging Other Ministries

Dower's report had been accepted in principle by the Ministry of Town and Country Planning. Now the next step was to sell National Parks to other government departments, many of which stood to be directly affected by them. Harold Vincent wanted to seize the initiative for the Ministry by setting up an official inter-departmental committee, to lead negotiations across the whole of government. But his superior, Lawrence Neal, characteristically chose to overlook the wood in preference for the trees. In a memorandum to the Permanent Secretary, Neal acknowledged that while current liaison arrangements were somewhat *ad hoc*, having been 'carried over from Ministry of Health days', this was 'something more than a good beginning, and capable of very satisfactory development into an effective but flexible system between us and individual departments... Personally, I should be inclined to leave it that we fit the decision to the needs of each case as it arises.'[144] The matter was referred to the Permanent Secretary, and eventually a compromise was agreed whereby there would be no formal standing committee comprising all affected departments (as Vincent had proposed), but a more informal committee where relevant departments could discuss those parts of the report that directly affected them.

Meanwhile, the pressure on Dower was becoming intolerable. He had undertaken extra missions for Vincent during the spring of 1943; drafted a report twice as long as had been anticipated; and was to revise it (three times) in response to comments by his colleagues. In preparation for the Permanent Secretary's meetings in September, he had prepared the nine-page digest of his report, and drawn up an agenda of the key issues to be discussed. At the same time, Vincent had been considering putting Dower in charge of all the 'amenity' work in the Ministry's Research Division. 'Apart from the desirability of considering National Parks

---

144 Neal to Whiskard, 3 May 1943.

133

as one element only of our amenity work,' he wrote to Neal, 'there are particular subjects which need attention – notably the treatment of buildings of historic and architectural importance, and the contact with the Ministry of Works on country houses and ancient monuments; contact with the Forestry Commission; Ministry of Health on water; provision of accommodation for holidays etc.'[145] (Author's italics)

Nevertheless, during the summer Neal continued to press Dower to finish the three detailed surveys of the Lakes, Snowdonia and the Peak District that had been promised for mid-May. He reprimanded Vincent for the delay. 'I feel that this timetable should have been under close watch in your Division. It is disappointing that still further delays now come to light...'[146] Neal's behaviour prompted a sardonic addition to Dower's 'gallery of Ministry clerihews':

> Lawrence Neal
> Prefers men made of steel
> Flesh and blood won't stand the strain
> Of so forceful a brain.

It was not long before Dower's patience snapped. He responded to Neal (via Vincent) that his original terms of reference to prepare detailed reports on the sample areas were simply 'out of date':

> The usefulness to the Ministry of such work is in its provision of a sound general picture and of significant examples for the development of a *general* National Parks policy and for the support of that policy in inter-departmental consideration. I have, in fact, already used a good deal of the information collected on my survey visits etc. by way of illustrative examples in my general report... In following up my general report it will I think be found that further study of related issues is more

145 Vincent to Neal, 8 June 1943.
146 Neal to Vincent, 8 June 1943.

urgently needed and will be more fruitful than the study of particular areas... I instance the Forestry Commission's proposals on post-war Forest Policy issued today which may have profound repercussions on N.P. policy, and which I propose to study immediately.

Neal back-pedalled, but sought to save face by insisting that he should get at least one regional report. 'I have re-stated my feeling that we should be wise to have the Lake District report completed at a really early date,' he wrote. So it was to be a report on the Lake District only, and a short one at that.[147]

There was some compensation for Neal: Dower had proposed to spend more time in London.

My health seems now to be well restored (subject to a word with my doctor). I don't think any harm would come of my being in London for a larger part of my time ... for between half and two-thirds of the working-days of each month (such days to include any spent on specific Ministry visits to other places): the balance of my time being spent at home on report writing etc. I have already made arrangements for semi-permanent lodgings in London which I can use as much or as little as required.[148]

In fact, the main reason for spending more time in London was to rally support for the implementation of his report. He started with the Minister himself, William Morrison. As a temporary civil servant, Dower was unable to go over the heads of his superiors and seek an audience directly with the Minister. However, he was able to organise a small deputation from the Standing Committee on National Parks. This was arranged for 14 September 1943 – the day before the key meeting of the Permanent Secretary's Committee. Dower briefed the chair of the Standing Committee, Sir Norman Birkett, on which key issues to focus on, and

147 Neal to Dower, 27 August 1943.
148 Dower to Vincent, 9 June 1943.

also Morrison himself, on what he should expect from the delegation. 'It may safely be assumed that the case for National Parks which the deputation will present will be the same in all essentials as that presented in my preliminary Report on National Parks,' Dower (unsurprisingly) informed Morrison. 'They are not likely to raise any issue which I have not opened and examined...'

The deputation comprised Sir Norman Birkett, Col. EN Buxton (the Vice-Chair) and the Revd. HH Symonds (who had assumed Dower's former role as the Hon. Drafting Secretary). Alongside the Minister were Dower himself and a departmental official to take the minutes. The conversation ranged widely, touching on the control and treatment of common land after the war; access over water-supply gathering grounds; afforestation; roads and traffic control in National Parks; the issue of compensation; and the regulation of land uses and developments by government departments and statutory undertakings.

The meeting seemed to be a great success on both sides. Morrison expressed his gratitude for having the opportunity to hear the Standing Committee's views, and stressed that 'no difference of principle' existed between him and the Committee 'either as regards policy or machinery'. He invited them to put forward suggestions for the delimitation of National Park areas, and an order of priority for designating them. He expressed the hope that the Standing Committee 'would keep in close touch with the department and would consider themselves free to make suggestions or to draw attention to any particular dangers or difficulties at any time.'[149]

Dower also sent a copy of his report to Stafford Cripps, then Labour Minister for Aircraft Production, formerly Leader of the House of Commons – and a good friend of Pauline's father, Sir Charles Trevelyan. A keen rambler himself, Cripps was anxious to see a copy of the report as soon as possible.

---

149 *Note on the Deputation from the Standing Committee on National Parks received by the Minister on Tuesday 14 September 1943*, HLG 92/51.

Predictably, the 'half or two-thirds' of working days each month offered by Dower were soon exceeded. From mid-August to mid-September 1943, he was in the London office for seventeen days, and in addition spent a long weekend lecturing at the Town and Country Planning summer school in Birmingham. During that month he spent no more than five days at home. And the consequence was that in early October he was once again laid low with what he described as 'flu'. He was ordered to bed for a week by his doctor, to be followed by a few days of 'taking it easy'. In the Ministry, Neal acknowledged that Dower's illness would 'hold up matters for a little time', but still pressed him on following up the Secretary's meetings in September. Dower replied that the revision of his report was 'well ahead, though not yet complete' pending the input of several of his colleagues.

In the event, Dower's editing was not completed until 21 October. He sent a long, handwritten memo to Vincent, setting out the details of no fewer than seventeen significant amendments he had incorporated in his original draft. Many of them reflected the views of his departmental colleagues – Hill, Pepler, and George Strauss, the Parliamentary Under-Secretary to the Minister. One of the most important of these changes was a big reduction in the number of proposed National Parks. Dower described it as 'a general overhaul of my area recommendations, with the effect (1) of making the National Parks claim a bit more modest and (2) avoiding any treading on the Forestry Commission's toes. I have also thought it wise to add an explanation of why the South and East play such a small part in the National Parks picture.' As a consequence, he was obliged also to revise his original hand drawn map.[150]

Optimistically, Dower expected that Vincent would pass the revised document straight to the Permanent Secretary, Whiskard, who would then sign it off for printing. However, the culture of the Civil Service demanded that hierarchies must be respected, and accordingly Neal made an additional seven amendments. It was therefore not until 12 November that the document was eventually passed to

---

150 Dower to Vincent, 21 October 1943.

the Permanent Secretary – but still only in order for him 'to form a judgement on publication'.

An important conclusion of the Permanent Secretary's meeting in September was that the publication of Dower's report 'need not be held up by full discussions in detail'. But after reading the report (with its revisions) Whiskard decided that the question of publication should be determined by the initial responses of other Ministries. The journey towards National Parks would clearly require many small steps – and some of them on tiptoe. So from early November 1943, Dower circulated his report to sixteen Ministries and agencies, and eight senior non-governmental stakeholders. Over the following weeks, he and Vincent held meetings with four government departments, two agencies and Professors Dudley Stamp and Patrick Abercrombie. 'Substantial replies' in writing were received from four further departments, Lord Scott and Professor JA Steers. By early February 1944, Dower was able to report that – with the possible exception of the Commissioners of Crown Lands ('who were not much concerned in the matter') all the people with whom they had made 'effective' contact had shown a 'thoroughly favourable reaction to the broad principle of National Parks.'[151]

*

Dower's optimism was premature. The Commissioners of Crown Lands were in fact very concerned in the matter, questioning the economics of imposing higher amenity standards on agriculture (e.g. in relation to the choice of building materials), and indeed the justification for *any* national expenditure on National Parks at all. The Duchy of Cornwall was equally disturbed. The Duchy was an important player in the National Parks debate, since it owned most of Dartmoor, much of the coastline of Cornwall and Devon, the Mendips in Somerset and also extensive holdings in Dorset.

---

151 Dower to Vincent, 9 February 1944.

From the Duchy's office in Buckingham Place, its Secretary, Clive Burns, wrote to Vincent expressing concern at Dower's proposals in relation to future land ownership. Dower had stressed that 'The system of ownership, whatever it is [in future], *will nowhere be allowed to stand in the way of a democratically determined allocation of the land to its best use in the public interest,* or of a full, efficient and seemly development and maintenance of the land for such use.' (Author's italics) Burns responded that this was a 'misapprehension' of the constitutional position of the Duchy. Unlike other public bodies, he wrote, 'the property of the Duchy of Cornwall is not dealt with under an Act of Parliament except by consent of the Duchy' and this applied whether the Possesser at the time was the Duke of Cornwall or the Monarch. In any event, he argued, Dartmoor could already be regarded as a public park in view of the free access granted to the unenclosed portion of the moor and the adjoining Commons owned by the Duchy. And the ancient laws and customs peculiar to Dartmoor and the Commons were 'jealously guarded by the local inhabitants and the Duchy is at all times concerned that these are not infringed.'[152]

But the biggest players had yet to be engaged. These were the Ministry of Agriculture, the Ministry of Health, the Forestry Commission, the War Office, the Admiralty and, above all, the Treasury. The Treasury was to be left until last, on the grounds that the crucial compensation and betterment White Paper had yet to appear (see below). Dower noted: 'We have held off asking for meetings with the Forestry Commission and the Ministry of Health (mainly on water catchment), with the idea of getting a common front with the Ministry of Agriculture first. That the Ministry of Agriculture *will* take a favourable view of the main issue we may reasonably expect from what Dr Stamp has told me.'

Dudley Stamp was an adviser to the Ministry of Agriculture and Fisheries (MAF), a firm supporter of National Parks, and a friend of Dower. However, he seriously

---

152 Letter from the Secretary of the Duchy of Cornwall to Vincent, 3 December 1943.

misjudged the position of MAF, for at a meeting in late March 1944 two of its officials accused Dower and Vincent of 'baiting the agricultural community during the war'. Farmers might be suspicious of the increase of organised hiking, while landowners would reject stronger control over buildings. They suggested that the report should not be published during war-time 'when the agriculturalists were being hard-pressed by the Government on food production. An easier time might come in a period of gradual relaxation of Government control, say after the war with Germany and during the concluding stages of the war with Japan.'[153]

Dower's strategy of forming an alliance with MAF was clearly in shreds. 'We may have to fight them,' he conceded, while seeking a note of optimism: 'If we can establish that they *alone* are holding us up, this should not be very difficult.'

Half Time

The spring of 1944 brought rumours of a major re-shuffle in the Ministry of Town and Country Planning. It involved the transfer of Harold Vincent's Research Division, where Dower was based, to George Pepler's Plans Division. More importantly, it involved the departure of Vincent himself to a post in Washington, overseeing Anglo-American co-operation on wartime production.

Vincent had been at the Ministry for four years, during which time he and Dower had formed a strong relationship of mutual support. Vincent had become increasingly reliant on Dower's expertise in the development of rural planning policy, *de facto* transferring to him more of his own responsibilities in the knowledge that he could always be relied upon to do a good job. In return, Vincent invariably supported Dower over the issue of his ill-health, and in the frequent disagreements he had with Lawrence Neal. So Vincent's departure – planned for September 1944 – must have come as a major blow. Dower had lost a friend and gained an even heavier workload.

---

153 Memo by Vincent, 28 March 1944.

There was some compensation. Dower was to be promoted to Assistant Secretary, with a 10 per cent salary increase, and was to be given a new Research Officer. He was John Bowers, a former colonial civil servant who had worked on political affairs in the Sudan. He was to prove hard working, loyal and efficient.

In the Ministry, uncertainty over the re-organisation, together with frustration at the slow progress over planning legislation in general and on National Parks in particular, depressed morale. In mid-May, Dower wrote a hasty note to Pauline:

> Arrangements for our Division of the Ministry very unsatisfactory and all my colleagues very restive. I await developments with interest, but a general feeling that the slow coaches have won this round and that the sensible thing to do is to take things easily and make no fuss for the next few months – expecting a more favourable chance of a return match in the autumn. I think I shall instruct myself to take a maximum of time on visits to National Park areas in the near future. At least I'll learn some practical geography etc at the Ministry's expense!

This was despite a mounting backlog of work. 'What with my own work and with satisfying the curiosity of my keen staff of three,' he wrote a few weeks later, 'I see myself with a vista of "behindhandness" stretching so far into the future that it's really idle to try to catch up!'[154]

He realised that his promotion would mean spending more time in London. Apart from his new line-management responsibilities, Pepler had instituted weekly conferences of the Plans Division every Monday morning, making it more difficult for Dower to spend weekends with Pauline at The Rookery. In London, he would need somewhere more comfortable and permanent to stay than his 'digs' with Mrs Mabbutt. His thoughts turned to their house on Haverstock Hill, which they had let to tenants at the beginning of the

---

154 Letters from Dower to Pauline, 12 May and 16 July 1944.

war. 'I'm thinking more and more that our best plan will be to go back there (into half the house if not the whole) and that the time may not be very far off,' he wrote to Pauline. 'It will be hard to find a better place for living in London, and I feel increasingly that London for most of the time is my most probable future.' Once again he downplayed the danger of German bombing. On 13 June 1944 the first flying bomb had fallen on London, and over the next few weeks 10,000 more were launched. Over 6,000 people were killed – mostly Londoners – and one and a half million people fled the capital.[155] The statistics were not made public, and even if they had been Dower would have downplayed them. 'The flying bombs are now (touch wood) so few, that I personally find no discomfort from them at all,' he reassured Pauline. 'I lose no sleep. And during the day I confine my reaction to moving from my chair facing the window to another with my back to the wall beyond the window whenever one of the things sounds at all near.'

But it was different in the case of Pauline. Dower had decided it was too unsafe for her to stay in the city for any length of time. Instead, he hatched the idea of swapping The Rookery temporarily for the houses or flats of friends and relatives nearer London. He welcomed the offer of a flat in Oxford – 'an excellent idea, provided it doesn't mean that you spend the whole of August frowsting in the close and noisy oven of Oxford itself (a notoriously enervating place in July and August). But if you are there or thereabouts from August 1-10, I will certainly spend the bank holiday weekend with you, and if trains are reasonable, come down for the night most of the working days.'

*

Apart from the Treasury, a major reason for the slow progress in publishing Dower's report was the war itself. The government departments with the greatest impact on access

---

155 AJP Taylor, *English History 1914-1945*, Oxford University Press, 1986, p. 584.

to the coast and countryside were the War Office and the Admiralty, but because of wartime secrecy and uncertainty, it was accepted that substantive discussions with them would have to wait until the war was over. The coast was the area of greatest sensitivity. Prof JA Steers had highlighted the extent to which the Service Departments had damaged the coast in a major report to the Ministry of Town and Country Planning, which he submitted in late October 1943. Overcoming wartime restrictions as far as he could, Steers had spent nine months surveying the entire coastline of England and Wales, sometimes accompanied by Dower himself.

His report pulled no punches:

> A very important matter is the future of the large military training areas such as Minehead, Studland, Foulness, Bosherston, and others... The magnificent coast between Stackpole and Linney Head is now a prohibited area. This is completely justified in war time. But it would be a great pity if after the war the public were not allowed to follow the cliff path at, let us say, weekends. Except where complete secrecy is demanded, an arrangement whereby the public have occasional access should not be difficult...
>
> The amount of [barbed] wire used for coastal defence has to be seen to be believed. There are also a good many miles of iron trellis-pattern tank defences which will not be easy to demolish. The numerous concrete bastions must also be removed or blown up. All this work will take time, and unless care is taken it will be easy to let it hang fire. There will possibly be small incentive to tidy the coast once peace comes. But unless the problem is fully tackled, the coast will be disfigured for a long time...
>
> It is essential that no indiscriminate building should be allowed. The local, must be controlled by a national, authority whose duty should include the power to refuse permission to build any type of building in unsuitable places, and also the supervision and architecture of any buildings they allow to be erected...

If we take the view that the coast is a national possession, it follows that the nation and not local authorities should look after it... In short, all authorities, whether the great departments of State on the one hand, or the rural district councils on the other, must regard the coast as one and indivisible. It seems logical that all matters affecting coastal development, except those dealing with national defence and certain details concerning the growth of towns and ports, should invariably come first before a National Committee whose main duty should be the preservation of the coastline...[156]

Vincent described Steers' report as 'an excellent document', and wondered whether it could be used for public relations purposes, despite military censorship. He thought that one way of getting coastal issues on the agenda might be to hold an academic event at the Royal Geographical Society in London, where Steers could present his report. An invitation to the Minister himself would also provide some added impetus. 'I have a feeling that it would be a sound beginning,' wrote Vincent. 'More dignified than much propaganda.' At the bottom of the letter, Tom Stephenson noted, 'I think we could set this little ball rolling.'[157]

And roll it did – albeit slowly. On the evening of 5 June 1944, Dower walked through the gates of Lowther Lodge, the Norman Shaw building housing the headquarters of the Royal Geographical Society (RGS) in South Kensington. He noted the great scars on the outside brickwork caused by fragments of a heavy bomb dropped four months before during a night-time German air raid. The outer doors leading to Kensington Road had been blown out with their frames; several inner doors were broken to pieces, and one door from the back of the Hall was found lying in the middle of the stalls. A large part of the roof was stripped of its tiles, and remained thus for almost two months. Emergency

---

156 General report by JA Steers, *Need of Preservation of the Coast*, HLG 92/80.
157 Letter from Vincent to Steers, 19 October 1943.

repairs resulted in the suspension of RGS meetings until April – and an inevitable delay to the Ministry's event.

Inside the Hall, Dower took his seat on the platform, alongside Steers and an august panel of professors. They included the ecologist, Arthur Tansley; Dudley Stamp; William Holford; the physical geographer RK Gresswell; the President of the RGS, George Clerk; and, encouragingly, the Minister himself, William Morrison.

Steers began his presentation by listing the wartime pressures on the coast, which were creating 'problems of control and restoration no less urgent than those arising from industry and unregulated shack building – but for obvious reasons comment on it at present must be limited to the minimum.' He emphasised that the coast was a national possession, and 'should be regarded as a unit, and should be used and enjoyed under the aegis of the Ministry of Town and Country Planning... Only such an organisation can visualise the whole, have access to complete and informative statistics about relative numbers visiting the various parts of the coast, assimilate and compare the data on different localities, and deal with the resulting problems impartially.'

For his part, Morrison endorsed the view that the coast was a vital national possession, and must be planned nationally. Diplomatically, he made no reference to the role of his own Ministry in this process, and avoided offending local authorities by stressing the need for 'a partnership of national and local initiative' wherein 'national action must not overrule local concerns or impair local initiatives'.

Dower chose to focus on 'a knotty and difficult problem' of roads along the coast. His surveys with Steers had been undertaken 'under the exceptional, and from our point of view ideal, condition that the war had virtually cleared the roads of all but military and agricultural traffic; but we remembered and contrasted the clutter of tourist cars in pre-war holiday seasons.' After the war, he argued, roads some distance back from the coastline should be improved to take heavy tourist traffic, but narrower and rougher lanes down to coves should be closed to all but local motor traffic, or 'later the traffic will throttle itself'. There should be a continuous footpath along the coast, made possible by requiring farmers not to cultivate their land right down to the water's edge in order to leave space for it. This 'coastguards path' should be linked back at intervals to the ordinary road and footpath system, the junctions providing good places for car parks.[158]

Unbeknown to Dower, the 'narrower and rougher lanes' all along the English south coast from Falmouth to Brighton that night were far from quiet. Nose-to-tail queues of tanks and troop carriers throbbed and thrummed and clattered along winding tracks as they carried some 150,000 men and their equipment down to the landing craft jostling and pitching as they awaited their departure to Normandy. It was the eve of the D-Day landings – the largest amphibious attack in history, and the beginning of the end of the war.

*

Ten days after D-Day, it seemed as though another road block to progress on National Parks might at last be shifting. The White Paper *The Control of Land Use* was published by the government – a much delayed response to the September 1942 report of the Uthwatt Committee on compensation and betterment.[159] The focus of the brief, fifteen-page White Paper was how to respond to the changes in the value of land that would be brought about by major post-war reconstruction. The Uthwatt Report had recommended that the state should nationalise the development rights of all land which had not yet been built up, so that whenever land was required for development, the state would buy it at a price reflecting its existing rather than potential use. So agricultural land on the edge of a town, for example, would not be valued on the basis of its likely future use for house building. All the land required for a major development project would be valued at a single sum, the proceeds of which would be shared out to the former landowners as

158 *Geographical Journal*, vol. 104, no. 1-2, July-August 1944, pp. 18-27.
159 *Control of Land Use*, Cmd. 6537, HMSO, June 1944; *The Uthwatt Report*, Cmd. 6386, HMSO, September 1942.

compensation. Subsequently, the developed land would pass in perpetuity to the state.

The issue of land nationalisation was highly contentious, and the Conservatives – especially the large number of Conservative landowners – were adamantly opposed to the Uthwatt proposals. By contrast, the traditional policy of the Labour Party (as determined by its party conferences) was to secure the outright nationalisation of land – going further than the quasi-nationalisation of the Uthwatt Committee. This left-right divide was so intense that Michael Foot MP later concluded that 'The question of the ownership of land was the real rock on which the coalition was broken.'[160]

The political deadlock left open many key issues. The Foreword to the White Paper explained that '(The government) present this Paper to Parliament in order to focus public discussion on the difficult issues involved and to assure themselves that there would be a substantial measure of public support for a solution on the lines proposed.' In effect, this was more a Green than a White Paper.

In the event, the White Paper rejected any nationalisation of land. Instead, it proposed that:

> (a) compensation would be paid to those landowners who were refused permission to develop land ring-fenced by the state for e.g. agriculture, green belts or National Parks, and (b) a 'betterment' tax would be levied on the windfall profits made by those landowners who enjoyed increased land values following major developments such as the building of New Towns, housing and industrial estates.

The White Paper noted that 'a substantial redistribution of value will result from *national* policies for the balanced distribution of industry; reclamation of derelict land; preservation of fertile agricultural land; and the establishment of national parks.' Because these changes would take no account of individual local authority boundaries, many rural authorities where development

---

160 Michael Foot, *Aneurin Bevan: A Biography Volume 1 1897-1945*, MacGibbon & Kee, 1962, p. 474.

would be constrained could face huge claims for compensation from frustrated landowners, while in other authorities – particularly on the fringes of towns and cities – land values would soar in anticipation of major building projects. Not only would this be unfair as between local authorities, but it would also encourage them to base their planning on maximising 'betterment', while seeking to minimise the establishment of green belts or National Parks within their areas.

To create a more level playing field, the White Paper proposed to set up a centralised Land Commission. This would standardise levels of compensation payments and betterment charges across the country, and take over from local authorities the financial management involved. The Land Commission would then eventually be in a position to balance national betterment receipts with national compensation payments, so that the system, in principle, would be self-financing.

The precise level of compensation payments and betterment charges was one of the many issues left vague by the White Paper. Compensation payable to a landowner as a result of a refusal of planning permission would be related to the reduction in the value of the land, compared with a baseline of 31 March 1939 (i.e. lower than current value). It would require a great deal of work to establish whether a plot of land had any development value at all, and if so, how it should be valued. The White Paper proposed that no compensation at all would be paid during the first five years after the Act came into force, to give time for officials to survey land holdings and determine the appropriate level of compensation.

As regards the level of a betterment charge, the White Paper proposed a figure of 80 per cent of the increase in the value of the land that was attributable to the grant of planning consent, compared with the baseline of 31 March 1939. Again, there would need to be a delay of five years to determine these values. 'The proposal has been framed,' noted the White Paper, 'on the assumption that the control of the use of land will be so managed that over a reasonable period of years, and over the country as a whole, receipts of betterment charge will broadly balance the payment of fair compensation.' An expert commission would be appointed before the end of the five-year period to recommend the appropriate percentages of payments and receipts.

It was all highly contentious. The government's Chief Scientific Adviser, Lord Cherwell, had attended the War Cabinet Committee which finally agreed the White Paper. He reported to Churchill that:

> There was immense difficulty in arriving at a compromise between the views of the Conservatives, who say that land should not be singled out for abnormal treatment, and the Labour Party who maintain that all increment in value is due to the community... Every line of approach has been explored. Each has great difficulties, and finally all sides agreed on this proposal, though nobody much likes it. Fortunately, the proposals are put forward in the most tentative manner for discussion...[161]

Dower was disappointed, but not surprised, that most of the key questions had been left unanswered. Local planning authorities would not know for several years the compensation costs of establishing a National Park in their areas; nor whether the proposed Land Commission would ever be created to take over the burden; and if so, what its relationship would be to the Treasury. It was clear that the gatekeeper to National Parks in Britain was, and remained, the Treasury. There was no point any more in putting off discussions with it, since the detailed financial information Dower had hoped for would not be available for some years.

It was time to grasp the nettle.

---

161 Letter from Lord Cherwell to Churchill, 15 June 1944.

10. A Turn for the Worse

The Treasury's response to Dower's request for a meeting was haughty and patronising. On 1 August 1944, a Treasury official, Herbert Gatliff, explained that his colleague, Herbert Usher, 'will be ready to see you about National Parks after the Bank Holiday – say Wednesday or Thursday of next week – but after that he will be away for a fortnight, and I shall be going away to Scotland for nearly 3 weeks before he comes back, so we had better get on so far as we can next week...'

In the event, the meeting was cancelled at Dower's request because he had fallen ill and was recuperating at The Rookery. 'We were very sorry to hear that you were away sick and could not come to talk about National Parks this week,' Gatliff wrote the following week, 'but while we appreciate that it is time we did get a little further with discussion, the matter is not one of very great urgency just at the moment, and no harm will, I think, result from our waiting until you get to London again, and Usher and I are both back... On most of the questions that arise we have not yet formed any view sufficiently clear to make it worth putting them to you before we can talk about them...'[162]

When the meeting finally took place at the end of September 1944, Usher used the uncertainty over the White Paper on the Control of Land Use as a further excuse to stall. In a follow-up note to Dower, he wrote: 'I feel myself that it is very difficult to apply one's mind to this problem until we have a clearer idea of the view Parliament takes of the White Paper, and therefore the prospects of [it] being implemented.' He also pointed to four issues on which the Treasury would require more information before agreeing to publication of Dower's report:[163]

(a) What adjustments to the Report would be made to relate it to the White Paper?

---

162 Gatliff to Dower, 1 August 1944, HLG 93/56.
163 Usher to Dower, 28 September 1944, HLG 93/56.

(b) What would be the administrative costs of setting up a system of National Parks?

(c) Was it practicable or wise to keep confidential from Parliament the provisional choice of National Park areas made by a proposed Preparatory Commission?

(d) Was there some inconsistency between the functions of a National Parks Authority relating specifically to National Parks, and those advisory functions, suggested in his Report, relating to the protection of the wider countryside?

Dower knew that questions (c) and (d) could be settled without too much difficulty, but answers to (a) and particularly (b) would be far more speculative and time consuming.

He was exasperated by the Treasury's delaying tactics. He decided that the only way to out-manoeuvre Treasury officials would be to go over their heads and secure a declaration by Ministers that his report should be published without delay. Two sympathetic MPs – Edmund Harvey (Independent) and Geoffrey Mander (Liberal) – tabled oral questions in the Commons, which were answered on consecutive days in mid-October. Henry Strauss, Parliamentary Secretary to the Ministry of Town and Country Planning, confirmed that the Minister 'hopes soon to publish a Report on the subject of National Parks,' while the following day, the Minister himself, William Morrison, told MPs that the report 'should be in the hands of Honourable Members, so that they may assist me with their views upon it'.[164] It was not exactly a commitment to 'action this day', but it was a step forward.

Dower was quick to seize the initiative. Within a few days he had sent Neal a five-page memo stressing that the Minister's statement was a green light which had 'put us under an obligation to proceed at once with preparations for publication'. He was therefore working on revisions to bring the report up to date as regards the White Paper, and

---

164 *Hansard*, House of Commons 18/19 October 1944, vol. 403, cols. 2381-2 and 2535.

to meet the points made by other departments. He needed final confirmation, however, that the report would indeed be published under his name, as an expression of his personal views and recommendations ('course (A)'), rather than as an anonymous civil service document formally presenting the policy of the Ministry of Town and Country Planning ('course (B)'). 'As the blushing author who would get some personal notice (and credit or discredit) if course (A) were adopted,' he wrote, 'I have up to the present confined myself to posing this question without showing any strong preference for either course. But now, as things have turned out, I don't hesitate to recommend strongly that course (A) should be adopted...'

There were good practical reasons for this choice. Turning his report into a formal Ministerial document, he argued, would require (a) a complete redrafting to move the text from the first to the third person; (b) the inclusion of firmer policy commitments of the kind expected in an official document – which in turn would require (c) the re-opening once again of discussions with all fourteen government departments and agencies over the details. Altogether, course (B) would therefore result in a considerable further delay in publication.[165]

But there was another reason, omitted from Dower's memo – his health. His illness in August lasted until the end of October, during which period he was recommended bed rest and the avoidance of extended periods in London. He reassured Pepler that while he stayed at Wallington he was able to do work nearby, surveying the Roman Wall; delimiting the boundaries of a potential Cheviots National Park; and visiting the War Office in Berwick upon Tweed. But on 20 October he confided to Bowers that he was again 'back in bed with a feverish chill'. Then from mid-December to early February 1945, he was prescribed a further six weeks of bed rest, to be followed by 'living as continuously as possible in the country for some time to come'. His plan to spend two-thirds of each month at the Ministry in London would have to be abandoned.

---

165 Memo from Dower to Neal, 25 October 1944, HLG 93/56.

*

Meanwhile, the Ministry of Agriculture (MAF) was also maintaining a veto on publication. After seven months' silence, the Principal Assistant Secretary, Charles Bosanquet, reaffirmed MAF's view that 'the publication of the Report without any accompanying statement as to the policy of the Government in regard to its recommendations would be likely to alarm all those who farm the areas for which it proposes such important changes.' In particular, he objected to Dower's maps which seemed to suggest that as much as 20 per cent of all the farmland in England and Wales would be designated either as National Parks, Reserve National Parks, or Conservation Areas. Bosanquet detailed his objections following a meeting with Pepler and Dower on 17 November 1944:

> I pointed out that it was by no means the case that the chosen areas were limited to hill land. They included a lot of farming land in valleys with crops, dairy herds etc and it was vital that nothing should be said to suggest that these farmers, who were being very hard driven to produce food in war-time, were suddenly to be subjected to the whims of an unknown National Parks Authority sitting in London... I fully recognised that anyone reading the report carefully could not fail to grasp the fact that JD proposed to base National Parks upon a prosperous agriculture. But the publication of the report would cause a great deal of alarm amongst all those who farmed or were connected with farming in the areas of the proposed National Parks. But because few of the farmers would ever see the original report, or even read a full summary of it such as the *Times*, or *Manchester Guardian* might publish (if the report was to be published at all), what was really vital was to see that a proper summary of it was presented by the penny papers. The best way to do this was probably to have a press conference and a carefully prepared hand-out

to make sure that the only map published was that showing the ten areas proposed for National Parks. The hand-out should, so far as possible, emphasise that the report was a personal one by JD, and that the Government had not made up its mind to introduce legislation to give effect to it.[166]

But the real reason for MAF's objections was that the proposed National Parks Authority threatened to trample on its turf. It therefore wanted 'modifications' to the National Parks Authority's right to manage and purchase farmland. Moreover, the Ministry was developing a new post-war policy on hill sheep, and there was an urgent need to 'discuss' how this would link with Dower's report.[167]

Dower was anxious to keep MAF onside, in view of the Treasury's obstruction. He was also personally concerned not to antagonise Bosanquet, who had been his contemporary at Cambridge and was now a neighbour in Northumberland. Dower's response was therefore emollient, stressing that apart from two or three points of detail, 'there is nothing I want to quarrel with...' He was willing to change the maps, and also adjust paragraph 72 (on the powers of the National Parks Authority to manage or purchase farmland) 'and anything consequential on it to meet your suggestions when I get them'. He also apologised for failing to consult MAF *before* the Minister responded to Parliamentary questions on the publication of his report.[168]

*

Joining MAF and the Treasury in opposition to publication was the Ministry of Health (MoH). The specific issue in contention was the alleged threat posed by ramblers to the purity of drinking water from upland water catchment areas to which they might be given access. Water-borne

166 *National Parks*, note from Bosanquet to Dower, 18 November 1944 (revised 4 January 1945), HLG 93/56.
167 Bosanquet to Pepler, 30 October 1944, HLG 93/56.
168 Dower to Bosanquet, 1 January 1945, HLG 93/56.

diseases, it was argued, could be spread through bathing or the deposition of rubbish, urine and faeces in these sensitive areas. Dower's report had complained about 'the considerable interference – amounting in some instances to a virtually complete depopulation of the whole catchment area by prohibition of rambling, closing of footpaths, and elimination of resident farming – where the water is surface-gathered and relatively untreated.' And at the same time there were numerous inconsistencies. On the one hand, water from some gathering grounds was fully treated, even though access was severely restricted (often in the interests of grouse shooting). On the other, freedom of access was widely enjoyed elsewhere, even though little or no treatment was applied (as in the Elan Valley in mid-Wales and Thirlmere and Haweswater in the Lake District).

Dower's solution to the problem was that all drinking water supplies which were surface-gathered should be made pure and safe by 'appropriate and thorough' treatment. This might take the form of sedimentation, pressure filtration, chlorination or ozonisation, or some combination of these. He pointed out that fully treated water from the heavily polluted Thames safely provided the bulk of London's drinking supply. 'Where adequate treatment already exists or is brought into operation, the National Parks authority must see that restrictions, both of rambling over uncultivated land and of farming, are removed without delay... It is important not to over-estimate the difficulties, which are often exaggerated by prejudice and irrelevance...'[169]

Dower would have been wise to show a little more sensitivity in dealing with the MoH. It was, after all, less than three years since responsibility for planning had been taken away from the MoH and given to the Ministry of Town and Country Planning – and now the new Ministry was encroaching on matters of public health. George North from the MoH pointed out to George Pepler that 'even if he (Dower) were a recognised expert in water and water treatment, which of course he would not claim to be, I would

---

169 *Rambling and Water Supply Catchment* (paras. 44-47), 11 January 1945, HLG 93/56.

still suggest that it would be, to say the least, bad tactics to approach the problem in such a provocative way.' North was adamant that most of the arguments in Dower's report on water catchment areas 'are in flat opposition to this Ministry's policy of the first line of defence against water-borne disease being to avoid pollution of the sources by restricting public access and controlling agricultural use so far as these are necessary. If you back Dower's argument that all that is necessary is treatment, and that, given treatment, pollution beforehand hardly matters at all, you can't expect to get away with it. Even if it were right from the risk point of view to rely wholly on treatment – which we do not admit – there is also the 'deadening' effect of treatment to be considered. London's water may be more pure bacteriologically than, say, Manchester's, but few people who have a live, agreeable water, such as Manchester has, are going to put up willingly with highly processed water instead.'[170]

*

While other departments were dragging their feet, Dower's own Minister was calling for more haste. In early January 1945, 'a bit of a bombshell' destroyed any chance that Dower could enjoy a few weeks' restful recuperation. A letter from George Pepler broke the news that the Minister, William Morrison, wanted to get through legislation on National Parks during the current parliamentary session – i.e. within just a few months. The reason for the hurry was the prospect of a general election – the first in ten years – that was expected as soon as victory in Europe had been secured. At the end of October 1944, Churchill himself had announced that it would be wrong to carry on the wartime coalition after the defeat of Germany, and the National Executive of the Labour Party had already confirmed that it would fight an election independently. It would be party politics as usual.[171] In preparation for the contest, Morrison was

---

170 North to Pepler, 27 January 1945, HLG 93/56.
171 Paul Addison, *The Road to* 1945, *op. cit.*, p. 254.

anxious to demonstrate the credentials of the Conservative Party in the area of social policy – and setting up Britain's first National Parks seemed just the initiative he needed.

Neal was not at all sympathetic to the burden that this would impose on his over-stretched staff, stressing the need for 'vigorous action on our part' to accommodate Morrison's wishes. He listed the tasks that needed to be finalised – and urgently:

1. Publication of the Report;
2. Financial issues, if legislation for national parks was to precede 'White Paper'legislation [on compensation and betterment];
3. The legislative programme itself, including the submission of proposals to the War Cabinet's Reconstruction Committee.[172]

Dower's response was to dash off a nine-page, 3,000-word memo to Neal and Pepler that fairly sizzled with anger. He was outraged at the unscrupulous hijacking of the National Parks project for the purposes of improving the public image of the Conservative Party – and even more at Neal's ready capitulation to his superiors, regardless of whether the proposal was practicable or not. He wrote:

It is now suggested that we should work to a reverse order – a National Parks Bill first (if possible this session) and the White Paper legislation afterwards (if ever). It would not be fair to myself or to the numerous people with whom I have collaborated or consulted, including officers of other Departments, if I did not say at once that this is emphatically against my judgement, both now, and as freely and frequently expressed over the last two years. It seems to me a plain case of the cart – or one main part of the cart – before the horse. My Report was finished some months before the White Paper came out, but it was based on the assumption that legislation to deal with the compensation and betterment issue, on

---

172 Neal to Pepler, 2 January 1945, HLG 93/56.

something like White Paper lines, should and would
come first... It was primarily for this reason that I
inserted the proposal of action in two stages, with an
Advisory Preparatory Commission, not requiring
legislation, set up at the first stage to establish the
purpose and prepare the way ...it has been implicit
or explicit in all relevant discussions since then,
including, particularly, recent consultations with Mr
Usher and others of the Treasury.

Dower's memo continued by painting a number of possible
scenarios following a National Parks Bill that was premature:

(A). A Bill on the lines of his Report would be brought
forward with *no provision for any compensation payments*
under the existing Planning Acts, on the assumption that
a White Paper Bill would follow soon after. 'The objection
to this course is essentially political', Dower observed.
'The present Government, whose months are numbered,
are in no position to promise or assume that White Paper
legislation will happen; or, alternatively, if they *are* in such
a position, they plainly ought to proceed with the White
Paper legislation first.'

(B). A National Parks Bill as under (A) might be tabled
in the hope that valid *compensation claims would be small*.
The National Parks Commission might try to persuade
all but a few black sheep to refrain both from undesirable
development, and compensation claims. 'A plausible case of
this sort (perhaps sweetened by a small compensation fund
to enable the Commission to deal with the few black sheep)
could doubtless be presented; but it would in my view be
based on entirely unjustified hopes and be incapable of
standing the fire of informed opinion either in Parliament
or outside.'

In the case of both A and B, the National Parks Commission
would be landed with a choice of evils. 'Either they would
have to let a lot of undesirable developments happen within
National Parks, damaging both to the Parks and to their
reputation; or they would have to limit their National Park
areas to land possessing substantially no development value
... leaving out all the land in and around the larger villages

and small towns contained therein.' Dower pointed to the Lake District, where substantial 'islands' with potential development value would have to be excluded from the National Park on the grounds of cost, such as around Keswick, Windermere, Ambleside, Coniston, Grasmere and other places.

(C). A third scenario might see an early National Parks Bill brought forward as in A and B, but with full financial provision for the *payment by the Treasury* of all the estimated compensation costs. Dower was convinced that this would be politically untenable. 'I can't see either the Treasury or Parliament being prepared to foot a bill,' he concluded.

(D). A fourth course might be to proceed by *outright purchase* of the land in National Parks. This was Dower's preferred option, if early White Paper legislation was unlikely to be forthcoming. Nationalisation by the compulsory purchase of the freehold would be cheaper than compensation for foregone development opportunities. However, he acknowledged that this would also be politically impracticable in current circumstances, given the extent of National Parks envisaged for England and Wales.

He concluded:

No-one wants National Parks more or sooner than I do, provided they are not too few or too small and the Commission is given a workable job on a reliable foundation and with sufficient funds. If someone can show me how – on one of the foregoing courses, or on some other course I have failed to see – to make a pre-White Paper National Parks Bill a workable proposition, both politically and in administrative substance, I shall be delighted. But I cannot see it for myself.

And he threw down the gauntlet.

As regards the relevant revision of my Report and the preparation of any further policy papers or more detailed studies of finance etc, all I can do is to ask for instructions. Is the idea of going for a National Parks Bill now, before White Paper legislation, definitely to be adopted as a working basis? If so,

what is to be the line on the compensation question
(A, B, C above, or something else)? And are there to
be any other material changes from the proposals
in my report? Until I get such instructions, there is
no point in my doing anything more about clearing
up outstanding points with the Treasury... I await
instructions also before considering how far the
new revised footing may require us to start again
with other Departments, particularly Agriculture.

'I don't propose to sit down under it, and I don't think it
can be made to work,' Dower wrote to Pepler in a separate
letter.[173] But like all good negotiators, Dower offered Neal a
way out. He proposed a detailed road map comprising the
following steps:

(a) Completion of his Report, making it even more
explicitly dependent on the White Paper, and
meeting outstanding points demanded by other
Departments (by early February);

(b) Submission of a paper to the War Cabinet's
Reconstruction Committee seeking authority to

(i) publish his Report, with the Government's
endorsement of it in principle;

(ii) initiate the two-stage procedure he had
recommended, by setting up, without legislation, an
advisory Preparatory Commission to establish the
purpose of, and prepare the way for, the second stage
(late February);

(c) Assuming that such authority was given, publication
of the Report would follow, 'with appropriate public
relations arrangements, including possibly a small
National Parks exhibition (March);

(d) Launch of the Preparatory Commission under
existing powers in the 1943 Town and Country
Planning Act, and the establishment at the same time
of the 'Wildlife Conservation Council' recommended
in his Report (April);

---

173 Dower to Pepler 4 January 1945.

(e) The Preparatory Commission to take charge of all further work, working with the Ministry of Town and Country Planning's lawyers on drafting a Bill, and with the Plans Division on surveys of proposed areas, and detailed administrative questions.

Dower concluded: 'I believe that such a line of action, firmly and clearly presented, would be acceptable to Parliament and the public as a sensible and – pending White Paper legislation – sufficient treatment of the issue. It would be important to give an assurance that the Minister, with the advice of the Preparatory Commission, would make full use of his powers under the existing Planning Acts to "hold the fort" in potential National Park areas, until further legislation both for the White Paper and for National Parks, could be secured.'

*

Neal knew he had been outsmarted, and that his over-enthusiastic acceptance of the Minister's wishes had been a mistake. But he chose to bluster, pointing the finger at Dower for the current situation. 'Distance can give rise to a lot of extra difficulties!' he wrote in a note to Bowers.

> Mr Dower's minute ... illustrates these difficulties at both ends. Of course, much of what he says ... had already been broadly evident to us; his warnings help by filling in some of the detail... For some time past I have been urging Mr Dower to complete the outstanding portions of his task:-
> (a) Negotiations with doubting or objecting Departments, especially MAF and MoH;
> (b) The furnishing of financial information to the Treasury. I believe Usher wrote about three months ago.
> (c) Revision of the Report in preparation for publication.

The desirability of *completing* all this is underlined
by the Minister's recently expressed wishes, and the
completion should go forward in exactly the same
form as has previously been contemplated (Usher,
for instance, will not expect otherwise)... I see that
he mentions early February [for completion of the
Report]. I had hoped that the work would have been
further advanced than this...[174]

As regards his point (b), Neal had completely overlooked
Dower's detailed, five-page draft paper to the Treasury on
the administrative costs of National Parks, a copy of which
had been sent to him two months before. In that paper
Dower had stressed that there were too many unknowns
for any reliable estimation of the cost of carrying out the
National Parks policy, but that the White Paper on the
Control of Land Use 'powerfully reinforces my assumption
that the compensation cost of prohibiting or restricting
development would not fall to any material extent on the
funds of the National Parks Commission'. Some estimate
could be made of the more tangible costs – the salaries
and wages of staff, and the overhead expenses associated
with their work. He had calculated that on the basis of ten
National Parks and sixteen National Nature Reserves, this
would amount to a total of about £425,000 over four years.
Additional 'development costs' – i.e. financial contributions
to Joint Planning Committees in the parks; landscape
improvements and land acquisition; compensation to
landowners for public access; and grants to local authorities
and the National Trust – would cost an additional £750,000
over five years. The figures supported Dower's view that
'the cost of a generous and progressive scheme of National
Parks, expressed as an average net annual charge on the
Exchequer, would be measured in hundreds of thousands
rather than millions.'[175]

The achievement of Neal's other points, (a) and (c),
depended not on the time and effort Dower might put

174 Neal to Bowers, 9 January 1945.
175 Dower to Neal, 10 November 1944.

into inter-departmental negotiations, but on the extent of the 'red lines' insisted on by other Ministries. Neal seemed not to understand this. His response to Dower's request for 'instructions' was ignored, and instead he threatened to hand some of Dower's tasks over to others. 'As much of [the work] as can be done by Mr Dower should remain in his hands, but the remainder should be pursued at HQ (rather than allow delay),' he concluded.

Fortunately, all his colleagues were to side with Dower. Ernest Hill, the Ministry's head of legislation, even questioned the public relations value of an immediate Bill. 'National Parks would benefit only a minority,' he told an internal meeting with the Permanent Secretary. 'The country would want to know why they had been given priority to the exclusion of wider and more important problems, such as the provision of Green Belts and Open Spaces.' In addition, there were several important questions of policy that still awaited decision in the department, so that even the outlines of a Bill could not yet be completed. And given the need for agreement of the War Cabinet's Legislation Committee, and drafting assistance from Parliamentary Counsel, it would not be possible for a Bill on National Parks to be introduced this Session.[176]

Alfred Valentine also supported Dower's view that it would be extremely difficult to persuade the Treasury to shoulder *any* compensation in advance of betterment, and Neal himself highlighted the particular problems this would create in relation to the control of mineral workings. Pepler and Hill seemed to have persuaded him that Dower's proposal for a Preliminary Commission would be a sufficient pledge of the government's good intentions. And it was finally agreed that this was the message that should be conveyed to the Minister.

*

176 *Minutes of a Meeting on National Parks and other Legislation for 1945*, 19 January 1945.

While he was fighting on two fronts, Dower was cocooned inside The Rookery in Kirkby Malham. From late December 1944 the weather was intensely cold over most of Britain, and deep snow had settled on the roofs, lanes and fields of the village – cutting him off from his colleagues in London even more than usual. His doctors had ordered six weeks of bed rest during December and January, but the pressure of work over Christmas and New Year had been unremitting: completing the revision of his report, settling outstanding issues with other departments, discussing publication details, working up an eventual draft Bill... He told a friend that his writing work for the Ministry had twice given him writer's cramp, while for over a fortnight when Pauline had mumps he was 'assistant household help (unpaid)' on top of all his official duties.

His mounting frustration with working under Neal was the trigger for a major personal decision: he would resign as a full-time civil servant. He had already accepted that for reasons of health and logistics, he could no longer make frequent trips to London, and so from the end of February 1945 he opted to become a consultant to the Ministry. He would be paid a retainer, and for most of the time would work from home. He would still continue to undertake around two-thirds of his former Ministry work, the rest being covered by his assistant John Bowers, and Alfred Valentine, Vincent's replacement as Principal Assistant Secretary. But he would have more autonomy, and a little more time.

That at least was the plan. But on top of everything else he decided to move house, while still managing to find the time to draw a special pen-and-ink Christmas card announcing to friends that he and the family were shortly moving from The Rookery, to Cambo House in Northumberland. Sir Charles Trevelyan had made the house available so that Dower could convalesce closer to the family, and in greater comfort.

The relocation involved hard, physical work. 'I packed up some 300 assorted packages of White Papers, Blue Papers, dockets, files, maps, lantern slides, card indexes and literary and sporting impedimenta (thus soon exhausting my supply both of expletives and of red tape),' he wrote soon after the move in mid-February. Then there were the decorators, carpenters and plumbers to navigate around,

Pen and ink Christmas card drawn by John Dower, 1944.

and innumerable books and pieces of furniture to sort out, all of which, he observed with some understatement, 'proved a bigger and longer task than I had visualised'.[177]

*

Back in London, opposition by other departments to the publication of Dower's report was gradually crumbling, albeit reluctantly. During February 1945, among the packing cases, Dower made a number of further revisions to the text. The Treasury welcomed the significant cuts made to the second part of the report, which removed most of the detailed financial arrangements he had originally included. But they still had reservations, particularly about the powers

177 Dower to Neal, 24 February 1945.

– indeed, the name – of the Preliminary Commission, with Usher insisting that the Treasury should see a draft before Morrison submitted a formal paper to the Cabinet's Reconstruction Committee.

The Ministry of Agriculture was no less grudging, complaining that it had been 'bounced' into agreeing to publication by Morrison's statements in the House of Commons. In a letter to Dower, Bosanquet demanded that the content of the press hand-out accompanying publication 'should be settled in consultation with us, and that it should be stated clearly that the report represents your personal views and that the Government is in no way committed to acceptance of the ideas and conclusions it expresses.'[178] And for its part, the Ministry of Health never formally withdrew its objections to publication – but as a relatively weak Ministry it was not in a position to push the matter further.

*

Discussions on National Parks had so far taken place only at the level of officials, but on 7 May 1945 Ministers in the War Cabinet had an opportunity of discussing the issue at a meeting of the Reconstruction Committee, chaired by the Lord President of the Council, Lord Woolton. Morrison tabled a memorandum giving notice that following consultations with other concerned departments, he wished to publish Dower's report as soon as possible.[179] 'It is most desirable,' Morrison noted, 'in view of the widespread popular desire for National Parks, both that some definite pledge of our intention to proceed at the earliest possible date should be forthcoming in concrete form, and that preliminary work should be put in hand at once – which will be necessary both for the formulation of proposals for legislation when opportunity offers, and for practical action

---

178 Bosanquet to Dower, 23 January 1945.
179 War Cabinet Reconstruction Committee, *National Parks: Memorandum by the Minister of Town and Country Planning*, March 1945.

at a later stage.' Morrison gave his colleagues this reassurance: 'It will be noted that the Report will be published as one made to me by a member of my Department who has special knowledge of the subject, acting personally in the capacity of consultant; and that accordingly its publication does not commit the Government to detailed acceptance of the views and proposals in it.'

The representatives of the Treasury and the Ministry of Agriculture on the Reconstruction Committee – respectively, the Chancellor of the Exchequer Sir John Anderson, and the Minister of Agriculture RS Hudson – were still far from satisfied. Their argument revolved around the arcane issue of whether the Preliminary Commission on National Parks should in fact be a Commission, or a Committee. Dower had argued that only a Commission would attract men and women of sufficient standing and experience to ensure a measure of independence from the Ministry of Town and Country Planning. A Committee, on the other hand, would be staffed with civil servants beholden to their superiors. He went on:

> To appoint a mere Committee will look like shelving the issue to a further round of inconclusive consideration. On the other hand ... a Preparatory Commission with clear status under the Act of 1943, will, I believe, be just enough to satisfy both general and specialist opinion, for some time to come. It would give substantial form to the Government's acceptance of National parks, and would look like getting on with the job... It will be a tough job to get the requisite schemes of action worked out with a sufficient measure of agreement and goodwill: and it will, I suggest, make a great difference to the success and speed of this work that a Commission with a bit of 'red carpet' rather than a mere Committee should be engaged in the requisite contacts with the Local Authorities.[180]

---

180 HLG 92/49.

But this was the very reason why the Treasury opposed a Commission. The Chancellor argued that to set up such a Commission would be contrary 'to the sound principle of administration, and might well be an embarrassing precedent' since it would be dealing 'with such large issues as land ownership and other matters, arousing perhaps 'acute political controversy'. This would closely involve the Minister and other government departments, and 'it would therefore be better entrusted to a committee appointed by the Minister than to a Commission'.

RS Hudson, the Minister of Agriculture, also opposed a Commission, for reasons already rehearsed to Dower by his civil servants. The time was inopportune; food production must have first priority for some years to come; new arrangements for developing forestry had only recently been announced; and hill sheep farming presented problems which must be solved (by MAF) in the near future. The Minister of Town and Country Planning should simply use 'existing powers to prevent the spoliation of areas suitable for use as national parks'.[181]

Morrison countered that he wanted a National Parks policy that was 'positive and not preventive'. He was mindful, however, of the imminent general election, and anxious that a new government should be presented with at least the framework of such a policy, rather than a blank piece of paper. He was therefore obliged to concede. The Preparatory *Commission* that Dower called for at the end of his report was in fact to be a Committee after all – albeit comprising members of some status, and not civil servants.

Dower submitted the final, much revised, version of his report to the Minister on 12 April 1945, and it was published as a command paper on Wednesday, 16 May – just over a week after the formal surrender of Germany on VE (Victory in Europe) Day.[182] The National Government resigned the following week, and on 28 May a general election was called for Thursday 5 July 1945. Parliament was to be dissolved on 15 June.

---

181 CAB 87/10.
182 Dower, *National Parks in England and Wales, op. cit.*

Despite the dissolution, Ministers of the Crown continued to hold office until a new government was formed. On 2 July – just three days before polling day – Morrison was still able to write to potential members of the new National Parks Committee asking if they would confirm (or not) their participation. With restrained understatement, he wrote: 'I should be most grateful if you could let me have your decision – which I greatly hope will be favourable – as soon as possible.'

In the event, it was not until 26 July that the result of the election was declared, partly because of delays in transporting the thousands of votes of overseas service personnel. Labour's unexpected landslide victory swept Morrison from office, and on 4 August, a new Labour Minister, Lewis Silkin MP, was appointed his successor.

11. Hobhouse

At 11am on Wednesday 1 August 1945, in a drab London office in St James's Square, the members of the new National Parks Committee (NPC) gathered for their first meeting. Both the small talk and the temperature in the stuffy room increased as the high-summer sunshine filtered through the windows, still taped against enemy air raids.

It must have been with mixed feelings that Dower looked around the table at his new colleagues. After a decade of orchestrating the campaign for National Parks, it seemed as though he was now handing over the baton: all his hard work would be scrutinised, and probably revised by these nine people. But on the other hand, he was no longer working for the Ministry of Town and Country Planning, nor was he beholden to Lawrence Neal (who was about to leave the Ministry to return to retailing). And he was a full, independent and equal member of the Committee, whose terms of reference clearly established the Dower Report as the point of departure for the NPC's work.

During the previous few months Dower had tried to ensure that the Committee included as many of his friends and colleagues as possible. He had proposed as Chairman CPRE's Honorary Secretary, Professor RS Chorley, with Clough Williams-Ellis and Leonard Elmhirst as members. His note on a future programme of work had sought to keep at arm's length the influence of the Ministry, in favour of allowing the Committee to 'feel that they are themselves determining by discussion the ways and means by which they tackle the job'. So all that was necessary at this first meeting was to circulate a single page setting out 'Suggested Main Heads for a Programme of Work' and a brief review of the Dower Report.

In the event, it was Sir Arthur Hobhouse – not Professor Chorley – who took the chair and welcomed the NPC's members to their first meeting. Chorley had to be ruled out as Chairman on the grounds that as a prospective Labour candidate in the forthcoming general election, he would be disqualified should he become an MP. Hobhouse was chosen by the Ministry primarily as being 'a sound chairman and a countryman, and secondarily as representing local authorities'. A fifty-nine-year-old ex-Etonian and graduate of Trinity College Cambridge, he was Chair of Somerset County Council, President of the County Councils Association for England and Wales, and Chair of the Ministry of Health's Rural Housing Committee. He was a safe pair of hands, less provocative to other Ministries than the high-profile admirals and air marshals put forward by Neal (among others) as strong figureheads who could champion the cause of National Parks among the public.

Dower welcomed Hobhouse's appointment, and he dined alone with him the evening before the Committee's first meeting. He briefed the new chairman on the respective backgrounds of the nine members. They had all been selected from the great and the good; all but one were male, and five had been to Cambridge (of whom three were from Trinity College). The sole woman was Mrs Lindsey Huxley from the Women's Voluntary Service, but following her untimely death, Mrs Ethel Haythornthwaite took her place.

Over dinner Dower and Hobhouse went through a number of the 'assumptions and suggestions' provided by the outgoing Minister, WS Morrison, as guidance for the NPC's work. These were:

- There would be National Parks;
- An appropriate Central Authority, probably in the form of a Commission, would be set up for their administration;
- There would be a solution to the problem of compensation and betterment;
- Dower's report would form the basis for its work – even though the government was not yet formally committed to it;
- There should be no direct negotiations with Local Authorities, but the Committee could hear evidence from them;
- The NPC should not make detailed recommendations on legislation required for National Parks, since this

was a matter for the Ministry, in consultation with the Association of Local Authorities. But the Committee could make *general* suggestions on the objects to be achieved by such legislation.

- The Committee should complete its work within one year.

BOX 5: Members of the National Parks Committee (England and Wales) ('Hobhouse Committee')

Sir Arthur Hobhouse	Chairman
Lt. Col. EN Buxton	National Trust representative on Standing Committee on National Parks.
John G Dower	Architect and town and country planner.
Prof RST Chorley	Executive Committee CPRE. Hon. Sec. CPRE; Exec Cttee National Trust.
Leonard K Elmhirst	Dartington Hall Trust, forester.
Richard B Graham	Headmaster Bradford Grammar School; mountaineer and naturalist.
Dr Julian Huxley	Zoologist; Chair of Wildlife Sub-Committee on Wildlife Conservation.
Mrs Ethel Haythornthwaite	Hon. Sec Joint Cttee for the Peak District National Park; member CPRE Executive Cttee. Replaced Mrs Lindsay Huxley November 1945.

Clough Williams-Ellis	Architect and town and country planner; Chairman CPRE Wales; Vice-Pres Ramblers' Assn.
Sir William Gavin	Chief Agricultural Adviser to Ministry of Agriculture
Secretary: John B Bowers	Ministry of Town and Country Planning

*

At its inaugural meeting, the Committee decided that its first task should be to decide on the areas which should be selected as National Parks; those that should be selected first; and their appropriate boundaries and special requirements. The Dower Report had identified a 'Division A' of ten priority areas:

1. The Lake District
2. Snowdonia
3. Dartmoor
4. The Peak District and Dovedale
5. Pembroke Coast
6. Cornish Coast (selected parts)
7. Craven Pennines
8. Black Mountains & Brecon Beacons
9. Exmoor & North Devon Coast
10. The Roman Wall

But despite Dower's careful preparations, it soon became clear that the Committee and its Chairman had minds of their own. Hobhouse immediately raised the question of amending, or extending, Dower's list. He suggested the addition of areas that might offer greater amenity, or a wider range of landscape types, or – for recreational reasons – proximity to London and Eastern England. Julian Huxley added a fourth category – those parts of the countryside in need of urgent protection from imminent building development (particularly in the South-East), or damage through continuing occupation by the armed forces. A list

173

of ten further areas was discussed at some length, including the Norfolk Broads, the Chilterns, the Dorset Coast and Heaths, the Berkshire and Marlborough Downs, and the North and South Downs.

In the event, the Committee added a further three to Dower's priority list of ten:

11. The Dorset Coast and Heaths
12. The Berkshire, Marlborough Downs, and Savernake Forest
13. The South Downs

Dower was wholeheartedly in agreement as regards the Dorset Coast and Heaths. 'Personally, I rank its landscape beauty and recreational values in the highest class,' he wrote. 'The local authorities and local interests are now badly in need of national aid to get back and make good the large areas in the Isle of Purbeck and near Studland which have been requisitioned and used for battle schools etc.' He had even considered removing Dartmoor from his own priority list in favour of Dorset, in view of the opposition of the Duchy of Cornwall to National Park status. The Duchy owned at least half the proposed Dartmoor National Park area, and had a protected legal status.[183]

Dower also accepted that the South Downs might be suitable as a National Park, in view of its proximity to London. But he regarded the Berkshire and Marlborough Downs, although attractive, as being insufficiently wild. Julian Huxley, on the other hand, drew attention to the good 'walking land' they provided, and the continuing threat to the landscape posed by the military. The US Army had been using the area for battle training, and a large ammunition dump had recently blown up in nearby Savernake Forest, inflicting considerable damage. In the end, the Committee agreed that the area merited at least a visit, and that the Forestry Commission should be consulted on its future policy towards the management of forests in potential National Park areas.

---

183 *Preliminary Notes on Selection and Boundary Delimitation*, 24 July 1945, Paper NPC 4, HLG 93/2.

As regards the management of the Committee's work, Hobhouse proposed that during the next two and a half months – until mid-October 1945 – separate small teams should spend five or six days undertaking surveys of each of their allocated areas and defining their boundaries. Either Dower or John Bowers (now the Secretary of the Committee) would accompany them. Dower would cover five areas in Northern England relatively close to his home (the Roman Wall, Snowdonia, the Lake District, the Peak District, and the Craven Pennines (later to be re-named the Yorkshire Dales)), working variously with Richard Graham, Clough Williams-Ellis, and Hobhouse himself. This would involve working continuously from 20 August to 10 September, and from 1 to14 October.

Dower and Bowers were also given responsibility for making the necessary contacts with local authorities and other stakeholders, as well as arranging itineraries and accommodation for their respective parties. Bowers was additionally asked to obtain official passes to admit NPC members to areas under the control of the Service Departments. And on top of all this, he was charged with investigating the (admittedly unlikely) possibility of using aircraft both for survey work, and for the transport of members from area to area.

*

Wildlife conservation was a major item on the NPC's first agenda. Dower took a strong personal interest in the conservation of Britain's flora and fauna, observing in his report that 'it cannot be said that we have yet got in this country any national policy for the conservation of wild life, nor have we made any definite and assured progress towards determining a policy...'[184] It was not a secondary issue to be considered only as an addendum to National Parks.

Dower had been able to do some private 'botanizing' during the state of 'purdah' following the announcement

---

184 *National Parks in England and Wales, op. cit.*, para 61.

of the general election. On 1 June 1945, Molly Trevelyan (Pauline's mother), *en route* to a local wedding, gave her daughter and son-in-law a lift to Billsmoor Park in Coquetdale, about nine miles north of Cambo. That day Coquetdale was 'at its best under a sunny blue and white cloud-castled sky'. Dower described the landscape, flora and fauna in his journal:

> Billsmoor, with its many streams and natural – probably quite native and spontaneous – scrubby woodland, is certainly very attractive, but I should not rate it specially high as a potential Nature Reserve, except in so far as its enclosing high stone wall (in excellent repair) might make it special, clear-cut and easy to control.
>
> ...The woodland is nearly all alder in the boggier places and along the streams, and birch with hazel underwood in the drier places. At the edges the wood passes into an open scrub of hawthorn mainly, with some gorse and willows (small bushes, creeping and dwarf – I think without being quite sure, that these were *salix caprea, salix repens,* and *salix herbacia*). I noticed also a few rowans, one or two dog roses, and some considerable patches of bog myrtle around the boggiest open patches among the alders.
>
> ...Quite as interesting as the woodland inside Billsmoor are several other patches of wood and scrub lying outside but fairly close to it. Grasslees Wood, immediately to the north, is a very natural looking mixture of oak (dominant) with some ash and alder (locally dominant in the damp corners) and with a sparse underwood of hazel, crab-apple and rowan: throughout the wood, birch takes an intermediate place contributing both to the taller trees and to the underwood...

That evening, back at Cambo, Dower made a neat list in two columns of the thirty species of herbaceous plants in flower that he and Pauline had identified. He also finished reading the 600 dense pages of *The Handbook of British Flora*, by George Bentham and Joseph Hooker, 'marking up all species I have found in Malhamdale (M), in the country around Cambo (C) so far, and elsewhere – including a few found today at Billsmoor not previously marked'.

The following week, he wrote at length to Professor Arthur Tansley about the choice of trees for 'amenity' planting – and more importantly, about his growing interest in ecology:

Besides the Ecological Society reports, I have read with enthusiastic agreement your *Heritage of Wild Nature* and, during the last few weeks, I have spent many hours reading in your *British Islands and their Vegetation*, of which I recently acquired a copy. I only wish I had the prospect of enough free time to go systematically through this, with other reference books at hand, and become a belated but whole-hog student of plant ecology. I find the broad concepts and the technical terms stimulating and comparatively easy to grasp; the labour is mainly in translating the Latin names of plants into English ones – it is only in the last three years or so that I have made any attempt to memorize the Latin names, and I find they don't stick very easily or reliably...

I have been especially interested in your passages on the ashwoods and oakwoods of the Pennines – the woodland type which I know best. Your account of Colt Park is the more vivid because of my visit to it last August. I attach my note about this, if only as a sample of the kind of note which I and one or two of my colleagues are putting on appropriate Ministry files as opportunities for survey visits occur...[185]

Dower insisted that urgent measures were essential to preserve Britain's threatened wildlife, and had to fight against the initial scepticism of the Ministry. Some senior officials feared that critics would 'ridicule our interest in such a side-line as the conservation of wildlife and protection of our native plant and animal populations at a

---

185 Dower to Tansley, 6 June 1945.

time when we appear to be doing nothing about our major problems. This is fiddling while Rome burns.'[186] Later, the Ministry compromised and proposed that a nature reserves sub-committee should be set up within the Hobhouse Committee. But Dower pressed for something grander – a Wildlife Conservation *Council*, 'a permanent organ of government' largely composed of experts in the relevant fields, with wider terms of reference and greater status.

But the key question was: who should take the lead in post-war nature conservation? Dower had concluded that responsibility for establishing national nature reserves should lie with a National Parks Authority, advised by a Council of wildlife experts. However, already on the scene was the Nature Reserves Investigation Committee (NRIC), a non-governmental organisation which had been established under the chairmanship of Sir Lawrence Chubb, the Secretary of the Commons and Open Spaces Preservation Society. With official encouragement from the then Minister without Portfolio, Sir William Jowett, it had worked on its own report since 1942 on the need for national nature reserves – but outside the framework of future National Parks.

Tansley himself was not a member of the NRIC, although several members of the British Ecological Society (BES), of which Tansley was Chairman, were. In corresponding with him, Dower could not ignore the issue. He explained:

> The best conclusion I could reach was that the idea of National Nature Reserves stood a good chance of substantial realisation, on sound lines and within the next five years, if it came forward in close association with the idea of National Parks – but little or no chance if it came forward on its own as a quite distinct matter. I gather from your letter that you also incline to this view, and do not object to a single Commission being administratively responsible for both National Parks and National

---

186 John Sheail, *Nature in Trust: The History of Nature Conservation in Britain*, Blackie & Son, 1976, p. 111.

Nature Reserves – provided that the policy and management of the latter are effectively determined and supervised by expert ecologists. I don't differ from this proviso at all, nor – though it does not go into much detail – does my report.

Dower proposed that there should be at least one 'all-round ecologically-minded naturalist' on a future National Parks Commission, and that the salaried staff should include a sufficient number of trained ecologists, 'both for managing National Nature Reserves and for the application of a thorough policy for Wild Life Conservation throughout the National Park areas. My hope and belief is that on such a basis the ecological view will become a keynote of policy right through the whole system.'

He received strong support from his former colleague at Political and Economic Planning (PEP), Max Nicholson. Nicholson had a major influence on who should sit on the new wildlife sub-committee, particularly after November 1945 when he became head of the office of the new Lord President of the Council, Herbert Morrison. Not only did he persuade Morrison that he (Nicholson) should himself be a member of the wildlife sub-committee, but he also secured the appointment of two of his former colleagues from PEP - Julian Huxley (as Chairman), and the ornithologist Richard Fitter (as Secretary).

Formal responsibility for setting up the sub-committee – now termed the 'Wildlife Conservation Special Committee' – rested with Hobhouse. He was concerned to keep the *Special* Committee firmly within the orbit of the future National Parks Committee, insisting there should be no direct representation on the Special Committee of existing organisations, such as the NRIC or the British Ecological Society. The appointment to the Special Committee of Julian Huxley and Colonel Buxton gave them a foot in both camps, alongside their existing membership of the Hobhouse Committee. Dower himself was not a member, but his good personal relations with several of the wildlife experts provided further links between the two committees.

But Huxley had misgivings both about this dual role, and

how much extra fieldwork would need to be undertaken by the Special Committee. In contrast to most of his Hobhouse colleagues, he 'suggested' that there should be no commitment to linking wild life conservation to National Parks 'if this was against the considered opinion of the sub-committee'. A meeting of the Hobhouse Committee wearily concluded that this was a 'fair assumption', without making clear what the practical implications of this would be. It was a fine example of civil service obfuscation which obscured the relationship between National Parks and wildlife conservation.

Box 6: Wildlife Conservation Special Committee

Chairman:	Dr JS Huxley
Members:	Lt. Col. EH Buxton
	Capt. C Diver
	Dr CS Elton
	Dr EB Ford
	Mr JSO Gilmour
	Mr EM (Max) Nicholson
	Prof JA Steers
	Prof AG Tansley
	Prof AE Truman.
Secretary:	Mr Richard Fitter

*

The Hobhouse Committee was to hold no fewer than eighty meetings (both formal and informal), undertaking seventeen survey tours, and consulting eighty-two stakeholders, including planning, amenity and wildlife bodies, as well as government departments. It produced over one hundred substantial papers covering surveys, conservation areas, the holdings of service departments, forestry, mineral workings, water pollution, coastal preservation, pylons, holiday and tourist services, park planning committees and financial matters. It was not surprising that the Committee was to take twice as long to complete its work than the estimated one year.

But in the summer of 1945 all this was still to come. Throughout the Hobhouse Committee's first meeting on 1 August, a black cloud of anxiety hung over Dower as he pondered the future. The problem was this: would he be physically strong enough to tackle such an ambitious work programme? A few days before the meeting, he had confided to Bowers that he was 'very lethargic and somewhat dispirited' at having had to spend a week in bed in Cambo. 'I'm not ill, but it seems pretty certain that there is a little TB activity. I shall probably know better by the time I come up to London whether further rest-curing is called for, since I am having an X-ray and examination... It may be that I shall have to cut out survey-touring for August, joining in on it in September – I don't think it will be worse than that.'

A week later, a TB specialist in Newcastle settled the matter. 'I am confined to bed at the moment by a passing chill, but shall be up and about again by Sunday,' he wrote to Hobhouse and Bowers, as usual downplaying his condition. 'The doctors' views on my health are on the whole, encouraging. My general condition is sound, and though there is still some TB activity in the lung, they think this will settle down if I go very quietly for a bit.' *How* quietly was demonstrated by the postponement of his first three scheduled tours of the Roman Wall, the Lake District and Snowdonia – with a further question mark over the Peak District. But he reassured Hobhouse that his doctors were confident that he would be fit enough to come to London for the October and subsequent meetings of the Committee.

In the event, Dower managed to attend the October Committee, but had to pull out of the November one with a 'heavy and feverish cold' contracted during a (delayed) survey of the Yorkshire Dales. He reported to Hobhouse (who had accompanied him on the Dales tour), via Bowers, that his doctor was 'emphatic that I must stay in bed for the rest of this week: otherwise a thoroughgoing bronchitis and several weeks in bed, with general 'set-back', would be only too likely.[187]

---

187 HLG 93/38 Dower to Bowers, 14 November 1945.

As a result, the programme for Northern England slipped badly. This was precisely at the same time that the new Minister, Lewis Silkin, was pressing for early results. He wanted legislation on National Parks 'at the earliest possible date'.[188] This served only to increase the strain on Dower and his colleagues. Leslie J Watson, a thirty-nine-year-old landscape architect, had to be seconded to the Hobhouse Committee from the Ministry, to lead several survey trips in Dower's absence. (Watson was also an accomplished artist.) Meanwhile, Bowers complained to Dower in September 1945 that he was still unable to find a suitable technical secretary for the Wildlife Special Committee, and was having to do the work himself. 'I am afraid that the pressure of work, writing up Surveys and preparing the Wildlife Conservation Special Committee's meetings is so high that I haven't a hope of getting away to see you before the Dartmoor survey tour' (scheduled for the end of September).

Dower's illness limited his attendance to only eight of the twenty-one two-day Hobhouse meetings in London. The last one was in April 1946, after which his input was through letters, telephone conversations and his colleagues' occasional visits to Cambo. He still managed to undertake some survey visits closer to home – but only with Pauline's assistance as chauffeur and typist. At home in Cambo he read, commented on, and revised almost all of the Hobhouse Committee's written outputs. But overwork and isolation gave rise to frustration. His communications – particularly with his friend and colleague John Bowers – were sometimes tetchy, for he was a man in a hurry. 'As regards my Finance Paper,' he wrote to Bowers in August 1946, 'if you haven't already mucked about with the figures in the Salaries table, I would rather you didn't do so, but added at the end a postscript as attached herewith. Please also correct the additional mistakes as noted... May I please have a copy of NPC 77? Also of NPC 34, Appendix A; NPC 34, Appendix B; and NPC 35 (which I asked for many weeks ago, but have not yet had).[189]

188 HLG 93/8 Memo from Neal to ES Hill, 17 August 1945.
189 HLG 93/38, Dower to Bowers, 3 August 1946.

12. Tanks on the Lawn

They stood there in stunned disbelief. Gathered around the noticeboard in the cramped post office, the locals refused to believe what they read. Only a few weeks before, the small Dorset village of West Lulworth had celebrated the end of hostilities on VE Day. Shreds of bunting still adorned the shop door. Yet the letter pinned in front of them spoke more of war than peace. It had been signed by a junior officer, Lieut. Pymm, on behalf of 'the Adjutant, Gunnery Wing, Armoured Fighting Vehicles School, Lulworth Camp', and it announced the permanent closure of roads on the Isle of Purbeck between Stoborough and the coast. 'Starting on 30 May1945, shooting will be taking place daily over the whole of the East Holme Range area,' it read. The effect would be to close permanently five miles of the loveliest part of the Dorset coast, including Mupe Bay, Arish Mell, Worbarrow Bay and the western part of the Purbeck Hills.[190] Nearby Tyneham would remain a ghost village, despite the Churchill Cabinet's promise to its 225 residents that they could go home as soon as the war was over.

Tyneham and the hills around West Lulworth were just a small part of the much larger area of Purbeck that had been annexed for tank training, gunnery and missile practice by the Army's Royal Armoured Corps. The terrestrial ranges covered over eighteen square miles of limestone hills, cliffs and heathland – with an additional 'outer sea danger area', stretching thirteen miles out into the English Channel.

Dower was unaware of the Army's pre-emptive strike as he drafted his paper proposing National Park status for the Dorset Coast and Heaths.[191] It was tabled at the first meeting of the Hobhouse Committee, and secured ready agreement that Dorset should be among the first wave of potential

---

190 Letter from P Thornhill to the *New Statesman and Nation*, 7 July 1945.
191 Preliminary Notes on Selection and Boundary Limitation of National Park Areas, NPC 4, 24 July 1945.

National Parks to be surveyed. Noting that it was 'at present in the hands of the Service departments as a battle training area', the Committee concluded it was 'of great importance that (Dorset) should be preserved from permanent use for this purpose, and reconstituted for public enjoyment.'

In the event, the Army's threat of permanent closure was withdrawn, although it would remain in force until further notice. The Adjutant promised that any related notices would no longer be signed by 'anyone less than a Lieutenant-Colonel'. For lowly Lieutenant Pymm had seemingly failed to take account of the new Requisitioned Land and War Works Act 1945, which had received the Royal Assent just a few days before his notice was posted. The Act sought to 'regularise' the situation arising from the emergency wartime requisitioning of land by the government. In many cases, the relevant government departments wished to retain these holdings, often because they had invested millions of pounds constructing roads, factories, airfields, camps, hostels and defence works of various kinds. The Act provided for the compulsory purchase of the land on payment of compensation to the existing owner, thus preserving for the government the value of the works it had undertaken, and – if it wished – opening the way to subsequent disposal of the land (with the works) at its full market value.

This presented both the Ministry of Town and Country Planning and the amenity movement with a dilemma. If the War Office could now make permanent its occupation of land temporarily requisitioned for wartime training purposes, it would deny the public access to some of the most beautiful landscapes in Britain. On the other hand, if it chose to 'de-requisition' the land, either returning it to its legal owner(s) or selling it on the open market, it might well be used for purposes that would devastate the landscape with industrial estates, mineral extraction or unsympathetic house building.

The dangers posed by the military to areas of high nature value were highlighted by Arthur Tansley in a letter to Bowers in September 1945. He emphasised that areas which came up for 'de-requisitioning' ought to be considered first of all for purchase by the state as nature reserves, rather than handed over to other government departments or private interests. Bowers had already received 'unofficial information' that in the case of Pembrokeshire, the War Office had offered the land back to its previous owner, Lord Cawdor, who had then promptly proposed to sell it back to the War Office. Tansley called for a list of all requisitioned land suitable for national or local nature reserves, and an early warning system which would inform the National Parks Committee and/ or the Ministry of Town and Country Planning if any of these were to be relinquished.

Landowners – and certain amenity societies – were given scope to appeal against the permanent acquisition or disposal of their land. The Requisitioned Land and War Works Act set up an independent War Works Commission to adjudicate disputes – but its powers were circumscribed. The decisions of its seven members could be over-ridden by a Minister within forty days, unless the House of Commons explicitly imposed a veto. Common land or former open spaces had greater protection, requiring a positive vote in both Houses of Parliament before they could be taken over permanently. But this would not apply if the Ministry of Town and Country Planning or the Ministry of Agriculture could offer alternative land 'not being less in area and being equally advantageous to the public'.[192]

*

On the morning of Thursday, 11 October 1945, Sir Arthur Hobhouse, Julian Huxley, Leonard Elmhirst and John Bowers assembled outside the sprawling, five-star Hotel Grosvenor overlooking Swanage Bay, and waited for the two large taxis that were to take them on an intensive four-day survey of the Dorset countryside. Hobhouse justified the extravagance by observing that 'it is usually better to be driven so that members can see more of the country.'[193]

---

192 *The Requisitioned Land and War Works Act 1945*, Butterworth and Co., October 1945.
193 Hobhouse to Geoffrey Clark, 14 September 1945.

Dower was absent for reasons both of geography and health, but he took great interest in the trip as a means to impress upon the group how serious was the threat posed by the military to the beauty of the Dorset landscape.

The practical arrangements for the survey had been drawn up by Geoffrey Clark, a local planning consultant to the county council. He proposed an anti-clockwise sweep of the entire county – through Dorset's marshy flats and heaths, to the chalk northern hills coloured brown on the Bartholomew map, and then south-west to the sea. First, the party was to head north towards Shaftesbury, and the following day, north-west to Cerne Abbas and High Stoy Hill, moving to the King's Arms Hotel in Dorchester for the last two days. The tour would then take in Abbotsbury, Weymouth and Portland, and finally Lyme Regis and the Marshwood Vale in the far west of the county.

Bowers was captivated by the Dorset landscape. His report of the survey trip noted:

> While Dorset offers no continuous wild mountain and moorland country comparable to the northern and western National Park areas, it does provide within a comparatively small area an unrivalled variety of exceptionally beautiful inland and coast scenery...
>
> The coastal scenery is of particular beauty, comprising the marshy flats and reed-bordered estuary of Poole Harbour, the sandy beach of Studland Bay, the chalk headland of the Foreland and Ballard Points, the bold Purbeck limestone cliffs from Durlstone Head to St Alban's Head, gentler cliffs and coves from Chapman's Pool to Kimmeridge, more Purbeck rock at Gad Cliff, fine chalk headlands west of Lulworth, the unique peninsula of Portland, and running north-west from its base, the twenty mile long pebble bank of Chesil Beach, and westward, marking the transition to the Devon coastal scenery, the colourful cliffs of West Bay, Charmouth and Lyme Regis...
>
> The northern limit of the area surveyed by the Committee is marked by the long sweeping range

of the chalk downs extending westward twenty or thirty miles from the Stone Gap at Blandford. This northern escarpment, which rises to a height of 900 feet, provides expansive views over the Blackmoor Vale, while to the South fingers of high downland extend into the arable country of the reverse slopes. South-westward the chalk broadens out into some fine upland country between Dorchester and the coast at Abbotsbury.

There are in the area many attractive villages, with notable Norman and medieval churches and cottages, roofed with thatch or the local stone tiles; and also many small towns of character and beauty – notably Dorchester, Wareham, Blandford, Beaminster and Lyme Regis. (Swanage is a seaside resort of little architectural merit, and behind the Georgian port at Weymouth lies extensive and squalid urban development...)

For the holiday maker the area provides varied facilities for seaside holidays, with good bathing and sailing, for the natural-scientist many features and areas of unique interest, while for the rambler there are very considerable though somewhat scattered areas of open land and an extensive network of footpaths, in a perfect setting of downs, heaths, hills and coast.[194]

But Bowers was also well aware of the hurdles to be overcome before much of Dorset could be designated as a National Park. The most intractable issue was, of course, the extent of the Service Departments' holdings, which, if they continued, could well 'nullify the creation of a Dorset Park'. Little hope had been forthcoming from a Principal Secretary in the War Office in his response to an earlier enquiry from the Minister of Food, Colonel (Lord) Llewellin (who also happened to be a Purbeck resident). 'Until the size, nature and role of the post-war Army and Navy is settled, it is impossible to be quite certain as to the extent of their training

---

194 Summary Survey Report, Dorset, 11-14 October 1945, NPC 12.

requirements,' he declared. In any event, Tyneham, the Arne Peninsula and the East Holme area of Purbeck would be retained. And the Admiralty could be expected to hang on to Studland Bay for the purpose of assault landing exercises. The Principal Secretary's advice to his superior, Secretary of State for War Jack Lawson, was to give Col. Llewellin 'the full picture'. 'I am sure no harm would be done so long as Col. Llewellin did not pass it on, and so encourage every local authority to think that by making enough clamour now, they can extract some implied promise that the Services are not going to disturb them in the post-war period.'[195]

How wrong he was. On 24 October 1945, a deputation of the great and the good travelled from Dorset to Whitehall, demanding that the War Minister derequisition the whole of the East Holme battle training area. The party of seventeen, led by Lord Llewellin himself, comprised a complete cross-section of the county's political, industrial, and amenity interests. They included one former, and three current, Dorset MPs; the three chairmen of respectively the Dorset County, Wareham District, and Poole Borough Councils; representatives of the National Trust and CPRE; the National Farmers Union; the Southern Sea Fisheries; local clay mines; and the Co-operative Holidays Association. Feelings were running high.[196]

*

Dorset was just one of several potential National Parks that were under threat from the military. In Pembrokeshire, the greater part of the south-west peninsula west of a line from Pembroke to Stackpole – some seventy-seven square miles – was in the hands of the War Department. In his capacity as Secretary to the National Parks Committee, Bowers wrote to Ernest Hill at the Ministry of Town and Country Planning informing him that

---

195 WO 32/2174, 12 March 1945.
196 Letter from the Clerk of Wareham and Purbeck RDC to the War Office, 10 October 1945, HLG 71/1618.

unofficial information leads the Committee to believe that the War Department intend to keep this area as a permanent training area for Armoured Fighting Vehicles. It has already been considerably devastated. There are no buildings or farms still standing, and the countryside is a wilderness of weeds and running with rabbits. It is an area of exceptional beauty with a coast line of great magnificence and particular geological interest and is undoubtedly one of the most important sections of the proposed National Park.[197]

But there was a growing feeling within the National Parks Committee and in the wider amenity movement that the Ministry of Town and Country Planning was unable and/or unwilling to assert itself against the claims of other, more influential, government departments. As early as July 1945, GM Trevelyan had written an exasperated letter to *The Times* in his capacity as President of the Youth Hostels Association. He declared:

How ominous are the facts – how ominous the weak position of the Ministry of Town and Country Planning, its lack of recognised status in such recent legislation as the Water Bill, the Forestry Bill, and the Distribution of Industry Bill. That the Ministry has been imported at all into the Requisitioned Land Bill is simply due to the constant criticism which has been directed in Parliament against the official policy, or rather against the absence of a policy. And the protection of good agricultural land rests on no sure foundation; the beauty of the sea coast, with which the English people have some concern, is just about as defenceless. One could prolong the mournful catalogue. Soon – in a few months maybe – the full tide of development will begin its levelling and destructive sweep over the green and pleasant parts of England which survive...[198]

---

197 Bowers to Ernest Hill, 26 September 1945.
198 GM Trevelyan et al, 'Planning the Countryside', *The Times*, 7 July 1945, p. 5.

Lewis Silkin, the new Minister of Town and Country Planning, entered the fray within a few weeks of his appointment. He presented a long memo to the Cabinet stressing the need for 'close scrutiny' of the activities of the Service Departments. He explained that in March 1945, the Services held no less than 1.2 million acres of land – 750,000 on requisition and 460,000 in their ownership. This amounted to some 2 per cent of the total area of the United Kingdom – a proportion that was far higher in the case of open country, where the whole or the greater part of potential amenity areas had often been requisitioned. Half the Isle of Purbeck was occupied from Poole to Lulworth Cove – an area eleven miles long, and eight miles wide. The public were becoming restive, and local authorities were being prevented from planning urgent reconstruction. 'What is necessary is that all of the Service Departments should as a matter of urgency consider their positive programmes as a comprehensive whole, and that the Minister of Town and Country Planning and other Departments affected should be fully consulted on them at an early stage,' wrote Silkin. 'It is my duty under Statute to see that the best choice is made between competing uses of land, and Local Authorities must be informed as soon as possible, in view of the importance of that knowledge to the discharge of their duty in planning properly for the future of their districts.'[199]

At Prime Minister Attlee's suggestion, a summit meeting was convened for 5 November 1945 bringing together the Ministry of Town and Country Planning and the Service Departments. A gold-braided delegation of the Secretary of State for War (Jack Lawson), the First Lord of the Admiralty (Albert Alexander) and the Secretary of State for Air (Viscount Stansgate), together with their respective officials, rather outgunned Silkin with his four civil servants. But unperturbed, Silkin forthrightly pointed out that every government department concerned with the use of land (for example, housing, roads or National Parks) was being prevented from developing a comprehensive programme for reconstruction because of naval or military procrastination.

---

199 HLG 71/1618, 9 October 1945.

Partly this was due to uncertainty over the future needs of the Service Departments, but the situation was made much worse by each Service Department acting individually, rather than working together. And it was of utmost importance that the British countryside's special 'jewels in the crown' should be released before they suffered (further) damage.

Across the table, the Service Ministers professed themselves perfectly prepared to work together – but their comments and body language suggested otherwise. The First Lord of the Admiralty argued that a co-ordinating committee should not be allowed to 'lay down the law', but should be 'consultative and advisory' only. Any differences of opinion would have to be referred to Ministers to resolve – inevitably a protracted procedure which would negate the purpose of setting up a committee in the first place. Moreover, he stressed that the Service Departments should not have to justify their continued occupation of special sites, because Service interests were national (and by implication, more important) while amenity interests were generally local. Thus it should be for local objectors to state and win their case (despite their considerable lack of resources), not the Services.

For his part, Lawson, the Secretary of State for War, drew attention to the extended time it would take the Army to identify, assess and, if necessary, relinquish its holdings. He produced a large plan of the whole of England and Wales showing areas over 1,000 acres which were either a) in War Office ownership, or b) requisitioned during the War and now intended for gradual release, or c) taken over during the war, and which the War Office proposed to keep.

It was clear from the map that the process of reviewing WO land holdings would take many years.

The meeting eventually concluded with the following decisions:

- It would be 'desirable' to set up co-ordinating machinery to deal with the use of land by the Service Departments, and this should cover all military land uses and not just training areas and ranges;
- The new co-ordinating machinery should be linked to the existing Cabinet sub-committee on Airfields;

- The Minister of Town and Country Planning should submit a list of areas whose early release was of outstanding importance, and the Service Departments would 'do their best' to give these priority. But the *quid pro quo* would be costly: 'Where necessary, the Minister of Town and Country Planning would help to find suitable alternative areas.'[200]

The Ministry lost no time in drafting and circulating its list of requirements for each of the three Services, in England and Wales, as follows:

War Office

Wareham and Purbeck – 'a special amenity area, where there is also great anxiety on behalf of former inhabitants to return to their homes and resume their agricultural work. Strong public agitation has been caused by its retention.'

Morfa-Harlech, Snowdonia, and Pembrokeshire (South of Castle Martin) – of which Harlech is regarded as the most urgent.

Ashdown Forest, Sussex – a tank training area of some 3000 acres, about which there has been much public and Parliamentary anxiety.

Grimsby – 47 acres urgently required by the local authority for housing.

Chesterfield – 11 acres required to address the lack of space for playing fields in the locality, and the high incidence of road accidents involving children.

Admiralty

Long Ashton – 245 acres urgently required to be developed as a mental hospital.

---

200 HLG 71/1618.

Pett Levels, Sussex – area flooded during the war for defence purposes. Now drained but not accessible, and needs to be reclaimed for agriculture.

Abinger, Surrey – land should be released for amenity reasons and 'obnoxious' buildings removed.

Air Ministry

Leith Hill (Radar Station) – a special amenity area. An ammunition depot on the Commons near Leith Hill should also be removed.

Other areas – being considered by a separate Cabinet Aviation sub-committee.

A brief for the Minister of Town and Country Planning concluded on a note of sheer frustration:

The question whether these isles are large enough for all the Service requirements inevitably arises, but insofar as land in this country is concerned it is vital that Service Departments should relate their demands to a definite post-war programme and should co-operate freely, frankly and fully with the Ministry of Town and Country Planning and other Departments involved, at the earliest possible stage, to ensure that (a) the demands are kept to an absolute minimum; and (b) they are decided not by 'military necessity' alone, by a proper and just balance of military and civilian needs...
...It may be added that derequisition of the areas given in the list should be accompanied where necessary by the full restoration of the land, and the removal of any objectionable buildings or defence works (eg barbed wire).[201]

*

---

201 HLG 71/1.

In the circumstances, it is perhaps not surprising that the War Office failed to respond for several weeks. It was not until Christmas 1945 that Lord Nathan of Churt, the Parliamentary Under-Secretary of State at the War Office, eventually wrote to Silkin with a languor totally appropriate to the festive season. He explained that he had been asked by the Secretary of State for War to undertake a survey of the 'whole position as regards War Office requirements of land etc, both actual and prospective', and this investigation would inevitably take some time. As a result, he was not in a position to give a definitive response to the Ministry's request for the early release of key areas at risk. Indeed, Nathan's reply entirely ignored Ashdown Forest and Leith Hill; was vague about how much of Snowdonia might be de-requisitioned; and simply gave false information about Wareham and Purbeck ('with the exception of the east Holme Range, all areas including Studland Bay will be released in the near future...').

As for the proposed co-ordinating machinery between the Service Departments, he confirmed that he was 'in communication with the Admiralty and the Air Ministry upon this subject, but so far there has been no reply; I am urging a reply...'

Silkin's prompt response barely concealed his irritation. He reminded Nathan that it had been the Prime Minister himself who had encouraged preliminary discussions with the Service Departments, and he wanted to announce to the public 'in the very near future' that the co-ordinating machinery was in place.[202] However, it was not until early April 1946 that what was now to be called 'The Inter-departmental Committee on the Correlation of Service Department and Civil Department needs in regard to Land Use' was formally established. Silkin was obliged to accept that the exact machinery for co-ordination would have to be a matter for the Service Departments themselves. The influence of the Ministry of Town and Country Planning over the Service Departments was to be rather less than Silkin had hoped, but at least it was to be the Ministry's Under-

---

202 HLG 71/1618.

Secretary, Ernest Hill, who would chair the Committee. This was welcomed by the Permanent Secretary, who noted in relation to the Service representatives that 'from what I know of them, there would be difficulties unless the chairman was of senior rank.'

But it was not just the Service Departments who were dragging their feet – some senior officials in the Ministry of Town and Country Planning itself were also obstructive, fearing competition from a future National Parks Committee. So Bowers – supported by Dower – pressed Hobhouse to use the 'ammunition' he had gathered on the situation in Pembrokeshire 'for an attack on the Ministry'.[203] Hobhouse quickly responded by impressing on Alfred Valentine, the Ministry's Permanent Assistant Secretary, that the threats to National Parks from the Services required 'some drastic and immediate action'. 'Many of our members are most apprehensive as to the position,' he wrote. 'In one or two cases it is likely that they will have to report that unless these occupations are removed, or very greatly reduced, they cannot recommend that the area should be designated as a national park'. He supported Tansley's call for the War Department to produce a map of all the areas it occupied, indicating those it proposed to retain permanently. And he stressed that the War Works Commission should give first refusal to the Ministry of Town and Country Planning when releasing old Service occupations.[204]

Pressed into action at last, Valentine arranged a meeting with two representatives of the Service Departments, Messrs Gaster and Millar. They agreed to produce maps of War Department holdings, but were reluctant to go much further than that. On the question of future RAF airfields, for example, Gaster considered that 'It may be dangerous to press individual amenity areas too far, since objection to a particular site might lead to the choice of another with even greater objections.' He quoted in evidence the substitution of Leith Hill by Gibbet Hill in the War Office's chain of observatories. Particular difficulties had also arisen in the

203 Bowers to Hobhouse, 15 May 1946.
204 Hobhouse to Valentine, 18 May 1946.

case of the Marlborough and Berkshire Downs, which the National Parks Committee had shortlisted as a possible National Park because it was within easy reach of London. The area included thirteen army camps and no fewer than ten airfields, the most important of which were Ramsbury and Membury.[205] The minutes of the meeting recorded Mr Gaster's view that these airfields were probably 'not objectionable in themselves' – subject to their being 'tidied up' and the replacement of war-time buildings 'properly built and sited'. The War Department rejected the view that the presence of an airfield in a National Park area was *ipso facto* objectionable, and favoured instead case-by-case investigations of flying use, and the number of personnel working there. In any event, Gaster pointed out, the land was agricultural, with few rights of way, and its distance from London (three hours' journey) – with the rival attraction at hand of the more accessible South Downs – made it 'of minor importance'.

Valentine's team from the Ministry of Town and Country Planning agreed. Moreover, it refused to give Philip Mansfield (the Assistant Secretary who had taken over from Dower in the Ministry) full representation on the Cabinet Committee reviewing the holdings of Service Departments. He was to be permitted to attend only when specific National Parks issues were being discussed.

*

Meanwhile, at the other end of the country in Northumberland, the Army's appetite for more training grounds continued to expand. In a Christmas letter to *The Times*, GM Trevelyan noted that

> A substantial area in the Cheviot Hills has, under the cloak of war, been compulsorily purchased as an extension to the Redesdale artillery range... The area affected includes the upper waters of the Coquet, the

---

205 HLG 93/4 NPC 44, *Service Department Holdings and War Works.*

Roman Camp at Chew Green – an outpost on the uttermost edge of the Roman Empire, and the hills between the Coquet and the Scottish Border. This part of the Cheviots has been recommended in the Dower Report as a potential National Park, and the final stage of the Pennine Way is interrupted by the present extension of the range... A mistake has been made in acquiring this land for so inappropriate a purpose...[206]

Trevelyan had a direct interest in the preservation of the Northumbrian landscape, for he had bought a farm next to Housesteads Fort, later giving covenants over it to the National Trust.

Northumberland was also Dower's home county, and alongside his former Ministry colleague Thomas Sharp, he loved 'those grassy hills with their soft, many-tinted, cloud-shadowed outlines, their sense of wide, unrestricted freedom, their clean free air...[207] Yet Dower had placed only parts of the county on the National Park reserve list, rather than in the First Division. The reasons for this were undoubtedly the extent of the Army's occupation, together with the hundreds of square miles of Sitka and Norway spruce being planted by the Forestry Commission in the valley of the North Tyne and at Kielder. He felt compelled to propose just the central section of Hadrian's Wall as a future National Park. The area was only a dozen miles from his home in Cambo, and it was from here on 1 November 1945 that he embarked on a two-day survey in the company of Lord Chorley, Hobhouse and LJ Watson. A few weeks later he reported that

...the Wall and its associated works form one of the finest ancient monuments in the world. As a frontier memorial it is the best surviving from the Roman Empire, and second only to the Great Wall of China... There is here a unique conjunction of

---

206 Letters to the Editor, *The Times*, 27 December 1945, p. 5.
207 Thomas Sharp, *Northumberland: A Shell Guide*, Faber and Faber, 1952, p. 14.

wild upland country with an ancient monument that even those not archaeologically minded can hardly fail to find impressive. The 'Military Road' constructed soon after the 1745 rebellion, which runs close to or along the line of the Wall from Newcastle to Carlisle opens up the whole length of the National Park area and provides a splendid scenic route for motoring visitors, while the National Trust property at Housesteads provides a fitting introduction to its inner attractions...

Dower argued that only designation as a National Park could fully protect the area. Large-scale quarrying of the Whin Sill crags had led to the progressive destruction of the Wall itself and its amenities. And although further quarrying along the line of the Wall had been permanently prohibited, there were still three quarries in operation, each of which had destroyed a quarter mile of Wall and crag, and two large crushing plants operating north of Haltwhistle. In addition to quarrying, the Forestry Commission's activities posed a potential threat to the open character of the country immediately north of the Wall, and some way to the south, as seen from the finest part of the Wall at Housesteads.

But there were formidable hurdles to overcome before the Roman Wall could be given National Park status. The proposed park covered a comparatively narrow strip of country – just thirty-three miles from east to west along the line of the Wall, and from three to nine miles from north to south. This amounted to just 193 square miles in all, considerably less than the 'extensive area of beautiful and relatively wild country' that Dower's own report had set as a key criterion for selection. Moreover, the Ministry of Works had already introduced a Preservation Scheme under the 1931 Ancient Monuments Act, which ensured the strict preservation of a mile-wide strip of land stretching fifteen miles along the Wall and Vallum, from Greenhead eastwards to just short of Chesters. Within it, all forms of development were banned apart from agricultural improvements and forestry. 'The main objective of the National Parks Commission has therefore been secured,' wrote Dower, 'and the continued preservation and management of this stretch of the Wall, together with the remaining parts of the National Park, will require the closest co-operation between the Commission and the Ancient Monuments Service.'[208] This raised questions about whether there was any need at all for a National Park along the Wall. But as a north countryman, Dower remained obdurate.

---

208 *Report of the National Parks Committee (England and Wales)* Cmd. 7121, Appendix C.9, The Roman Wall, July 1947.

13. Into the Trees

Dower's direct role in attempting to prise Britain's finest scenery from the grasp of the Service Departments was relatively limited. This was partly because most of the negotiations were taking place hundreds of miles away in Whitehall. But – more importantly – during the winter of 1945-46 Dower needed to devote much of his time and energy to an equally crucial challenge – forestry. Any land that might be retrieved from the military was still in grave danger of being absorbed by an expansionist Forestry Commission.

Dower had noted in his report that

> ...the policies and activities of the Forestry Commission and the National Parks authority should be closely and continuously co-ordinated... The two bodies are potentially rival claimants over large areas of upland country, in some at least of which it is unlikely that both could operate successfully... It is to be hoped that (the Forestry Commission's) policy with its emphasis on the production of softwood timber and its disregard of secondary consequences, will be replaced, at the close of the present war, by a much more comprehensive policy which gives hardwoods a larger share in the planting programme; which treats the amenity values of trees as of no less national importance than their strategic and economic values; and which makes positive provision for the integration of silvicultural, agricultural and recreational development...[209]

He proposed a long-term plan earmarking 'areas for landscape preservation, agricultural development, recreational use or wildlife conservation, to the more or

---

209 Dower, *National Parks in England and Wales, op. cit.*, paras. 76-77.

less complete exclusion of any further conifer afforestation, while leaving suitable scope for replacement of existing woodlands, and some additional hardwood planting.' Existing forests in National Parks should be subject to negotiated 'amenity restrictions' – and without financial compensation. 'If any large piece of potential National Park land must, by Government decision, be mainly devoted to conifer afforestation,' he wrote in a letter to Arthur Hobhouse, 'then it should, in my view, be excluded from the National Park.'[210]

Dower looked forward to 'a mutually beneficial relation' and 'sufficiently early, frank and close consultation' between the Forestry Commission, the National Parks Authority and the Ministry of Town and Country Planning. 'If such basic planning is sufficiently thorough,' he wrote, 'I personally have little fear of any serious difficulties or controversies in subsequent execution and administration.'

Such apparent optimism was only to be expected in a Government White Paper. In reality, Dower had real concerns about the Forestry Commission's ambitions. These had been set out in a 1943 blueprint *Post War Forestry Policy*, in which the Commission had called for a huge expansion of afforestation and replanting to build reserves of standing timber as quickly as possible.[211] This was mainly for strategic reasons. The success of German submarines in sinking Allied shipping during both world wars had exposed the recklessness of relying on imported timber. Britain's housing, industry and mining depended upon it. In addition, the Forestry Commission argued that a systematic plan for afforestation would bring into production large areas of poor under-utilised land, and provide jobs in healthy rural surroundings for returning servicemen.

The Forestry Commission's paper called for no fewer than five million acres of state-owned land for timber production over the next fifty years – two million acres from existing forests, and three million from new afforestation.

---

210 Letter from Dower to Hobhouse, 17 November 1945, HLG 93/24.
211 Forestry Commission, *Post War Forestry Policy*, Cmd. 6447.

More immediately, during the first ten years, the state should acquire 1.85 million acres of new land, 900,000 acres of which would be planted, while 400,000 acres of existing woodlands would be re-planted. Meanwhile, it was hoped that private forestry would contribute an additional 200,000 acres, encouraged by a state-supported 'Dedication Scheme'. The stage was being set for a massive expansion of Britain's forests.[212]

The new Labour government did not immediately accept all of these proposals, but the Forestry Act of June 1945 considerably strengthened the Forestry Commission's hand. As a mere 'Commission', it had suffered in negotiations with other government departments from the absence of a sponsoring Ministry, but the new Act for the first time made it an agency of the Ministry of Agriculture. Henceforward, the Agriculture Minister would speak in Cabinet on the Commission's behalf. The Act also gave the Commission powers of compulsory purchase. Thomas Williams, the Minister of Agriculture, made a short statement to the House of Commons at the end of November 1945 stressing that the government was 'seized of the great importance of pressing on, as a matter of urgency, both with a large programme of new afforestation, and also with the replanting of our felled woodlands. We intend to prosecute both these tasks with the utmost vigour...'[213]

*

Two months later, on 1 February 1946, the Forestry Commission's Chairman Sir Roy Robinson, with his Deputy Mr WL Taylor, appeared before the Hobhouse Committee.[214] Robinson was a formidable figure, a tall, burly Australian

---

212 Douglas Pringle, *The first 75 Years: A Brief Account of the History of the Forestry Commission, 1919-1994*, Forestry Commission, 1994.

213 HC Deb. series 5, vol. 416, cols. 1779-84, 30 November 1945.

214 National Parks Committee (England and Wales), *Record of Oral Evidence from the Forestry Commission*, 1 February 1946, NPC/45, in HLG 93/24.

and a Rhodes Scholar who was determined to achieve his objectives, come what may. Dower had crossed swords with him ten years before over afforestation in the Lake District (see p. 48), and so he made a particular effort that day to come to London to meet him.

Sir Roy was quick to point out to the Committee that a large number of potential National Park areas were already 'in the possession' of the Forestry Commission, and the extent of such areas was set to expand. He listed some of the targets. On Dartmoor, the Commission wanted between three and four thousand acres; in the Black Mountains and Brecon Beacons it had identified 40,000 acres that might be planted; and in Northumberland, a very large forest (Keilder), comprising 40-50,000 acres, was in the process of formation north of the Roman Wall. When asked by Sir Arthur Hobhouse if it would be possible for the Forestry Commission to find the necessary acreage *outside* the 'first priority' National Park areas, Sir Roy expressed doubt that sufficient alternative land could be found in England and Wales, and stressed that he could not commit the Commission to avoiding any particular area.

Evident throughout the exchanges was the underlying tension between the Committee and the Forestry Commission. The key question was: who should have primary responsibility for management decisions within the Parks, particularly over amenity issues and their financial implications. Col. Buxton suggested that it would be natural for the Forestry Commission, as experts in woodland management, to take responsibility for managing all woodlands, including those primarily of landscape value. Sir Roy, however, stressed that the Commission could not devote itself to such 'refinements' until its more 'fundamental requirements' were satisfied.

Sir Arthur Hobhouse went straight to the heart of the matter. Did Sir Roy regard National Parks as a threat to national forest policy, and would he object in principle to National Parks legislation? 'Only if it was assumed that conifers were inadmissible in national parks,' was his reply – a response in direct opposition to the Dower Report. Sir Roy offered 'close co-ordination of policy' between the administration of National Parks and the Forestry Commission's own National Forest Parks. But as Dower had already pointed out in his report, National Parks were not National Forest Parks, where 'recreational use and landscape preservation are not dominant but secondary purposes – conditioned by, and subsidiary to, the planting, forest management and timber production which are the Commission's *raison d'être*... Wherever it establishes new plantations on previously open and uncultivated land, it reduces by so much the actual or potential opportunity for rambling access.'[215]

Sir Roy had few allies among the Hobhouse Commissioners – with one major exception. Leonard Elmhirst had produced in the weeks before the February meeting a number of lengthy papers for the Committee clearly supporting the Forestry Commission's views.

Elmhirst was an agricultural economist and philanthropist who, with the financial support of his American wife Dorothy, had bought the Dartington Estate in south Devon in 1925 as an experiment in rural regeneration. His entry in *Who's Who* noted his sole recreation as 'Care of Trees', and he afforested much of the estate both as a commercial venture and a research undertaking. In 1946 he was to become President of the Royal Forestry Society of England and Wales, and was the architect of a 'dedication scheme' to support private forestry.

For Elmhirst, 'the key problem for the National Park Authority will be how to assist and promote sound forestry', rather than advance the cause of countryside amenity. And he asked Robinson a question that was clearly planted. 'In what particular respect did the Forestry Commission find the protagonists of "Amenity" particularly vexatious'? he enquired. Sir Roy replied that criticism was frequently levelled by those who had failed to look at the problem. People were prejudiced against afforestation by the inevitable unattractiveness of forests in their early stages. But he believed that when the forests came to maturity they would be found 'to enhance the attractions of the country'.

---

215 *Forestry and National Parks - Synopsis*, November 1945, NPC 23.

The interest of a wood or forest was to be derived not from its landscape value, but 'from exploration of its interior'.

Elmhirst's position had already been challenged at the Hobhouse Committee's meeting on 15 January 1946. Sir William Gavin asked him to explain why he was so interested in the productivity of woodlands, when that was surely the duty of the Forestry Commission, not of a future National Parks Commission. Dower himself had comprehensively dismissed an early synopsis of Elmhirst's views in a letter to Hobhouse. 'I find myself in disagreement with, or in doubt about, much of its content,' he wrote, 'more especially in application to the upland country of the North of England, which I know best.'[216]

It was sadly ironic that from November 1945 to January 1946 the discussion of Elmhirst's papers should have taken place at 16 Queen Anne's Gate in Westminster, the headquarters of Political and Economic Planning (PEP). Over a decade before, it was here that Dower had worked closely and harmoniously alongside Elmhirst, setting up a PEP Land Group and writing a number of papers on agriculture policy.[217] Now, the two men were diametrically at odds. An indication of the distance between them was evident in a barely coherent note by Elmhirst on *Hedgerow Timber and Amenity*:

> Hedgerow timber can be, and often is, a curse to the farmer and serious economic disbenefit to the farm... The roots of a tree can soak up moisture and reduce fertility over a quarter to half an acre, and the foliage prevents the sun exerting its beneficent influence on crop, soil and bacteria. The roots interfere seriously with the plough...
>
> Amenity to the countryman is so often directly associated with utility in a way that the urban mind can neither endure nor understand. The smell of well-rotted manure, of the pig-sty, or of silage can arouse the sense of 'Bisto' in a farmer's nose, but

216 Letter from Dower to Hobhouse, *op. cit.*
217 See p. 39.

may turn the stomach of the townsman. There are and have been nearly as many passing fashions in the conception of amenity as in the field of women's hats and waistlines... Again multiplicity of small fields and the miles of fence or banks prevalent in days when labour was cheap and machinery non-existent, are a curse to the farmer...

Any tendency on the part of a Parks staff to try and conserve this or that redundant hedge, fence or hedgerow tree is bound to involve not merely compensation for 'restraint', but the opprobrium of farmer and countryman... Now that motoring or bus riding has offered to thousands a means of enjoying the countryside vista that only the hunter or horseman could easily enjoy before, there is a real case for studying the amenity of roadside views and viewpoints, and of planning or clearing to meet it.

Dower responded to these 'interesting notes' by pointing out that landowners and farmers were nothing like 'so purely utilitarian and self-interested, and so regardless of public amenity' as Elmhirst had made out:

The appreciation, conservation and creation of landscape beauty is *not* a monopoly of visiting townsmen! Nor is landscape amenity anything like so much a matter of passing fashion as Elmhirst suggests. The qualities and features which Wordsworth most valued in the Lake District 140 years ago are precisely what its more sensitive lovers, both resident and visiting, most value there today.

The Hobhouse Committee eventually agreed that the promotion of sound forestry should indeed be a priority for individual National Park committees – but only insofar as the Forestry Commission itself failed to do the job. Each National Park should appoint an expert landscapist with a knowledge of forestry, but their function should be 'to represent the claims of amenity upon all forestry operations' and 'to define certain areas which shall be termed amenity woodlands, and to see these are operated on sound principles of management, but with the specific aim of amenity and public enjoyment rather than of maximum profit.'[218]

*

But by the end of October 1946, Sir Roy Robinson had got most of what he wanted. In a full day's debate in the House of Commons, the Minister of Agriculture Thomas Williams moved 'That this House approves the policy of His Majesty's Government for Forestry as announced by the Minister of Agriculture and Fisheries on 30 November 1945'.[219] He urged the Forestry Commission to prepare for 'large scale action', announcing that the Chancellor of the Exchequer had boosted the Forestry Fund by £20 million for the five years between 1946 and 1950. This would provide a first instalment of 365,000 acres for afforestation or replanting, on state land. Additional planting would also come from the private sector.

The six-hour debate illuminated the extent to which the government's forestry policy was now dominated by the Ministry of Agriculture. In over 40,000 words of parliamentary debate, National Parks were not mentioned once. When the need for recreational facilities in the countryside was raised, the Minister of Agriculture referred 'naturally' to the National Forest Parks: Argyll, Glen Trool, Hardnott, Snowdonia and the Forest of Dean. Discussion of conflict with other land uses was limited to references to agriculture alone. 'Apart altogether from potential agricultural land,' Williams declared, 'there are scores of thousands of acres in this country simply crying aloud for afforestation at once, where nothing but trees could be produced in those areas...' A national survey of land suitable for afforestation had been established with the intention to protect the interests of farmers (not amenity),

218 Discussion of Elmhirst's paper *Forestry in National Parks,*
  NPC 31, HLG 93/4.
219 HC Deb. series 5, vol. 428, cols. 51-154-84, 24 October 1946.

and it would be the Ministry of Agriculture that would take the final decisions in England and Wales if any conflicts arose.

Despite the government's official policy, the members of the Hobhouse Committee (all bar one) remained staunchly intransigent. And Dower's stamp was clearly visible in Hobhouse's final report when it was published in July 1947:

> The protection of landscape beauty and the claims of public enjoyment in National Parks will demand in some cases the complete exclusion of planting from certain areas, in others its exclusion on hill tops and ridges, in others the substitution of hardwoods for conifers – and, in yet others, a judicious admixture of hardwoods, the planting of hardwood fringes, the provision of paths, open clearings or unplanted fair-ways, and the avoidance of hard straight lines in rides and at plantation edges.

The report proposed that plans giving owners of private woodlands financial support for planting in National Parks by means of the Forestry Commission's 'dedication scheme' should first be referred to the National Parks Commission before they became effective. And if these plans proved to be insufficiently specific, the Forestry Commission should be required to produce more details.[220] At the same time, the local Park Committees in the National Parks should identify areas where planting new woodlands would require their consent – and 'reasonable conditions' could be attached, including how these woods should be laid out, and the types of trees to be planted. 'Suitable' compensation would be made available to landowners if consent was refused, together with a right to appeal to the Minister of Town and Country Planning (but note – not to the Ministry of Agriculture).

But no such radical proposals found their way into the 1949 National Parks and Access to the Countryside Act. The

---

220 Report of the National Parks Committee (England and Wales), Cmd. 7121. Report of the Hobhouse Committee, paras. 127-32.

priorities set out in the Hobhouse Report were inverted, with the importance of amenity sidelined in just thirty-four words, headed *Protection for Agriculture and Forestry*:

> In the exercise of their functions under this Act it shall be the duty of the [National Parks] Commission, the Nature Conservancy and local authorities to have due regard to the needs of agriculture and forestry.[221]

---

221 National Parks and Access to the Countryside Act, 1949, chap. 97, para 84.

14. Planning in the Parks

Choosing which areas of England and Wales should be designated as National Parks was difficult enough – but it was only the first step. Deciding how each of them should be planned and managed, and by whom, was just as important and no less contentious. It was an issue that was to dominate the Hobhouse Committee's agenda for over a year, from November 1945 to February 1947. Setting up a new system of countryside planning raised fundamental questions over differing perceptions of democracy; the design of new administrative structures; and what we would now call the issue of 'subsidiarity' – that is, which level of government was most appropriate for dealing with which types of problems.

The Scott Committee Report had answered this latter problem by proposing that a future National Parks Authority (later, the National Parks Commission) should take complete control over local planning in each of the Parks, for all purposes, and to the exclusion of local councils. The Dower Report, too, had stressed that 'National Parks, if they are to be worthy of their name and purpose, must be *nationally* selected, provided and supervised by a specific *national authority* primarily concerned only with National Parks and National Nature Reserves.'[222] (Author's italics)

Lord Chorley reinforced this view. In a memo to his colleagues, he wrote:

> Actual experience of local authority planning has been such as to suggest that to leave them in charge of it would imperil the whole National Parks scheme... Local authorities are too apt to regard all such matters from the point of view of rateable values. They are anxious to attract new industries and to build up old ones, and in the event

---

222 Dower, *National Parks in England and Wales, op. cit.*, para. 84.

of a conflict between amenity values and rateable values, they are almost certain to prefer the latter.[223]

RB Graham also questioned the competence of local authorities. 'The attitude of some of them is plainly hostile,' he wrote, 'and their nominees are not likely to be of high quality, nor to be inspired by the right ideals.' He argued that councillors often did not represent the people who actually lived in the proposed Parks, and were instead most sensitive to the demands of the more numerous city dwellers.[224]

It was Chorley's conclusion that the supervision and control of both strategic planning and day to day management in the National Parks should rest centrally with a National Parks Commission. And to ensure this, a two-thirds majority of the members and chairs of each of the Park Planning Committees should be appointed centrally by the Minister of Town and Country Planning.

But Arthur Hobhouse took entirely the opposite view. As Chair of Somerset County Council and President of the County Councils Association, he championed local authorities. He would not concede that a National Parks Commission – or even a sub-Committee of the Commission – could handle, centrally, the large volume of problems that would arise across all National Parks. The minutes of the National Parks Committee record that 'While he (Hobhouse) agreed that local authorities were variable in quality and often slow to start, they were often tenacious and persevering when they set themselves to a task. He did not want to see National Parks operated in the face of local authorities' antagonism.' For him, it was 'a difference between centralisation and de-centralisation, and between bureaucracy and democratic administration.'[225]

Hobhouse therefore proposed that in each National Park a key 'Special Joint Planning Committee' (i.e. the Park

223 *Park Planning Committees*, memo by Lord Chorley, NPC 84, 14 August 1946.
224 RB Graham, *Park Planning Committees - Constitution and Numerical Composition*, NPC 72, 9 July 1946.
225 Arthur Hobhouse, NPC 27, 20 November 1945; and NPC minutes, 9 August 1946, in HLG 93/3.

Planning Committee responsible for local development control) should include no more than one-third of national representatives, the remaining two-thirds majority being appointed by the local authorities operating within the boundaries of each Park. Separately, a 'Local Park Committee' (composed not of elected councillors, but local volunteers to cut costs) would be responsible for the day-to-day management and development of the Park. Only the Chief Executive Officer (responsible for appointing and deploying staff) would be appointed centrally by the National Parks Commission.

Dower found himself half way between Hobhouse and Chorley. While stressing that National Parks were a national asset, he was also strongly in favour of giving local authority representatives the leading role on the Park Planning Committees. He was concerned that if hundreds of local councillors across England and Wales were to be in a permanent minority in the governance of large swathes of the counties they represented – at a time when they had been promised increased powers in the forthcoming Town and Country Planning Act – they might well oppose the passage of National Parks legislation altogether. Dower sought to square this circle by advocating joint action between national and local authorities, working together. He proposed that local authorities should normally have a majority (up to two-thirds) on the Park Planning Committees, while national priorities would be secured simply by giving the Minister of Town and Country Planning in Whitehall (advised by the National Parks Commission) strong fall-back powers. For example, the Minister would be able to increase the proportion of national representatives, or even in extreme circumstances take over the Park Planning Committee altogether. And if the National Parks Commission were to be outvoted, the Minister would be able to put the decision on hold while it was 'reconsidered'.[226]

The arguments over the balance of power between local and national representatives flowed back and forth during the first six months of 1946. By August, Hobhouse was in a state

---

226 Minutes of the NPC, January 1946, HLG 93/4.

of desperation. He decided that arbitration was the only way out of the impasse, and turned to his friend Sir Cecil Oakes, the Clerk of East Suffolk County Council. Oakes had a wide knowledge of local and central government and had according to Hobhouse been 'outstandingly successful in promoting the co-operation of local authorities in Suffolk and the Eastern Counties'. But even so, the plan that Oakes eventually put forward was not at all what Hobhouse had in mind. Hobhouse (with Dower) had proposed that two committees were essential to deal separately with the two major functions of National Park administration – on the one hand, the more negative process of regulating potentially harmful development, and on the other more positively – providing recreational facilities in the Parks for the benefit of the public. But Oakes favoured bringing together these two functions into a single Park Planning and Management Committee – and he proposed that this committee should be dominated by a majority of national representatives. There would, however, be two sub-committees, A and B, to feed into its work. Sub-committee A would deal with the management and development of the Park, and this would have a majority of local representatives, while B would cover strategic planning and development control, where local councillors would be in a minority. The most crucial planning decisions, therefore, would be in the hands of central government representatives, rather than officials who lived and worked in the area.

Most of the Hobhouse Committee members – including Buxton, Elmhirst, Gavin, and Ethel Haythornthwaite – grasped the Oakes proposal with great relief as a way out of the deadlock. But not Dower. In early September 1946, he wrote to Hobhouse acknowledging that the Oakes plan was 'ingenious', but giving the National Parks Commission majority control of local planning in the Parks would invite 'bitter opposition' by the local authorities. 'I do not think for a moment that they will be taken in by the expedient of giving them a majority on a sub-committee, any decision of which can be reversed or varied by the Commission majority on the main Committee.'[227]

---

227 Dower to Hobhouse, 2 September 1946 HLG 93/38.

Dower was prepared to compromise a little in a bid to secure a consensus. Instead of a two-thirds majority of local authority members on Park Committees, he conceded that '50:50 representation of the county councils and the National Parks Commission might be the most satisfactory solution,' with the Chairman chosen from within the Park Planning Committee. In the event of a stalemate, the matter could be referred to the Minister. Dower was also adamant that Oakes' plan of a single Park Planning and Management Committee would not work. The development and management of each Park would require significant expenditure on staff and facilities, which local authorities could ill-afford. Therefore, responsibility for this function should lie entirely with the National Parks Commission, with Park staff appointed and managed by an overarching Chief Executive, who would himself be appointed by and answerable to the National Parks Commission.[228]

*

Such arguments within the Hobhouse Committee about Park Planning Committees inevitably delayed the completion of the Committee's Preliminary Report to the Minister, Lewis Silkin. He was pressing for a National Parks Bill as soon as possible, but the Secretary to the Committee, John Bowers, who was responsible for translating the Committee's often tortuous discussions into successive drafts of the report, was feeling the pressure. He explained to Dower that he had been 'stricken with what appears to be a recurrence of malaria, which I thought had cured five years ago when I left Abyssinia.' However, the fever rather conveniently 'only hits me in the evenings so I have been able to get off the urgent (national park) business and hope to get cured in good time for the next series of meetings.' Then a week later, his assistant resigned with a duodenal ulcer.[229]

---

228 Minutes of the NPC, 18 November 1946, HLG 93/5.
229 Bowers to Dower, 27 September 1946, HLG 93/38.

The pressure eased somewhat when it became clear that there was, anyway, no space in the current Parliamentary session for the introduction of a National Parks Bill. Moreover, it was decided that the circulation around Whitehall of a substantial Preliminary Report would be politically unwise. Max Nicholson, the Head of the Office of the Lord President of the Council (and member of the Wild Life Special Committee) advised Hobhouse that if other government departments had early sight of a draft, 'there might be some danger that (they) would raise objections which would force the Minister to require us to re-consider our Report and to water it down before the final version was published. There might even be a danger that this proceeding might hold up the final publication for several months.' Instead, there should be informal discussions with the Ministry of Town and Country Planning alone, and it would then be up to the Committee 'to consider any suggestions for modification or omissions', rather than other departments.[230] As a result of Nicholson's intervention, the focus now shifted to completion of the *final* report, and ensuring that when it appeared, it had maximum public impact.

Bowers prepared an amended draft in preparation for the Committee's meeting, just before Christmas 1946. Most of the Committee had adhered to the Oakes proposals they had welcomed in September, but Bowers chose to incorporate Dower's proposal of a 50/50 local/national split in the Park Planning Committee. The major difference was that a Chairman should be appointed by the National Parks Commission from outside the Committee, the effect of which would be to give the national representatives an inbuilt majority of one.

Dower was again unable to attend the December meeting in person. His letter was dictated to and written by Pauline, and signed in Dower's wavering left hand. 'I unfortunately had a slight haemorrhage yesterday and have to keep in bed and be lazy today and tomorrow,' he informed Bowers. 'I am still plainly not well enough for a trip to London.'[231]

---

230 Bowers to Hobhouse, 28 August 1946, HLG 93/36.
231 Letter from Dower to Bowers, 17 December 1946, HLG 93/38.

His continuing absence was unavoidable, and it sometimes had unfortunate consequences. From 300 miles away he was unable to argue his case face to face with his colleagues. Instead, his views were channelled to them via letters, or telephone calls to Bowers – and on receipt were sometimes misunderstood. Even Bowers himself misconstrued some of Dower's positions, much to Dower's irritation. 'I strongly object to the passage,' he wrote, 'which purports to describe a reservation I have not yet written, and thoroughly mis-describes the difference between myself and the rest of the Committee. Indeed, the whole passage is quite unnecessary, and it would be sufficient and much more dignified to confine the reference to my reservation to a footnote...' And Dower was also assiduous – indeed pernickety – in searching out errors of style, punctuation and printer's errors in the drafts that Bowers sent him.

> First, you will notice I have struck out quite a number of phrases and a few sentences which seem to me unnecessary and either (a) tautological or (b) sententious or (c) mere glimpses of the obvious...
>
> Secondly, you should still watch the use of Caps. throughout... The particular case I have most noticed is that of 'Order' (meaning a Statutory Order); this should, I suggest, always have a capital 'O'...[232]

A clarificatory telephone call usually calmed the waters. Bowers suggested to Dower that it was 'not entirely hopeless that if your reservation was circulated as a convincing document before the next meeting, the Committee might be persuaded to adopt it'. Hobhouse, too, wrote to Dower on New Year's Eve, in this case pleading for him to fall in line with the rest of the Committee:

> I feel that it is most important to avoid reservations if this can possibly achieved. Or, where members find themselves compelled to record reservations, that these should be kept to a minimum of

---

232 *Ibid.*

disagreement. In the case of our Report, I cannot but feel that a really substantial disagreement indicated by you would weaken the Report's effectiveness, as it would indicate that the Committee were not unanimous and would give anyone hostile to National Parks an argument for their opposition. Any disagreement on the recommending body would be quoted as a reason for opposing our proposals generally.

Sensing what the response would be, Hobhouse ended his letter asking Dower to state his bottom line. He should set out clearly 'the proposals for local organisation which you feel *must* be voiced by yourself.'[233]

Bowers was despatched to Northumberland early in the New Year to engage in what he described as 'a little low-grade diplomacy'. He was expected by the Committee to be a neutral go-between, but he and Dower were friends as well as colleagues, and Bowers privately agreed with Dower that the Oakes proposals gave too much power to national representatives. The best solution therefore was an equal split in the Park Planning Committees – although, as Bowers wrote later, 'I still have a personal liking for a local authority majority...' He was well aware, however, that Graham, Buxton, and Ethel Haythornthwaite wanted to reduce local authority representation to just one-third. Indeed, Graham made it known that if the Committee were to agree to a 50/50 split, he, too, wished his dissent to be recorded in the final report.

Bowers and Dower talked into the night in front of the log fire at Cambo, while outside the temperature plummeted. Inside, some progress was made. 'It was, as always, refreshing to get away from an atmosphere of expediency and compromise, and hear some honest, straight thinking,' Bowers wrote on his return to London. 'I'm only sorry if in my invidious mission I seemed to have the smell of that atmosphere hanging around me...'[234]

---

233 Hobhouse to Dower, 31 December 1946, HLG 93/38.
234 Bowers to Dower, 13 January 1947, HLG 93/38.

By the end of January, Dower had managed to send to London a number of his detailed amendments, two of which were fundamental in seeking to establish a balance within the Park Planning Committees, between local authority representatives and national appointees. But he did take a small step towards a compromise:

> My proposal as you know was 50/50 membership [of the Park Planning Committee] and the Chairman to be chosen by the National Parks Commission from among the members of the Committee. The text now makes the Chairman additional, and impairs my intention of genuinely equal shares in the representation. If the Committee decide on the Chairman being extra, I wish my disagreement to be recorded – but again *I don't propose to make a reservation on the point.*

Dower's second amendment concerned situations where a Park Committee faced a conflict between local and national interests on which they were unable to reach a decision. He believed that in such a case, the matter should be determined by the Minister. This was opposed by several Hobhouse Committee members who wished to reinforce the power of the local representatives. But Dower was adamant:

> I regard the content of this paragraph an essential part of the scheme of local organisation as it now stands, and I trust the Committee will decide to retain it. If they omit it, I shall think it necessary to submit an Addendum (*not a reservation*) covering the content of the paragraph.[235] (Author's italics)

*

In the event, Dower's view on the role of the Minister won the day, but he was forced to concede that the Chairman of a

---

235 Dower to Bowers, 26 January 1947, HLG 93/38.

Park Committee would be appointed by the National Parks Commission, and not from among the local representatives on the Committee, thereby giving the national representatives an advantage of one. But in a gesture to the local authorities, the final report of the Hobhouse Committee stressed that the national representatives 'should mainly be persons resident within or near the National Park, with understanding of local traditions and interests and of the purposes of National Park policy...' Moreover, Park Committees would be able to appoint sub-committees from among members of the Park Committee exclusively, or through the co-option of others 'who would contribute valuable knowledge or represent the views of lower tiers of local government, or of voluntary bodies...'

Dower had sought and secured compromise, and in the event no reservations appeared in Hobhouse's final report.

15. Fighting over the Wall

The time had come for the National Parks Committee to take some decisions. By Easter 1946, the ten members had completed their surveys of the candidate National Parks proposed by Dower in his report. And the Minister of Town and Country Planning, Lewis Silkin, was pressing for legislation at the earliest feasible date, and wanted a Preliminary Report on progress as soon as possible. A key meeting on the choice of National Parks was scheduled for 1-2 April in London's St James's Square, but it was touch and go whether Dower would be well enough to make it. In early March, he had fallen sick once more and was confined to his bed, remaining there for most of that month. As a result he missed the Annual Conference in Derbyshire of the Ramblers' Association, where he was to be elected President to succeed Arthur Leonard, the Grand Old Man of the open-air movement. Dower's Presidential Address calling for greater education and understanding – particularly between ramblers and farmers – had to be read to the conference in his absence. From Cambo, he wrote to John Bowers that work on 'promised stuff like the Heads for a National Parks Bill' had to be put to one side because of his illness, but the onset of spring lifted his spirits. His bed was moved alongside the wide-open study window, overlooking the still-melting snow outside. 'Spring is in the air, buds are on the move, and everything points to a little day-dreaming contemplation,' he wrote. 'Tell LJ (Watson) that I bask in the fragrance and beauty of a glorious magenta-red hyacinth – one of those he gave to Pauline...'[236]

In the event, Dower's health improved sufficiently for him to join his Committee colleagues in London after all. According to the terms of reference of the National Parks Committee, its point of departure in selecting the Parks was to be Dower's list of ten set out in his report. However, over the previous nine months several new considerations had

---

236 Dower to Bowers, 9 March 1946, HLG 93/382.

emerged. To begin with, Dower's list had prioritised areas of wild country, but these happened to fall in the north and west of the country, leaving the more populous south and east of England without a National Park. Dr Julian Huxley, himself a Londoner, tried to redress the balance and pressed for the inclusion of the Berkshire, Marlborough and South Downs. Although they were very different from the more mountainous regions in the north, Huxley argued that downland areas were comparable in quality to wilder country, 'exhibiting typical English landscape and providing much open rambling land'.

As Chair of the Wildlife Conservation Special Committee, Huxley's priority was nature conservation rather than just the protection of landscape, and as such he supported the inclusion of the Norfolk Broads in the shortlist. The 200 miles of East Anglian waterways represented one of the greatest and most varied areas in Britain for biodiversity, as well as providing opportunities for sailing and boating. Richard Fitter, the Secretary of Huxley's Committee and himself an accomplished ornithologist, had written in December 1945 a Memorandum for the Hobhouse Committee pointing out the threats to the Broads posed by uncontrolled boating, silting of the waterways and 'bungaloid' ribbon development. 'The Broads are definitely in great need of some control, which nothing but a body such as a National Parks Administration or the National Trust would be in a position to provide,' he wrote. 'The existing authorities are too numerous and un-coordinated to be capable of a unified, directed effort which the situation demands.'[237]

The Norfolk Broads were to be surveyed on 10-13 May, and by a considerably larger group than usual, including Col. Buxton, Leonard Elmhirst, Lord Chorley, Sir William Gavin, Clough Williams-Ellis, John Bowers and Richard Fitter. But Dower remained housebound – and sceptical. The Broads did not fit his definition of a National Park:

237 Richard Fitter, *Memorandum on the Inland Waterways and Broads of Norfolk and Suffolk*, 19 December 1945, NPC 41, HLG 93/4.

they would have been more suitable, he suggested, 'if the motor boat had never been invented'.[238] And as regards the southern downlands, he pointed to the wartime expansion of arable land and the potentially serious impact on farming of the thousands of ramblers attracted by a National Park. However, the Committee concluded that the Berkshire and Marlborough Downs should be recommended, subject to a survey of wartime developments, and their 'absorptive capacity'.

A further key issue in choosing National Parks concerned coastal areas. Dower's report had included in the first instalment (Division A) 'selected parts' of the Cornish coast – consisting of the Land's End and Lizard Peninsulas, and the stretch from Padstow Bay northwards towards Westward Ho!. Hobhouse found it difficult to envisage a coastal National Park in Cornwall because of the serious administrative problems it would raise. The long, narrow coastline, divided by arbitrary local authority boundaries, would be 'most difficult and complicated'. Even so, he believed that at least sections of the Cornish coast should become a National Park (or Parks) since it 'ranked especially high in popular esteem and was in great need of protection'.

The only other proposed coastal National Park was Pembrokeshire, which attracted the support of both Dower and Huxley on the grounds of its unique beauty, and the addition of the 'valuable hinterland' of the Preseli Mountains. Dower also suggested that its designation 'might improve the possibility of evicting the Service Departments'. JA Steers, however, was far more ambitious than such piecemeal tinkering, arguing that the entire coast of England and Wales should be protected and managed as a single unit by a central Coastal Advisory Planning Committee. Hobhouse, meanwhile, was concerned that yet further expansion along the coast would undermine the role of the fledgling Ministry of Town and Country Planning, since the proposed National Parks and Conservation Areas (see below) already covered over one-third of the English and Welsh coastline.

---

238 Minutes of the NPC, 1-2 April 1946, HLG 93/4.

*

Dower remained well enough to participate in three supplementary surveys in late April and early May 1946 of the North York Moors and Coast; the Yorkshire Dales and Howgill Fells; and the Peak District and Dovedale. Although conveniently close to home, the work stretched over a period of almost three weeks, and for Dower this was a step too far. On 18 May he once more wrote to Bowers from his bed that 'a sharp fever' had laid him low 'with a headache and temperature, unfit for any sustained work'. His doctor had forbidden for the foreseeable future any further visits to National Park Committee meetings in London. By early July, Dower could report to Bowers that 'I continue to mend and am now up and about in my study half the day, and making progress with a heavy arrears of correspondence etc. I have even had a couple of strolls around the garden, but I am still very washed out physically, and I have no doubt at all that the doctor is right in asking for at least a month more of quiet rest cure here...'

In fact, the meeting early in April 1946 of the National Parks Committee was the last that Dower was able to attend. He managed to stay engaged with its work only by letter or telephone, and the occasional visit to Cambo of a Committee member. His enforced absence from London put him at some disadvantage in the arguments over the selection of Parks. Moreover, writing became increasingly difficult 'on account of my rheumatic elbow, which is tiresomely worse, doubtless through inactivity and general poisoning during the last four weeks in bed'.[239] He soon discovered that the stiffness and pain was caused by a tubercular infection of the joint, which needed to be put in plaster. 'I shall doubtless find it inconvenient at first to have a stiff elbow,' he wrote to Bowers, with some understatement, 'but it will not incapacitate me from any working point of view.' His previously neat handwriting became erratic, so he taught

---

239 Dower to Bowers, 19 June 1946.

himself to write with his left hand. Even so, he became increasingly dependent on Pauline as his amanuensis and typist.

*

On 8-9 July 1946, the National Parks Committee considered a second draft of its Preliminary Report to the Minister. This now proposed thirteen potential National Parks to be designated in three instalments. The list included the Cornish Coast, the Roman Wall, the Berkshire and Marlborough Downs and the Norfolk Broads – but the Roman Wall and the Broads were bracketed 'with a view to omitting one of them'.

Most of the Committee, including Hobhouse, had concluded that they should propose no more than twelve National Parks. Already, together they covered an area of some 5,000 square miles – almost 10 per cent of the total area of England and Wales – and the administrative burden of creating and managing any more was considered too great. And Col. Buxton also pointed out an additional reason: the need 'to guard against probable superstition in the public mind by avoiding a recommendation of thirteen Parks'.

Dower was appalled at the prospect of the Roman Wall being dropped, and wrote to Hobhouse insisting it must be included. If any area was to be omitted, it should be the Broads, he argued. He did not want a future National Parks Commission to be 'involved in the complex and expensive work of planning and managing the Broads, entailing issues of land drainage, navigation, water supply and reclamation'. And he also proposed the exclusion of the Berkshire and Marlborough Downs. If necessary, the South Downs would be a preferable candidate.

Dower's letter divided the Committee. At its next meeting on 14 August 1946, Col. Buxton, Richard Graham and Ethel Haythornthwaite favoured the Roman Wall, while Sir William Gavin and Leonard Elmhirst championed the inclusion of the Broads. So in a sleight of hand, Hobhouse proposed that the Broads might be given a special status as a

'National Reserve', a novel category that reflected its unique features. But it should be designated at the same time as the first instalment of National Parks, to counter any impression that it had been relegated to the second division.

The list and timing now looked like this:

First Instalment (1948)
The Lake District
North Wales (Caernarvon and Merioneth Mountains)
The Peak District and Dovedale
Cornish Coast

Second Instalment (1949)
Yorkshire Dales
Pembrokeshire Coast and Preseli Mountains
Dartmoor
Berkshire and Marlborough Downs

Third Instalment (1950)
Roman Wall
North York Moors and Coast
Brecon Beacons and Black Mountains
Exmoor

For Special Treatment (concurrently with First Instalment)
The Broads

Julian Huxley was not directly involved in the horse trading, as he was heavily committed in setting up the United Nations Educational, Scientific and Cultural Organisation (UNESCO) in Paris. But on reading the minutes, he immediately wrote to Hobhouse firmly opposing the designation of the Broads as a 'Special Area', or 'National Reserve'. 'First, because though the Broads is in some ways different from other areas, it is important that we should be able to apply the concept and name of "National Park" to as wide a range and type of country as possible. We have already gone some way in this direction by including coastal parks and, of course, a [possible] South Downs Park would be of very unusual type – practically a scarp strip.'

Huxley agreed that there should be no more than twelve Parks – so if the Broads were to be designated, one of the Committee's proposed list would have to go. 'I feel strongly that the Broads should be included and the Roman Wall excluded,' he wrote. 'The Roman Wall could be put high up on the list of areas which might be recommended later, but personally I have always felt that it is better treated as a Conservation Area in which the central feature, namely the Wall itself, would be specially protected as an ancient monument, or in any way that might seem fit.' He ended the letter with a warning: 'I do not feel that I could put my name to a proposal for what makes virtually thirteen National Parks, or for one which would include only twelve but leaves out the Broads.'[240]

Deadlock between the two men with the greatest authority within the Committee presented Hobhouse with a difficult dilemma. Both Dower and Huxley could seriously undermine the impact of the Committee's recommendations if either one of them insisted on including a major reservation in the final report. Even worse would be a resignation. It appeared to Hobhouse that the only way of squaring the circle was to appease both of them: (a) agree with Huxley that there should be no 'National Reserves' alongside National Parks; (b) include the Broads; and (c) retain the Roman Wall to placate Dower. Something had to give. After several days of contemplation, Hobhouse proposed yet another plan.

> If the Committee recommends three types of landscape areas for separate treatment – national parks, national reserves, and conservation areas – there is likely to be criticism that our recommendations are too complicated. I therefore feel that the reference to National Reserves would

---

240 Letter from Julian Huxley to Hobhouse, 22 August 1946, NPC 92.

be a mistake, and that it is also undesirable to depart from the round figure of twelve National Parks.

As the Committee is divided in the choice of the Roman Wall and the Broads (each of which are strongly backed by some members) I think the only solution is to omit one of the *other* areas provisionally selected for a National Park. Of the other areas, I suggest that the North York Moors is the best choice. Although this area is undoubtedly of high landscape value and also serves Middlesbrough and adjoining towns, it is not at present especially vulnerable to development and the North Riding County Council has an exceptionally good planning organisation to protect it. Also, our information indicates that there is no desire in the area for the creation of a National Park... Accordingly, I would like the Committee at their next meeting to consider the adoption of twelve National Parks, including the Roman Wall and the Broads, and excluding the North York Moors.[241]

But Richard Graham, supported by Lord Chorley, wanted to retain the North York Moors, both for the quality of its landscape and architecture, and to block the construction of a proposed reservoir at Farndale. Graham also wished to keep both the Roman Wall and the Broads, and therefore demanded a return to thirteen rather than twelve National Parks.

Most of the Committee were anxious to close this particular Pandora's Box, and so threw their weight behind Hobhouse's new proposal. Huxley, however, continued to insist that the Roman Wall should be excluded 'as being in little favour and in least danger'. In the end, Hobhouse was obliged to call for a vote, and Huxley's view prevailed: the Roman Wall would be excluded from the recommended areas, and as a small concession to Dower, the South Downs would replace the Berkshire and Marlborough Downs.

---

241 Chairman's Note on Selection of Areas, 7 September 1946, NPC 93, HLG 93/5.

It fell to John Bowers to break the bad news. On 14 September, he reported to Dower the conclusions of the meeting:

> It was felt by certain members that a simple reservation over your signature advocating the inclusion of the Roman Wall would not seriously detract from the strength of the Report. However, it was the general view of the Committee that a reservation carrying the weight of your signature, which advocated the inclusion of the Roman Wall *and* the exclusion of the Broads from our recommended areas, would be a much more serious matter... The terms in which your reservation is worded rests of course in your discretion, but I undertook to communicate the Committee's views to you by letter so that you should have ample opportunity to consider them. I greatly hope that we shall have the opportunity of discussing this and other matters before the Report takes final shape...

Dower pondered his position over the following two weeks. He was well aware that the authority of the final report would be seriously compromised if the Committee's unanimity were to be broken by his reservations. But he was equally adamant that after all the years of work he had devoted to the cause of National Parks, his beloved Northumberland should not be the only northern county left without one. He had to secure the Roman Wall at all costs. This would require sacrificing one of the other proposed Parks, even though omitting any one of them would be a high price to pay.

*

Also fighting for Dower's attention in August and September 1946 was the issue of Conservation Areas. The term 'Conservation Area' applied to Divisions B and C in the Dower Report – that is:

- areas reserved for possible future National Parks
- other amenity areas that were unsuitable in view of their limited extent or wildness
- the intensity of local land-uses such as forestry and arable farming
- their close proximity to country of still higher quality (as in the case of the Howgill Fells).[242]

Their value was that they formed a reservoir of possible future National Parks, often providing links between one Park and another to create long chains of protected landscapes. For example, southwards from the Cheviot and Rothbury Forest in Northumberland, a combination of National Parks and Conservation Areas stretched almost unbroken to Stoke on Trent. The Howgill Fells and Silverdale Conservation Areas linked the Lake District and the Yorkshire Dales National Parks. And of the proposed fifty-two Conservation Areas no fewer than nineteen of them protected coastal areas which fell outside most of the National Parks.

However, in early September 1946, Dower wrote to Bowers that it was 'very important not to let the number of Conservation Areas get out of hand i.e. to retain a reasonably high standard for inclusion in the list and in particular to exclude areas which, however interesting, fall below a minimum size of about 20 square miles... The danger here comes from (JA) Steers, with his additional coastal areas, most of which in my opinion ought not to be included in the Conservation Areas list... I have, however, adopted a few of Steers' additional areas, including them in new or adjusted Conservation Areas of my own.'

Dower had begun to revise their boundaries – particularly those in the north of England with which he was well acquainted, and in Wales. This was undertaken with a meticulous eye for detail. 'I don't see why you take a kink in at Llanerfyl,' he wrote to Bowers. 'The valley west of Llanerfyl seemed to me rather dull but the hills around

---

242 Dower, *National Parks in England and Wales, op. cit.*, paras. 10-11.

it are quite good, and the little hill east of Llanerfyl is an attractive feature with a steep eastern slope that rounds off the boundary...' But once again failing health interrupted his work. On 7 September he wrote to Bowers that he had been having 'slight but persistent haemorrhages for the last five days, and it has become plain that I must stay flat and inactive in bed till they cease. Even if they do so at once, it would still be too much of a risk to come to London so soon.'

*

On 2 October 1946, Dower wrote to Hobhouse asking whether the Committee would consider keeping the Roman Wall, but excluding either the Cornish Coast, Exmoor or the North York Moors. Five days later, at the fifteenth meeting of the Committee, Sir William Gavin proposed that they should adopt the first option. He was supported by Richard Graham, Clough Williams-Ellis, Col. Buxton and (reluctantly) Ethel Haythornthwaite. Lord Chorley was the most sceptical, and considered that omitting the Cornish coast would disappoint a large number of people. And the arguments for excluding the Roman Wall were just as compelling. Huxley meanwhile was absent in Paris, and Leonard Elmhirst was away in the north of England with the Footpaths and Access Committee.

Long and difficult negotiations resulted only in continued deadlock. After the Committee meeting, Ethel Haythornthwaite made clear to Hobhouse her fear of yet further delay – and she was particularly concerned that the whole Committee had been invited to dinner with the Minister, Lewis Silkin, in just ten days' time. 'Postponement of legislation seems the most serious blow to our whole work and aims,' she wrote, and 'immediate protective measures' were needed in all the potential Parks.'[243]

Elmhirst happened at that time to be physically the nearest Committee member to Northumberland, and he

---

243 Letter from Ethel Haythornthwaite to Hobhouse, 17 October 1946, HLG 93/37.

used the opportunity to visit Dower in Cambo to try to broker a deal. He had previously pressed for the exclusion of the Roman Wall on the grounds of its small size, its existing level of protection, and (for him) the welcome prospect of unfettered expansion of forestry in the area. Even so, he sympathised with Dower as a friend and colleague from PEP days – and he realised the seriousness of his illness.

Surprisingly, he had never visited the Roman Wall, and so while Dower retired to his bed after lunch, Elmhirst took up Pauline's offer of a scenic tour. During a brilliantly sunny autumn afternoon, she drove almost ninety miles, impressing on him both the beauty and uniqueness of the landscape, and how crucially important it was to Dower that it should be protected as a National Park. The friendly persuasion had its effect: Dower later reported to Bowers that Elmhirst was 'greatly impressed' with what he (Dower) now proudly called 'the Roman Wall National Park'.[244]

On his return to London, Elmhirst reported back to Hobhouse on his tour and his discussions with Dower and Pauline. Hobhouse then contacted Huxley, who readily agreed to support the inclusion of the Roman Wall and omit the Cornish Coast. Subsequently, Hobhouse was able to confirm with Chorley that he was also in agreement. In a letter to Ethel Haythornthwaite, Hobhouse concluded: 'I am taking it that this will be the Committee's unanimous and final view, and the map department has been given instructions to proceed on these lines.'[245]

'To my mind,' he explained in a memo to the Committee, 'there are three important and conclusive reasons for our final decision:

- **Unanimity**... The public is looking to our Committee for guidance on a very difficult matter of choice. It is by no means certain that Parliament will be unanimously behind National Parks, *still less as many as twelve.* Any indication of doubt or disagreement on the recommending body would be quoted as a reason for

244 Dower to Bowers, 14 October 1946, HLG 93/38.
245 Hobhouse to Haythornthwaite, 14 October 1946, HLG 93/37.

departing from the full proposals. Incidentally, I have just heard from Elmhirst who was with Dower in the North when he got the news of our final agreement, that he was greatly pleased and in his present state of health, it has probably given him considerable stimulus.

- **Variety** I think that our proposals, *especially for so many parks as twelve*, are greatly strengthened by the inclusion of so unique an historical feature as the Roman Wall. We now have in our selection every type of outstanding area – mountains, moorland, downs, coastal areas, inland waterway and a great historic area.
- **Conservation Areas**… By including the Cornish coast [as a Conservation area], which should be enlarged by the inclusion of practically the whole of the south-west coastline from Exmoor to Poole Harbour, the importance of Conservation Areas can be immensely emphasised. I feel that if it is made clear in our Report that the Cornish coast is not excluded from National Parks for reason of any inferiority in landscape value, but because of administrative difficulties and the difficulty of distinguishing between different portions of this coastline, there can be no reflection on this beautiful area. Moreover, we must in our proposals for Conservation Areas include sufficient powers and finance to make their protection a certainty…' (Author's italics)

Subsequently, the Committee confirmed that their final report should make a very strong case for regarding Cornwall 'as a Conservation Area of first class importance, no less in landscape value to many National Parks'; and it was essential that despite its exclusion, Cornwall should become 'a beacon' that would showcase the effectiveness of Conservation Areas.[246]

But the final choice was rather too hastily agreed to be considered a rational approach to policy making. Both Hobhouse and Elmhirst realised the great importance of

---

246 Minutes of the NPC, 7-8 October 1946, HLG 93/5.

securing an agreement before the Committee met with the Minister. Including the Roman Wall would be a 'win-win' situation: it would settle the matter, while giving Dower a 'considerable stimulus' and renewed commitment to finish his remaining work. And the concessions made by Huxley, Chorley and other members of the Committee were not as generous as they might seem. To begin with, the formal designation of the Roman Wall would be some years down the line – and possibly never. Hobhouse's references (above) to the large number of proposed Parks foreshadowed the possibility of an eventual exclusion of the Wall – and most of the Committee knew that Dower would not be around long enough to challenge it.

But as Elmhirst had reported, this final agreement had given Dower a noticeable boost. On 23 October 1946, he wrote to Hobhouse confirming that he was 'entirely satisfied with the choice of both Parks and Conservation Areas as it now stands'.[247]

247 Dower to Hobhouse, 23 October 1946, HLG 93/38.

16. Journey's End

The winter of 1947 was the coldest Britain had experienced in three centuries. From mid-January to mid-March, hundreds of villages across Britain were cut off for weeks; over 300 main roads were rendered unusable; stockpiles of coal were frozen solid, immovable in mines and depots; power stations were forced to shut down. Millions of people imprisoned by snow drifts up to twenty-three feet deep faced hunger, cold and misery. On the coast, the ferry service from Dover to Ostend was suspended as pack ice drifted through the Channel – a vivid reminder to Dower of that bitter winter he had spent in Dover seven years before.

From Northumberland, he wrote to Bowers in late February: 'We are still deep in snow. Each blizzard cuts us off temporarily from all but telephone connection with the outer world. Nothing got through yesterday, but the post forced a way through today by using horseback for the last lap.'[248]

For Dower, this was no excuse for putting aside the detailed work of amending and proof-reading Hobhouse's draft report and its associated papers. From his bed he went through in forensic detail Tom Stephenson's report on Footpaths and Access to the Countryside, parts of which he considered 'disconcertingly unsatisfactory and requiring extensive re-writing...' In early March, he found the Summary of Recommendations in the Hobhouse Report 'appallingly long – and reading it was nearly the death of me...' By mid-April, the remorseless pressure of work was taking its toll. He upbraided Bowers on his punctuation and verbal clumsiness, and his failure to spot printers' errors, observing impatiently that 'two "we's" and two "therefores" in a couple of lines are distinctly uncomfortable...'[249]

Even at this late stage, there were still substantive policy differences with some of his colleagues. For example, he insisted that there should be a clear allocation of roads and

---

248 Dower to Bowers, HLG 93/38, 27 February 1947.
249 Dower to Bowers, HLG 93/21, 18 April 1947.

tracks within National Parks between motorists and walkers, with 'almost all green lanes and mountain and moor cart tracks banned to motorists, except for access to households and farms'.[250] At the same time, he objected to waymarking long-distance walking routes within the Parks. 'The idea of a stream of walkers all going the same way home from Shap to Ravenglass and from Ulverstone to Penrith, with sleeping accommodation laid on, fills me with alarm. Not my notion of a National Park at all!'[251]

*

At that time there was no effective medication available in Britain to tackle tuberculosis. In the UK, foreign exchange scarcities meant that by November 1946, a mere fifty kilos of the effective drug Streptomycin were imported – and this was to be distributed to fifteen- to thirty-year-olds, not older chronic cases where the infection was too far established.[252]

By now Dower had completely lost the use of his right leg and arm, and was teaching himself to write with his left hand. His increasing frailty was evidenced by his wavering signature, and it was left to Pauline to decipher his notes and amendments and type fair copies of his letters. He knew he was dying, and during the summer of 1947 he discussed the matter dispassionately with sixteen-year-old Susan, home from her boarding school in York. By now he had a bed in a converted chicken hut on the front lawn, where in the summer he could be in the fresh air while watching the boys from a safe distance. Meanwhile he continued to smoke his favourite Four Square tobacco in his favourite pipe – possibly an indication of his acceptance of the inevitable.

He was not generally a man to complain, but his troubled state of mind was apparent in his poetry. In April 1947, as spring flowers once more carpeted the fells above Ilkley, he yearned for his treasured walk on High Moor Edge:

250 Dower to Bowers, HLG 93/21, 10 March 1947.
251 Dower to Bowers, HLG 93/38, 16 February 1947.
252 Helen Bynum, *Spitting Blood: The History of Tuberculosis*, Oxford University Press, 2012.

Pen and ink drawing of
John Dower by his wife
Pauline.

JOHN DOWER

No, I do not forget thee, favourite walk
Of all my boyhood – and young manhood too,
But now, alas, these fifteen years enjoyed
Only in memory or in image swift
Of a rare dream; as chance the other night...

His earlier poem 'Winter Night' was a cry for comfort, an
expression of bleak isolation and regret:

I woke to deepest night
As if one called my name,
And listened for some sound;
    But no sound came.
Of wind to stir the trees
There was no faintest breath;
Under deep snow all earth
    Lay mute as death.

Each minute seemed an hour
As the tense silence grew...
At last an owl's clear hoot
    Broke the strain through!

Then soon an answering hoot –
Some wakeful farm dog's bark –
Faint stir of roosting bird –
    Peopled the dark.

Till the church clock struck three,
And with its bell-voice deep
Closed my strange lullaby
    In easy sleep.

*

Back in London, the final draft of Hobhouse's report was completed by 15 March 1947, and published four months later on 18 July, alongside Huxley's report of the Special Committee on Wildlife Conservation. The sub-committee on Footpaths and Access to the Countryside reported later in September.[253] While it was Dower who had done much of the editing and correction of the draft Hobhouse Report, the daunting task of pulling it all together fell to John Bowers as Secretary to the Committee – and he was on the brink of collapse as he typed the final pages. This did not go unnoticed by his colleagues, and in late April Leonard Elmhirst sent Bowers a letter of thanks for his commitment and hard work. 'I only hope your energies won't have been so drawn that you will not have any left for creating and establishing the parks themselves. If you don't lend a hand, who will? John Dower looks like being an almost total loss, in the field at any rate...'[254]

But Dower felt he could relax at last, secure in the belief that his life's work was done. Pauline remarked that during this period he was 'so content and confident, and seemed

---

253 Cmd. 7121, 7122 and 7207 respectively.
254 Letter from Elmhirst to Bowers, 20 April 1947.

to have no worries or anxieties'.[255] But late in September he appeared to lose ground rapidly. In the early morning of Friday, 3 October, Pauline looked into the bedroom to find her husband still asleep, and so as usual went down to the kitchen to make a pot of tea. When she returned a few minutes later, Dower had died, quietly and alone. Mary Trevelyan reassured Herbert Griffin in a letter the following day that 'he had no suffering, and never realised how ill he was…'[256]

For the next few weeks, Pauline was in a state of shock, unable to take in that her husband had died. Her three children were away at their respective schools, and although they were all told within a few hours of their father's death, only Susan, the eldest, was allowed to come home for the funeral. It was a few days before Pauline could visit Robin at his prep school in Ilkley, and Michael at The Leys School in Cambridge. Throughout their childhood she had kept them apart from their father as much as possible, for fear of their contracting TB. Michael complained bitterly that he had hardly seen him for seven years, and now he was being deprived of a last goodbye.

Only a few close friends and relatives attended the funeral service at Newcastle Crematorium, but it was not long before the news of Dower's death appeared in the national press. Inevitably, all his obituaries drew attention to the Dower Report. *The Times* observed that

> Dower's many qualities combined to produce a classic of its kind: its combination of strong but not extravagant idealism with much practical wisdom is illuminated by a clear and forceful prose style, and it has all the virtues of a short work written by one who has all the details at his finger tips.[257]

Others focused on his dedication and capacity for sheer hard work. Professor William Holford, one of his colleagues in the Ministry, observed:

---

255 Pauline Dower to Elmhirst, 3 November 1947.
256 Mary Trevelyan to H Griffin, 4 October 1947.
257 *The Times*, 8 October 1947.

Gradually, and in spite of periods of enforced rest, which he must have known were insufficient to bring him back to health, he concentrated more and more on his great objective. He wrote continuously and with increasing decision, as if he felt that the project could only be hammered out at white heat. Yet, curiously enough, he continued to penetrate at the same time a maze of detail which was all put in order and added to the argument. He was an administrative and technical committee in one...[258]

LJ Watson, one of Dower's colleagues at the Ministry and a distinguished artist, focused on his personality and values.

Those that were fortunate enough to know John Dower will remember his charming personality and the stimulation which his company invariably gave, for he had an extraordinary faculty for inspiring others with his own enthusiasms. There was something large and generous about his outlook. He wanted passionately to see the countryside properly cared for, but he also wanted other people to have the facilities for discovering the enjoyment which he had himself discovered in the appreciation of nature. During his lifetime he certainly did all he could to help to achieve these facilities, but the full fruits of his work will remain to be seen. Should they be achieved, there could scarcely be any a finer memorial to him.[259]

Some days later, Pauline and Arthur, her brother-in-law, drove from Cambo to Ilkley through a damp October mist. On arrival they followed Wells Road out of the town, continuing uphill along the edge of Ilkley Moor to Woodhouse crag, and the favourite walk Dower had yearned for in his unfinished verse 'The High Moor Edge'. They scattered Dower's ashes over a gritstone outcrop –

---

258 Prof William Holford, *Journal of the Royal Institute of British Architects*, vol. 55 (1947-48), pp. 38-9.
259 LJ Watson, in *Out of Doors*, Winter 1947, p. 39.

the ancient Swastika Stone with its intriguing designs, carved four thousand years before. Below them, glimpses of Dower's boyhood home, his prep school and his local church emerged periodically through the thickening fog hovering over the town.

Epilogue

Eighteen months later, on 31 March 1949, the Minister of Town and Country Planning, Lewis Silkin, rose to his feet in the House of Commons to open the second reading of the long-delayed National Parks and Access to the Countryside Bill. He declared: 'In 1945 the late Mr John Dower issued a report on National Parks in England and Wales. He was a great champion of the open air, and it is a source of deep regret to us all that he has not survived to see the fruition of his efforts; but his work lives.'[260] In fact, Silkin and his senior civil servants must have been relieved that Dower was no longer around to fight against what can only be described as the unravelling of the Dower and Hobhouse Reports.

The weakening of the commitment to National Parks was largely a consequence of the 1947 Town and Country Planning Act, which had come into effect on 1 July 1948. It introduced a radical reorganisation of the planning system in England and Wales by:

- requiring planning permission for all land development (with the exception of agriculture and some government initiatives);
- cutting the number of planning authorities from 1,400 to 145 (to be formed from county and borough councils);
- requiring a comprehensive development plan for each of these areas;
- financing a 'compensation and betterment' scheme (see p. 146 ff).

The Act gave local authorities wide-ranging powers to undertake the redevelopment of land themselves, or to use compulsory purchase orders to buy land and lease it to private developers. Extensive central government grants were made available to local authorities to tackle significant

---

260 House of Commons Debates, 31 March 1949, vol. 463, col. 1464.

war damage. They were also given powers to control outdoor advertising, and to preserve woodland, as well as buildings of architectural or historic interest – the forerunner of the modern system of 'listing'.

But the strengthened role of local authorities in countryside planning raised fundamental questions about the overlap with future National Parks. In late January 1948, Silkin was asked in the House of Commons whether the 1947 Act alone was sufficient to protect National Parks, without the need for any additional legislation. Silkin replied that this was 'fundamental to the whole question on national parks, which I am at present considering'. By July 1948, he was still considering, and declared that he was 'not in a position to make any statement on this matter'.[261]

The reason was that, behind the scenes, government plans for National Parks were being diluted. On 1 June 1948 Silkin presented a five-page memorandum to his ministerial colleagues proposing that responsibility for all planning in the Parks should be handed over to the county councils rather than a National Parks Commission. 'The more I think of it,' he told the Lord President's Committee, 'the more convinced I am that it would be wrong to take planning powers away from County Councils… within a few months of their acquiring the powers. In several cases the (national park) areas will amount to a substantial proportion of the whole county.' The areas to be defined as National Parks should therefore be proposed in the first instance by the county councils themselves – and not by the National Parks Commission. The selection of Parks would be restricted to extensive areas only of beautiful and relatively wild country of special value for public enjoyment and recreation (Dower's original formulation) – which by definition would exclude other areas short-listed because of their proximity to centres of population, such as the South Downs, or for their antiquity, such as the Roman Wall.[262]

---

261 National Parks etc. Bill, Second Reading 31 March-4 April 1949, HC vol. 463, cols. 1461-1668.
262 Memorandum by the Ministry of Town and Country Planning to the Lord President's Committee, LP 48, 1 June 1948, CAB 124-444.

Silkin's memorandum went on to discuss the 'right to roam' across uncultivated land. 'I do not propose to make it obligatory on planning authorities to define all uncultivated land for this purpose,' Silkin wrote. 'That would be a vast and unnecessary undertaking, and the Ministry of Agriculture and the Forestry Commission have both represented that it would be exceedingly difficult to define with any certainty land where unrestricted public access would *not* be harmful to the agriculture and forestry interests. I am myself not convinced that *any* provision is needed to facilitate public access to uncultivated land in private ownership... The public is already accustomed to wander over a very large part of the uncultivated land in this country without any legal right to do so, and it seems to us unfortunate to cast doubts on the present practice...'

Nevertheless, Silkin had to acknowledge the long history of agitation, particularly among Labour supporters, for access to the grouse moors of Derbyshire. 'I propose accordingly to enable planning authorities to declare a public right of access to specified areas of uncultivated land, including beach and foreshore, where there is reason to think that the public are unreasonably excluded; and I would propose to provide for compensation...' The right to roam would therefore be in the hands of local planning authorities and not the National Parks Commission. The provision of open access would not be compulsory, and where it was, could be withdrawn at the instance of the Ministry of Agriculture or of the Forestry Commission, 'where that was necessary in the interests of agriculture or forestry'.

The effect of such proposals would have been to reduce the role of the National Parks Commission to a mere watchdog, restricted to commenting on local plans, and reviewing any development projects likely to conflict with the main purposes of the Park. Instead of taking the lead on planning in the Parks, the Commission would be given various day-to-day management tasks, such as:

- acquiring land to facilitate public enjoyment
- initiating works such as the opening up of waterways

- providing assistance for hotel and catering accommodation
- removing unsightly developments
- preserving and planting woodlands
- burying overhead cables underground
- subsidising the use of more expensive building materials.

Compared with the proposals in the Dower and Hobhouse Reports, this amounted to a considerable demotion. In compensation, Silkin sugared the pill by giving the National Parks Commission 'certain limited functions' *outside* the Parks – the protection and preservation of Conservation Areas, for example, and the protection of any area of natural beauty in the wider countryside. 'The Commission would thus be a Commission for the Care of the Countryside, or a Commission for the Protection of Rural England and Wales,' he declared. His clumsy (probably inadvertent) annexation of CPRE's name underlined dramatically how far the status of the National Parks Commission was being reduced to that of a mere pressure group.

*

It would be wrong to blame Silkin alone for putting the brake on twenty years of progress towards National Parks. He was a relatively weak Minister steered by his senior civil servants – and in particular, Evelyn (later Dame Evelyn) Sharp. She was tough-minded, direct and decisive – a 'can-do' civil servant concerned to bring solutions to Ministers rather than just problems. The Chancellor of the Exchequer, Hugh Dalton, described her as 'the best man of them all, with tremendous energy, first-class administrative brains, and a capacity for trampling through and over obstructions of all kinds'.[263] As the Number Two (Deputy Secretary) in the Ministry of Town and Country Planning, she had played a major role in the framing of the 1947 Town and Country

---

263 Kevin Theakston, *Leadership in Whitehall*, Palgrave, 1999, p. 135.

Planning Act. She continued to maintain close working relations with local authorities, seeking to strengthen their independence, influence and capacity for initiative.

Her superior at the Ministry – the Permanent Secretary Sir Thomas Sheepshanks – was rather less dynamic than Dame Evelyn, but was as committed as she was to minimising the role of government and keeping a grip on public expenditure. In April 1948, he had written to Silkin questioning the need for *any* legislation on National Parks, and especially the establishment of a National Parks Commission:

> I more than ever have the feeling that the case for legislation is very weak, and that so far as administrative merits are concerned an informed critic could demolish most of our arguments pretty easily... I feel bound to repeat the warning that I have given you before, that this might quite possibly prejudice the future existence of this Department. As you know, we are inevitably regarded by many of the older Departments as a fifth wheel in the coach. It might be said that a *sixth* wheel in the shape of an independent Commission for country or amenity planning would be quite intolerable. The concluding argument might be that amenity or country planning is the one function which justified an independent defender of its own, and it would be better that that defender might be the proposed new Commission and that the Ministry of Town and Country Planning might therefore cease to exist.[264]

However, Silkin had to accept that public expectations had been raised and National Parks legislation – including the establishment of a National Parks Commission – was unavoidable. But in an almost apologetic letter to eleven other government departments, Evelyn Sharp made it clear that the Ministry of Town and Country Planning 'proposed to stop some way short of the full Hobhouse plan'.

---

264 Sir Thomas Sheepshanks to Minister, 22 April 1948, vol. 259G.

We visualise that the National Parks Commission would be entitled to be consulted and to express a view on plans prepared by County Councils as they affect National Park areas; and on major projects for development – whether by Government Departments, local authorities, statutory undertakers, or private developers. This cannot be welcome to Departments, but if we are to legislate at all – and in our paper we give our reasons for thinking that we must – we do not think that we can do less than this. I ought to say that we shall pretty certainly be pressed to give a good deal more than this; the Hobhouse Report went a good deal further; but we are assuming that this is as far as Departments would think we should go, and that we can count on your support for trying to limit the right of the Commission to be consulted, to major projects...'[265]

*

Continuing delay in presenting a draft Bill to Parliament fuelled fears among MPs and amenity groups that the entire enterprise might be dropped. The Future Legislation Committee of the Cabinet had given Silkin a deadline of 31 May 1948 for including a National Parks Bill in the 1948-49 legislative programme. However, a meeting of the Lord President's Committee on 23 April concluded that 'the Minister's proposals had not been adequately worked out, and the Minister was invited to discuss outstanding points with the Departments concerned...' This would involve yet further consultations with the Home Office, the Ministry of Agriculture, the Board of Trade, the Ministry of Transport, the Service Departments and, particularly, the Treasury. Inevitably, the 31 May deadline slipped, and Silkin was obliged to accept Herbert Morrison's proposal that the introduction of the Bill should be put back to February 1949.

After Silkin had refused for a second time MPs'

---

265 Letter from Evelyn Sharp, 4 May 1948, in CAB 124-444.

demands for a statement on progress, no fewer than eighty-one members of the Parliamentary Labour Party (one-fifth of the total) signed a letter to the Minister demanding the introduction of a National Parks Bill during the next formal Session of Parliament. The letter noted that there was within the Labour Party 'a strong body favouring this course'.[266]

The amenity societies were equally angered by official foot-dragging. The Standing Committee on National Parks was 'alarmed and despondent' at the direction the Ministry of Town and Country Planning was taking. At a meeting with Silkin and Sheepshanks at the end of December 1947, a deputation from the Standing Committee made clear their fundamental opposition to the Minister's proposals. Lord Birkett, Chairman of the Standing Committee, expressed his disappointment and frustration in a follow-up letter to Silkin:

> Ten years ago we interviewed the Minister of Health. We were told to go away and educate public opinion. In this we have had some success. And those who, since then, have formed the idea of a new and special planning category for National Parks, and have come to value it and work for it hopefully, will feel it as a blow to the usefulness and power of the Ministry of Town and Country Planning that it had now decided to let this opportunity go by, in which it could have played an open and emphatic part in building up a national system of National Parks. For not only did you reject our proposals for giving, as we think, true effect to the underlying intention, in matters of planning, of the Hobhouse Report: you also rejected the proposals, in these matters, of the Hobhouse Report itself...
>
> The first duty of the National Parks Commission is in planning (protection), not in 'management'. It should have the right to review the decisions of the Park Committee if they should offend against the

---

266 Letter to Lewis Silkin from Parliamentary Labour Party, 27 July 1948.

national standards laid down by the Commission; and in the case of other Departments of Government – which by law can and will override the local planning committee – the Commission should have the clear right to refer the questions of conflict to some recognised tribunal of appeal.[267]

The most influential champion of National Parks at this time within the government was EM (Max) Nicholson. As Head of the Lord President's Office, he played a decisive role in managing the government's overall business, was an accomplished ornithologist and an active member of the Wild Life Conservation Special Committee, making recommendations on national nature reserves and the launch of a new 'biological service' of professional naturalists. Nicholson regarded with disdain the weakness and procrastination of the Ministry of Town and Country Planning, which he made quite clear in a long memo to the Lord President, Herbert Morrison, on Silkin's dilution to his own draft Bill.[268] He wrote:

In detail, the proposals are extremely shadowy. The Minister does not suggest, for instance, what the name of the proposed [National Parks] commission should be, how it should be composed, what sort of staff it should have, or whether it will be given definite guidance about the extent and choice of national parks. There is still an enormous amount of work to be done before anything precise enough for presentation to Parliament emerges and it is impossible at this stage to say whether the eventual detailed Bill will not reveal serious weaknesses and difficulties at present fluffed over in the paper.

Nicholson proceeded to demolish many of Evelyn Sharp's proposals to hand over the planning of National Parks to individual county council planning committees. He was

267 Letter from Lord Birkett to Minister, 18 January 1948, file 95249/35/2.
268 Nicholson to Lord President, 1 July 1948, CAB 124-444.

adamant that the selection of the Parks should not be left to county councils, and 'the Minister should make it clear that he intends to instruct the Commission to adopt as a basis the twelve national park areas in the Hobhouse Report ... while observing the right to add two or three more. In every national park there should be one body looking at the planning as a whole – and even where only one authority is concerned, that authority should set up a special National Park Committee co-opting the necessary people to make the administration of the national park a success.' The county councils, he insisted, should at least consult the National Parks Commission on persons to be co-opted to the Parks Committee, to ensure that they would 'have in mind the national significance of the Park'.

But of most concern to Nicholson personally was the absence of any measures to advance nature conservation.

> It is essential that whatever bodies are running national parks should have expert biological advice in order to conserve the natural resources in such matters as maintenance of water levels, burning of vegetation, planning, drainage etc... It is important that provision should be made for the functions recommended for the Biological Service in respect of national parks to be covered by the Bill. The Bill should provide for certain powers in respect of national nature reserves, in particular the inclusion of nature reserves in the objects for which compulsory powers of acquisition can be exercised; the inclusion of protection of sites of essential importance among objects for which grants should be given; and the requirements by which the National Parks Commission can be consulted in all appropriate cases by national and local authorities concerned.

Nicholson convinced Herbert Morrison that there had to be a National Parks Bill in the 1948-49 parliamentary session, and this was later confirmed in the King's Speech on 26 October 1948. Under fire from several directions, Silkin was obliged to concede that local authorities should after all be required to set up special committees to plan and manage National Parks in their areas (or joint boards where a Park was in the area of several local authorities). He also accepted the principle that a proportion of the members of such committees should be non-elected, and co-opted by the local authority after consultation with the National Park Committee (rather than with the Minister himself). 'On the whole,' Silkin wrote, 'I prefer "Commission" to "Minister" as I want to give the Commission as much power as I can. I think that nomination to a local authority can only result in friction, and that the non-elected members will be in a much stronger position if co-opted by the authority instead of being forced on them.'[269]

*

The National Parks and Access to the Countryside Act eventually received the Royal Assent in December 1949 – a full twenty years after Ramsay MacDonald had set the ball rolling with the establishment of the Addison Committee. During the Second Reading of the National Parks Bill in the House of Commons, the former Minister of Town and Country Planning, William Morrison, made a generous acknowledgement to John Dower 'whose report is with us today as a memorial to his own great knowledge, taste and zeal in the public interest...' He referred especially to the benefit various amenity societies had gained from 'his untiring labours and skilled perception'. But Morrison was deeply disappointed by the Act. 'This is a very different conception of the status and functions of the National Parks Commission from that recommended by the Dower and Hobhouse reports,' he declared. 'I have no doubt that [the amenity societies] feel that, to the Commission recommended by the Dower and Hobhouse Reports, *this* Commission bears about the same relation as what is called a baby's comforter bears to a real feeding bottle. It may by

---

269 Letter from Lewis Silkin to Herbert Morrison, 27 November 1948.

superficial resemblance attract and sooth the innocent, but it stops short and there is nothing behind it.'[270]

Disappointing though the Act was, between 1950 and 1957 the National Parks Commission made designation orders for ten of the twelve Parks recommended by the Hobhouse Committee. These first Parks covered 7.3 per cent of England, and 19.7 per cent of Wales – overall, 9 per cent of the total area of England and Wales. But after 1957, there followed a hiatus of over thirty years before the next Park (the Broads) was designated – largely reflecting the opposition of Conservative governments, sceptical local authorities and large landowners.

National Park	Date designation was confirmed	Area (square miles) at December 1974
Peak District	17.4.51	542
Lake District	9.5.51	866
Snowdonia	18.10.51	840
Dartmoor	30.10.51	365
Pembrokeshire Coast	29.2.52	225
North York Moors	28.11.52	553
Yorkshire Dales	12.10.54	680
Exmoor	19.10.54	265
Northumberland	6.4.56	398
Brecon Beacons	17.4.57	519
		TOTAL 5,253 square miles

What was missing from this first tranche was the Roman Wall, for which Dower had fought fiercely within the Hobhouse Committee. He had described it as 'one of the finest ancient monuments in the world. As a frontier memorial, it is the best surviving from the Roman Empire,

270 National Parks etc. Bill, *op. cit.*, vol. 463, cols. 1487-96.

and second only to the Great Wall of China.'[271] He was determined that Northumberland should not be the only northern county without a National Park, and that this should be as close as possible to Wallington and his home in Cambo. However, the Roman Wall was the smallest of all the proposed National Parks (194 square miles), and was already protected by a Preservation Scheme. Julian Huxley, amongst others, wanted to exclude it as 'being in least favour and in least danger'.

Enter Dower's widow, Pauline. Following her husband's death, in 1950 Pauline was appointed a member of the National Parks Commission. (Later, she was also to become Deputy Chair of the Commission, and President of the YHA.) She was as active and obdurate as her husband, and took over his mantle, including securing the Roman Wall as a National Park. She realised, however, that it was too small within its proposed boundaries, and would be better incorporated within a larger Northumberland National Park. This would have no mountains comparable with Snowdonia, nor lakes comparable in size or range of scenery with those of the Lake District. Moreover, it was the least populated and visited of the ten Parks. Yet it had many other attractions – the variety of form and colour of its hills and valleys, wide horizons, its rich flora and fauna, a romantic history, and solitude in a remote landscape.

Establishing its boundaries, however, was not straightforward. Incorporating Northumberland's unsurpassed coastline, for example, would have entailed the inclusion of a large area of flat farmland and the A1 trunk road. Similarly, including most of the Roman Wall would have crossed the border into Cumberland (already a major partner in the Lake District National Park), and also into industrial Tyneside to the east. Kielder Forest to the west was owned and administered by an unsympathetic Forestry Commission, and to the north the Ministry of Defence Otterburn Range occupied thousands of acres.[272] But in the event, Pauline's

---

271 HLG 93/3, 20-21 November 1945.
272 Mervyn Bell (ed.), *Britain's National Parks*, David & Charles, 1975, p. 128.

tireless lobbying succeeded in creating a Northumberland National Park, with its long and irregular boundary shadowing much of the Pennine Way. Stretching forty miles from north to south, and on average ten miles across, it was a bold compromise which linked the fine scenery of the Roman Wall with the great dome of the Cheviot. And it was exactly twice as large as John Dower's dream for a Roman Wall Park.

Appendix 1

The Hobhouse Committee Report
(Report of the National Parks Committee (England and Wales) Cmd. 7121, July 1947, 140 pp.)

The Hobhouse Report recommended establishing **twelve National Parks**, immediately following the passage of the required legislation. There would be four parks designated each year over a period of three years. The twelve parks selected would include nine of the ten originally proposed by Dower in his Report (the exception being the Cornish Coast), plus the South Downs and (crucially for Dower) the Roman Wall. The total area to be covered by the twelve parks was 5,682 square miles.

Hobhouse proposed that overall responsibility for National Parks policy would lie with a **National Parks Commission**, consisting of a Chairman and nine members, all appointed by the Minister of Town and Country Planning. The Commission would be a legal entity established by statute, financed by the Exchequer, and empowered to regulate its own proceedings.

Each park would be managed by a **Park Committee**, acting as the local planning authority within the area of the park. It would be responsible for drawing up development plans and for granting or refusing planning permission. The Report stressed that the administration of National Parks should be for the *nation's* benefit – 'the parks should be national in fact as well as name'. Accordingly, the Chairman of each Park Committee would be appointed by the National Parks Committee. Of the remaining members, 50 per cent would be appointed by the county councils and county borough councils falling wholly or partly with the Park, and the other 50 per cent would be appointed by the National Parks Commission. The latter would be national appointees, but they would also be mainly persons living in or near the park with an understanding of the locality, as well as the wider purposes of National Park policy. Any serious conflict between local and national interests would be decided by the Minister of Town and Country Planning.

Development Control

All proposed development on land within the National Park would require planning permission from the appropriate Park Committee. Exceptions would apply to government departments, statutory undertakers (e.g. the Forestry Commission) and local authorities where they were supported ('sanctioned') by the relevant government department. Without such support, the normal planning controls would apply. Another major exception would be agriculture (see below).

The Hobhouse Report was particularly forthright in demanding the co-operation of all government departments in respecting the needs of National Park policies. It noted:

> Government Departments should be asked to inform the National Parks Commission of all proposed use or development of land in National Parks which they intend to carry out or to sanction, and the Commission should refer to the Ministry of Town and Country Planning for consultation with his colleague in the appropriate department, any matter in which a conflict of interest cannot be resolved between the Commission and the department concerned.
>
> Where any existing development or use of land by a government department seriously conflicts with the amenities of a National Park, the Commission should negotiate for its removal or modification, or if necessary, refer the matter to the Minister of Town and Country Planning for consultation with his colleague in the department concerned.

Where such inter-departmental consultation failed, the matter would ultimately be decided by a permanent Committee of the Cabinet, or by the Minister.

The Armed Services

The Report pulled no punches in listing the damage to the landscape inflicted by the military. Such damage included:

- Disturbance of gun fire over wider areas than just those that are appropriated
- Disfigurement by camps and military buildings
- Serious detriment to agriculture
- Interference with wildlife
- Defacement of the land and destruction of vegetation by tracked vehicles
- Danger from military traffic on narrow roads

  'It would be no exaggeration to say that the appropriation of a number of particular areas now listed for acquisition by the Service Departments would take the heart out of the proposed National Park areas in which they are sited, and in certain cases render our proposals for the designation of individual National Parks entirely nugatory...'

Hobhouse recommended that permanent machinery should be established to undertake periodic reviews of all existing Service Department holdings of land within National Parks. These should be relinquished when no longer a national necessity. The disposal of such land should be notified in advance so that the National Parks Commission could stake a claim. Proposed new acquisitions by the Service Departments should be communicated in advance to enable the National Parks Commission to put forward objections in inter-departmental discussions

Forestry

Park Committees would be empowered to specify areas in National Parks where the planting of new woodlands would be subject to their consent. They would be entitled to attach conditions in relation to the layout of new woodlands, and the types of trees planted. All new plans under the Forestry

Commission's Woodlands Dedication Schemes would be referred to the National Parks Commission 'so that reasonable requirements to promote or safeguard landscape beauty or recreation may be incorporated into the plans'. The Commission should also have power to purchase existing amenity woodlands, and carry out programmes of planting and management.

Agriculture

In stark contrast to its proposal to regulate the activities of the Service Departments and the Forestry Commission, the Hobhouse Report adopted an arms-length approach to the management of agriculture. It acknowledged that in National Parks there were indeed potential conflicts with farming, including:

- New agricultural buildings
- Extensive conversion of moorland into pasture
- Eradication of hedgerows and banks, and their replacement by wire fencing
- Occasional interference with views by high banks and tall hedges.

However, Hobhouse proposed that changes in agricultural land use should not be subject to planning control (other than for new building), on the grounds that such problems were 'not serious'. Co-operation between the National Parks Commission and farmers, landowners and agricultural authorities would be essential for the integration of landscape, recreational and access requirements with agricultural policy. 'Reliance should rather be placed on the goodwill of agriculture owners and farmers, and the good relations which we feel sure will be established and maintained between them and the Park Committees...'

Conservation Areas

The Hobhouse Report acknowledged that there were many areas of fine country and coast which had not been selected as National Parks, but which nevertheless contributed to the wider enjoyment of the countryside, as an 'essential corollary of our National Park scheme'. Fifty-two of these potential 'Conservation Areas' (termed 'Amenity Areas' in Dower's earlier report) were selected according to a variety of criteria. These might include the limited extent or wildness of the area compared with a National Park; intensive land use preventing rambling access; or closeness to adjacent countryside of still higher quality. Many of the proposed Conservation Areas also offered easier access for town and city dwellers remote from National Parks, or in some cases access to areas of outstanding wildlife and scientific value.

Within twelve months following the necessary legislation, local authorities in proposed Conservation Areas would be required to draw up detailed boundaries for approval of the Minister of Town and Country Planning. Following formal designation, the local planning authority would set up an Advisory Committee – or Joint Advisory Committee where two or more local planning authorities were concerned – which would have the right to be consulted on the drawing up of development plans for the Conservation Area. Hobhouse proposed a large measure of state control over major developments: 'The impact of large-scale uses of land upon the unspoilt country of the Conservation Areas will be considerably mitigated by judicious allocation of the land *on a national scale* to its appropriate uses...' (Author's italics)

In day-to-day planning, the Advisory Committees would have special regard to the siting and appearance of all new buildings; to the conservation of amenity woods 'and the place of commercial forestry in the landscape'; to the location and appearance of reservoirs and waterworks; to mineral workings; to the siting of electricity pylons; to the treatment of highways; to the control of outdoor advertisements; to the regulation of camping; and to preserving archaeological sites and historic buildings. The Hobhouse Report noted: 'Wise control of development will be of national concern throughout all Conservation Areas.'

Members of the Advisory Committee would be drawn both from the local planning authority, and from representatives of the National Parks Commission. Unlike in National Parks, the number of members nominated by the Commission, and indeed the size of each Advisory Committee, would be flexible, and determined by the Minister. The local planning authority, however, would always have a majority. The designation of Conservation Areas was to be staggered, according to their individual importance. The National Parks Commission would carry out an early survey, in close collaboration with the Ministry and the local planning authorities concerned, of all proposed Conservation Areas, to draw up an appreciation of their relative requirements, followed by a programme of work and expenditure. Preference would be given to those areas 'particularly vulnerable to misdevelopment or (which) have already suffered extensive disfigurement, and to those which will make the most valuable contribution to the nation's health, enjoyment and recreation, and are in need of positive provision for these purposes.' The Cornish and Devon coasts should be given the highest priority for the Commission's attention.

Appendix 2

Footpaths and Access to the Countryside

Footpaths and Access to the Countryside: Report of the Special Committee (England and Wales) Cmd. 7207, 23 September 1947, 64 pp.

The Footpaths and Access to the Countryside Report was drawn up by a sub-committee of the main National Parks Committee. It was chaired by Arthur Hobhouse, and comprised five members of the National Parks Committee (including John Dower), and five additional co-opted members representing agricultural interests, ramblers and local authorities. It was an ambitious, even radical document, reflecting the views of Tom Stephenson, Francis Ritchie and Dower himself. However, many of the measures it proposed depended on action and/or consent by local planning authorities, government departments, or the Minister of Town and Country Planning.

The terms of reference of the report were:

To consider, with due reference to agriculture, forestry and other essential interests, the measures necessary for:

(a) The preservation and maintenance of existing rights of way; the provision, where required, of new rights of way over both land and water (but not to include rights of way enjoyable by vehicular traffic); and the provision of long-distance and coastal footpaths;

(b) The provision of access for the public to mountain, moor, heath, down, cliff and common land, and uncultivated land generally, with particular reference to the recreational use of the countryside by the public.

Footpaths

The report proposed comprehensive surveys by county and county borough councils of all rights of way within their areas (covering footpaths, bridle paths and drovers' roads). These were to be completed within a period of four years, and would include full consultations with the public and interested parties. Any path used by the public continuously for twenty years would in all cases be deemed to have been dedicated as a highway. Legal disputes would be referred to Courts of Quarter Sessions, and to the High Court if necessary.

Local Highway Authorities would also be required by law to repair and maintain all rights of way, and to prosecute anyone obstructing a right of way. This would include 'serious damage to the surface by vehicles' or the erection of barbed wire fences too close to walkers. 'The turning out of bulls over 12 months old in any field traversed by a right of way' would also be illegal. Local authorities would be permitted to create new rights of way, if necessary through compulsory purchase. Affected landowners would be entitled to claim compensation.

Long-Distance Rights of Way

The report was strongly in favour of establishing long-distance footpaths, including 'the re-opening of the old coastguard paths as a right of way for walkers around the whole coastline of England and Wales'. It proposed six inland long-distance paths:

- The Pennine Way – 250 miles from Edale to the Scottish border
- The Chilterns to the Devon Coast – 200 miles from near Cambridge to Seaton (taking in the Ridgeway)
- The Pilgrims Way from Canterbury to Winchester (120 miles)
- The South Downs, from Eastbourne to Salisbury Plain (110 miles)
- Offa's Dyke, from Prestatyn to Chepstow (150 miles)
- The Thames Path from Teddington to Cricklade (136 miles).

The National Parks Commission would be responsible for drawing up proposals for long-distance and coastal footpaths where these fell within the boundary of a National Park and/ or Conservation Area, and also where the path crossed more than one planning authority. As regards the coast, the report proposed that all beach and shore should be designated as access land, apart from foreshore vested in the Crown, where access should be by negotiated agreement. 'Full consideration' should be given to providing footpaths leading to the sea.

The approximate length of all existing coastal footpaths *within* proposed National Parks and Conservation Areas (not all of them rights of way) amounted to 687 miles. The length required to complete footpath routes along the coast within these areas would require a further 198 miles. This would still leave 1,866 miles to complete a continuous long-distance path around England and Wales.

Access to Uncultivated Land

The report defined 'access land' as all uncultivated land 'whether mountain, moor, heath, down, cliff beach or shore', together with suitable stretches of inland water. Responsibility for designating access land would lie with the local planning authority, in consultation if necessary with the Ministry of Agriculture's Land Utilisation Officer, who would settle the definition of 'uncultivated land'. A draft map of access land would be submitted by each relevant local authority to the Minister of Town and Country Planning within one year after legislation. Following consultations, the Minister would make an Order confirming the (possibly amended) Draft Maps, following which the local planning authority would publish a definitive Statutory Map.

Planning authorities would be able to withdraw land from designation where the land ceased to be uncultivated, subject to a local enquiry. Moreover, on the initiative of the County Agricultural Executive Committee, the planning authority would be empowered to withdraw land on agricultural grounds for up to three years. In addition, and in exceptional cases, the planning authority could request the Minister to withdraw land 'on the grounds that serious or recurrent damage was being caused as a result of its use as access land' – in which case compensation would be payable by the planning authority to the owner or occupier. (This proposal was opposed by a minority of the members of the Footpaths and Access Committee, including Dower, Tom Stephenson and Francis Ritchie. They rejected the view that access by a 'sympathetic urban public' was incompatible with farming interests, arguing that 'no statutory safeguards can ever be so effective as an informed public opinion in upholding good standards of behaviour'.)

Some land would automatically be exempt from public access, including:

- Buildings of all types, including any adjacent land, 'in the interests of privacy or safety'
- Land used for storing or testing weapons
- Agricultural land
- Plantation woods
- Nature reserves
- Archaeological sites
- Parks, golf courses, shooting ranges
- Local authority parks and playing fields

In relation to the controversial issue of sporting rights (e.g. grouse and deer shooting) on proposed access lands, the planning authority would be empowered to suspend public access for a maximum of twelve days during any shooting season. The landowner would be required to warn the public of shooting days, and to provide alternative routes.

No exemption would be granted to Forestry Commission land which was unsuitable for planting – for example, mountain tops and steep hillsides. Water catchment areas would also be open to the public, except where special restrictions were necessary to protect springs, intakes and feeder streams close to reservoirs. The Report noted that there was inconsistency between the rules of different water undertakings, and considered that there was a strong argument for the purification of *all* drinking water. 'There is no alternative today but to use thorough and scientific treatment of drinking water... Great Britain is much too small a country to be able to tolerate drastic restrictions on public access for reasons which can no longer be considered necessary... Public access to water catchment areas for the purpose of air and exercise should be permitted,'

In relation to land taken over by the Service Departments, the report noted that a forthcoming White Paper on Land Requirements of the Services was expected to recommend the requisitioning of around one million acres. However, the report proposed – ambitiously – that public access should be secured over all Service training grounds not used for training with live ammunition. In respect of artillery ranges, local planning authorities should seek to secure access when firing was not in progress.

In conclusion, the report considered that its proposals were 'an effective contribution ... to the health and well-being of the nation, and an important step taken towards establishing the principle that the heritage of our beautiful countryside should be held in trust for the benefit of the people.' But at the same time – and as a gesture to farmers, landowners and local authorities – it emphasised the importance of establishing a 'country code' which would 'evoke a better all-round standard of responsible behaviour in the countryside and ... instil a greater appreciation of the ways and needs of rural life and the interdependence of town and country.'

Onwards and upwards: campaigners in 1948 lead parliamentarians along the route of the Pennine Way to convince them of the need for tougher National Parks legislation. (Ramblers Association)

Acknowledgements

The author and publisher would like express their gratitude to the following individuals and organisations for their support of this publication.

Kevin Bishop, Chief Executive National Parks UK

Michael Dower
Robin Dower
Dame Fiona Reynolds
Sandra and Richard Brown
Adrian Phillips
Paul Hamblin, National Parks England

The following have offered invaluable practical assistance:

Wendy Breach and Peter Rodger
Roger Clegg
Kathryn Wilkinson
Tom Wilkinson
Hannah Madsen

Index

People

MacDonald, Ramsay 3, 20, 29,
31, 33-4, 45, 52, 78, 250
Macmillan, Harold 34-5, 95
Morrison, Herbert 37, 179, 246,
248-50
Morrison, WS 108, 110, 135-6,
145, 151, 156-7, 166-9, 171, 250

Nathan, Lord 194
Neal, Lawrence 37, 100-2, 108,
110-13, 127-37, 140, 151, 157,
160-4, 171, 182
Nicholson, Max 35-7, 179-80,
215, 248-9
Nye, Archie 19, 63-6, 72

Oakes, Sir Cecil 213-15, 217

Pepler, George 12-13, 17, 27, 32,
71, 81, 86, 89, 100-1, 128-9,
131-2, 137, 140-1, 152-7, 164
Portal, Lord Wyndham 37, 97

Reith, Lord 75-9, 81, 90-2, 97
Robinson, Sir Roy 48-50, 202,
204, 207

Scott, Lord Leslie 92, 138
Sharp, Dame Evelyn 44, 244-5,
248
Sheepshanks, Sir Thomas 245, 247
Silkin, Lewis 169, 182, 190, 194,
214, 220, 230, 241-50
Spence, Kenneth 20, 42-6, 48, 50-
1, 53, 56-8, 67, 85, 97, 104, 107
Stamp, Professor Dudley 104-5,
138-9, 145
Steers, Professor James Alfred
vii-xi, 113, 119, 138, 143-5, 180,
222, 229
Stephenson, Tom 47, 109-10, 131,
144, 234, 260, 262
Symonds, Revd. HH xii, 44, 48,
50-3, 56-8, 89, 97, 116-19, 136

Tallents, Sir Stephen 37, 109-10,
130-1
Tansley, Sir Arthur 123, 145, 177-
8, 180, 184-5, 195

Thompson, William Harding 27,
31, 72
Trevelyan, Sir Charles 3-4, 19-20,
22-3, 25-6, 45, 63, 95, 105, 136,
165
Trevelyan, GM 1, 5, 9, 18-20, 24-
6, 30, 44, 49-50, 55, 189, 196-7
Trevelyan, Molly 24, 26, 176

Usher, Herbert 150, 158, 162, 166

Valentine, Alfred 163-4, 195-6
Vincent, Harold G 78-81, 83, 86,
89, 92, 100-3, 105-8, 110-13,
126, 128, 130-1, 133-5, 137-40,
144, 164

Watson, Leslie J 182, 197, 220,
239
Whiskard, Sir Geoffrey 37, 112,
127, 131, 133, 137-8
Williams, Thomas 202, 207
Williams-Ellis, Clough 26, 56,
105, 107, 170, 173, 175, 221, 230

York, Archbishop of 52-3

Places

Black Mountains 117-18, 173,
203, 225
Brecon Beacons 117, 173, 203,
225, 251

Cambo 22, 24, 164, 176-7, 181-2,
197, 217, 220, 223, 231, 239,
252
Cambridge vii, 4, 9-13, 16, 18-20,
52, 83, 85, 154, 171, 238, 261
Cheviot Hills 63, 117, 152, 196-7,
229, 253
Chilterns 18, 119, 174, 261
Cornwall vi, viii, 31-2, 100, 112,
117-19, 173, 222, 224-5, 230-2,
254, 259
Craven Pennines 67, 117-18, 173,
175

Dartington 36-7, 172, 204

Organisations and Legislation

Crown Lands 56, 138

Dower Report, *see* National Parks in England and Wales
Duchy of Cornwall viii, 138-9, 174

Footpaths and Access to the Countryside Report (1947) 230, 234, 237, 260-4
Forestry Act (1919) 48
Forestry Act (1945) 202
Forestry Commission 20, 48-55, 118, 120, 134-5, 137, 139, 174, 197-8, 200-8, 243, 252, 255, 257, 263
Friends of the Lake District xii, 5, 20, 42-6, 48-53, 55-6, 58, 67, 101

Hobhouse Committee (1945) 132, 170-233, 251
Hobhouse Report (1947) 199, 208-9, 219, 234, 237, 241, 244-7, 249-50, 254-9
House of Lords 51-2, 62, 76-7

Joint Committee of Open Air Organisations 52, 56-8, 116

Lake District National Reserve Committee 42-5
Land Commission 148-9

Ministry of Agriculture and Fisheries 79, 104-5, 107, 125, 139, 153-4, 166-7, 173, 185, 202, 207-8, 243, 246, 262
Ministry of Defence 252
Ministry of Health 12, 33, 38, 41, 79, 81, 83, 86, 91, 96, 132-4, 139, 154-6, 166, 171
Ministry of Town and Country Planning vii-viii, x-xi, 37, 44, 108-10, 113, 119, 126-31, 133-5, 137, 140-1, 143, 145, 151-2, 155, 161, 163-4, 167, 170-3, 177-8, 182, 184-5, 188-90, 192-6, 201, 215, 222, 239, 242, 244-5, 247-8, 255, 259
Ministry of Transport 79, 122, 246

Ministry of Works and Buildings/ Planning 6, 78-80, 91, 96-7, 100-1, 108, 116, 118, 134, 198

National Nature Reserves 62, 123-4, 162, 178-9, 184-5, 210, 248-9, 263
National Park Committee Report (1931), *see* Addison Report
National Parks and Access to the Countryside Act (1949) 1, 208-9, 241, 250
National Parks Authority (projected) 56, 122-5, 128, 131, 151, 153-5, 178, 200-1, 210
National Parks Bill 61, 116, 157-8, 159, 214-15, 220, 246-7, 249-50
National Parks Commission 127, 132, 158, 162, 179, 198, 205, 208, 210-15, 218-19, 224, 242-7, 249-52, 254-7, 259, 262
National Parks Committee, *see* Hobhouse Committee
National Parks in England and Wales, Report by John Dower (1945) 1-2, 25, 113, 168, 170, 173, 175, 197, 200, 203, 210, 228-9, 238
National Trust ix, 1, 23, 30, 46, 49-50, 53, 56-7, 59-60, 102, 127, 163, 172, 188, 197-8, 221
Nature Reserves Investigation Committee (1942) 122-4, 178-9

Political and Economic Planning (PEP) 5, 27, 35-42, 81, 96, 102, 179, 205, 231

Ramblers' Association vi, 32, 44, 47, 60, 110, 173, 220, 264
Requisitioned Land and War Works Act (1945) 184-5, 189
Royal Engineers 6, 10, 64, 70, 72-3
Royal Geographical Society 144
Royal Institute of British Architects 4, 15, 17, 26-7, 32, 131, 239